Healing
Hearts

Healing Hearts

Meditations for Women
Living with Divorce

JAN JOHNSON DRANTELL

BANTAM BOOKS
New York Toronto London Sydney Auckland

HEALING HEARTS

A Bantam Book / September 1993

All rights reserved.
Copyright © 1993 by Jan Johnson Drantell.
Book design by Ann Gold.

For information address: Bantam Books.

Library of Congress Cataloging-in-Publication Data
Drantell, Jan Johnson.
    Healing hearts : meditations for women living with
divorce / Jan Johnson Drantell.
        p.   cm.
    ISBN 0-553-35172-9 : $8.95
    1. Divorced women—Prayer-books and devotions—
English.   2. Devotional calendars.   I. Title.
BL625.9.D58D73   1993
242'.6433—dc20   93-9637
                                                    CIP

Published simultaneously in the United States and Canada

Bantam Books are published by Bantam Books, a division of
Bantam Doubleday Dell Publishing Group, Inc. Its
trademark, consisting of the words "Bantam Books" and the
portrayal of a rooster, is Registered in U.S. Patent and
Trademark Office and in other countries. Marca Registrada.
Bantam Books, 1540 Broadway, New York, New York 10036.

PRINTED IN THE UNITED STATES OF AMERICA

FFG   0 9 8 7 6 5 4 3 2 1

ACKNOWLEDGMENTS

During the course of recovering myself at the end of my marriage, I was extremely fortunate to have the support and love of many people. They continued to be part of my support network during my work on this book. I couldn't possibly mention them all by name. The people here, and others, helped me specifically by providing quotes, offering parallel books from their personal libraries, and sharing their own experience.

Lynn Quade, Penn Garvin, Dee Ready, Loretta Chietti, Amy Brokering, Margaret Welshons, Amity Buxton, Gilda Iriate, Lauren Artress, Katherine Schoen, Nancy Mootz, Jean Powell, Sandra Lewis, Mary Montgomery, Mary Lou Flandrick, Greg Brandenburgh, David Gibson, Anne Wilson Schaef, Gloria Karpinski.

I am particularly grateful to Miriam Frost and Christin Lore Weber for their expert editorial help at the beginning and the end of this project.

Thanks to Jonathon Lazear and his staff at The Lazear Agency. And thanks to Toni Burbank and Michelle Rapkin at Bantam for everything.

And finally, thanks to my daughter, Addie Johnson, who lived through lots of days with me. She provided quotes, clerical help, understanding, and love.

INTRODUCTION

I wrote this book because I wish I'd had one like it to read when my seventeen-year marriage ended. Even though I never thought of myself as a woman who was defined by her marriage, I found that I had somehow lost my center. I still had friends, family, meaningful work. But I wasn't who I had been. I felt angry, hurt, bewildered, and lost. I felt awkward in social situations. I found much more of my time was being consumed in everyday chores. Having one adult instead of two in the house made a big difference. I frantically tried to keep up with being a mom, being a worker, and being me, although there was scarcely time for the latter. And there was one small problem. I didn't know who me was anymore.

Shortly after my separation I realized that I was seeing the world through gray-colored glasses. Everything was dingy, dreary, dark, and bleak. At other times in my life, when some things seemed bleak, I could at least look at lively colors in other corners of my life. I could rely on myself to solve problems, to entertain and delight myself, to get me through the bad patch, one day at a time. At worst, I could always find the black humor in whatever it was that was making the world seem dark. Now I could not. So I set about writing this book as one way to allow myself to see color in my life again.

As women we are often vulnerable to losing sight of who we are and what we want, to losing our own centers, if you will, to definitions provided by our relationships with others. Many of us would blanch at saying we are defined by our husbands. Yet, in part because relationships are so important to us, we do tend to lose track of who we are.

When we divorce, we always become somebody else—in our own eyes, in the eyes of our friends and families and the world at large. Our lives change rapidly and dramatically. Even if we chose to be single again and feel we are embarked on an exciting new course in our lives, the rapidity and intensity of changes can make our lives feel out of control. Most of us have any number of people in our lives telling us what our lives should be. The trick is to listen to ourselves, to discover who we are.

Whether we're ending a marriage of long standing, one in which we were mostly happy or mostly miserable, or a shorter relationship, we need to grieve the ending. We need to allow ourselves the time and space to heal our hearts.

Daily reading and meditation with this book can help you discover who you are and create a space in which to nurture yourself in the present moment. You can use the reading assigned to each day's date, or you can look for a reading that addresses a topic that is "up" for you that day. Use the topic index or browse through the book to find a meditation that fits your need. However you use this book, it will most likely work best for you if you use it every day.

The essence of *Healing Hearts* is living in the here and now, each day, one day at a time. Healing ourselves, which is another way of saying finding ourselves, is not dwelling in the past, stuck in the morass of what might have been "if only" or impaled on the edge of recrimination. What if I had been kinder, smarter, wiser, more understanding? What if I hadn't picked fights? What if I hadn't put my needs first? What if I had? What if? What if? What if? Then would I still be with my spouse?

Nor is healing our hearts trying to live today by planning for or worrying about a host of future what ifs. What if I can't take care of the house? What if my kids grow up damaged? What if I can't do my job? What if I never fall in love again? What if I do? What if I never feel happy again? The knife of future what ifs cuts us off from our feelings, our lives, our selves, and can kill us. It surely kills our ability to live in today.

When I live in today, I live where I am, with myself, accepting my past, opening to my future, and living in the present. I allow myself to feel my grief, anger, depression. And I allow myself to feel my joy, humor, and hope. Today is where I look to my Higher Power and to the life force within me to:

Grant me the serenity
To accept the things I cannot change,
The courage to change the things I can,
And the wisdom to know the difference.

JANUARY 1

A new year can begin only because the old year ends.
—Madeleine L'Engle

We mark many new years during a year—the new calendar year, turning a year older, religious festivals, spring. Each of these marks our hopes and expectations for what is coming and our letting go of what has passed. Some things—winter, for instance—are easier to let go of than others. Clearly one of the hardest new years is the year that begins our starting over as single.

For some of us this year seems to start in the bleakest winter of our lives. Everything seems dead. It's hard to let go of the old year of our marriage. And it's even harder to see how anything new might come of it. Others of us who have endured a bad old year of marriage may look with relief on this new year of starting over single. Yet the bad is sometimes as hard to let end in our lives as the good.

When we embark on starting over as single people, each day is for us a new year. When we let an old day, an old year, an old way of life end, we can be open to the surprises, sorrows, and joys of a new year.

Letting go of the old, I wish myself "Happy New Year" today and every day.

JANUARY 2

Faith needs her daily bread.   —Dinah Mulock Craik

And so do we. Faith or belief in ourselves and in the power of a Higher Power, whatever name we call God, needs to be nurtured. Our faith will nurture us if we keep it alive and if we are alive to it, on a daily basis.

Being alive to faith is not memorizing a list of rules and regulations. Being able to rattle off a complicated theological argument for the existence of God is not being alive to faith, nor is reasoning or bargaining with God that we'll do better when things get better. To be alive to faith doesn't mean we don't have moments, hours, days, weeks, years of doubt.

Being alive to faith every day is setting aside time to be. It can be as simple as breathing in and out, reminding ourselves and our God that we're here in the present breathing in and out. There are things in our life we simply can't figure out. They don't make sense. They give us only pain. When we're simply being with ourselves, the idea is not to think up solutions based on some bolt of lightning from above. The idea is to turn ourselves over to the power of our Higher Power moving within us.

When I feed my faith with daily bread, I keep myself alive.

JANUARY 3

*Our daydreams—and our nighttime dreams as well—can
allow impossible wishes to come true. And they can, in
fact, make a difference in how we feel. . . . Our waking or
sleeping fantasies that satisfy less permissible desires may
reduce the urgency of those desires.* —Judith Viorst

Dreams are free. They don't cost anything, and
in them, night or day, we can give free rein to our
imagination and our subconscious or unconscious
resources. Dreams are freeing.

We might dream impossible wishes. Dreaming
alone doesn't make them come true. Yet dreams
can help us set our sights on our heart's true
wishes. Dreams can, quite literally, affect how we
feel. Who hasn't awakened after a nightmare with
a sense of uneasiness or discontent? Or after a
particularly satisfying dream, feeling, if just for a
minute, better about life?

Dreams, if we pay attention to them, can provide us with a wealth of information about ourselves. Dreams have a way of pointing the way,
especially during transition times when we're lost
in a morass of conflicting feelings or trying to
deny bad feelings. Daydreams or night dreams let
us take the perfect revenge, come up with the perfect retort, launch new careers, make new homes.

Following my dreams can lead me to myself.

JANUARY 4

Since our values are linked to our conscience through feelings, we feel guilt when we are dishonest to our own values. When our guilt rises, we must first tune into ourselves and ask whose guilt it is. —Marilyn Mason

There's nothing intrinsically wrong with holding family, community, or church values. Yet unexamined values lead to neurotic, overwhelming guilt, like day leads to night—inevitably.

Suppose I feel guilty about not meeting my exspouse's needs. Whose standards am I living by? Suppose I feel guilty about wanting to begin a new intimate relationship because if I do I might not give my kids or my job or my friends or my community work enough of my time. By whose clock am I measuring?

Folk wisdom about guilt implies that we don't feel guilty unless we have something to feel guilty about. That's true as far as it goes. But often what we have to feel guilty about is that we're not meeting somebody else's values about what we should be doing, saying, or thinking. So maybe when we're feeling guilty about that, what we ought to feel guilty about is that we're not meeting our own standards.

I can use my guilt in the service of bringing my actions in line with my values.

JANUARY 5

Boredom helps one to make decisions. —Colette

Boredom is nature's nag. Boredom is our heart's way of telling us it's time to make some changes. Yet, when we act primarily from boredom, we may stir things up without considering whether the changes are for the best. When we act solely from boredom, we may try to smother or silence our boredom with food, activity, alcohol. We don't hear ourselves saying it's time to make changes. We simply try to get rid of the boredom. Feeling bored? Clean the closet, wash the dishes, rearrange the furniture. Mindless tasks are somehow supposed to be a cure for boredom.

Boredom may have caused us to leave our marriages in the first place. Bored to death with a way of life we could no longer tolerate, we made a dramatic change. However, if the changes aren't to our liking, somewhere inside us boredom waits to be heard from again.

Having become single again, we quite often find ourselves being bored with feeling awful, sad, depressed, disgusted, angry. When we get bored enough with these feelings, we can make the decisions and take the action that wakes us up to renewed interest in living.

Feeling bored is a clue that I need to make changes.

JANUARY 6

What loneliness is more lonely than distrust?
                                                —George Eliot

Most of us who are separated or divorced know that we can be lonely in a relationship. And we almost surely know distrust in a relationship. What distrust could possibly be more lonely than not trusting ourselves?

When we're single again, we need to rely on ourselves to make decisions and take care of the business of daily living in new ways—alone. For some of us this is exhilarating, for some scary; for most of us it's probably both. As we take care of the "stuff" of daily living—owning our successes and our mistakes—we build our trust in our abilities, and ourselves.

When we're feeling lonely, it's hard to trust ourselves. When we trust ourselves, even though we're alone, we don't feel as lonely. When we face our feelings of grief, anger, and loneliness, and let ourselves feel and express them, we are trusting ourselves with the truth. We're trusting ourselves to choose being alone rather than being lonely in distrustful relationships.

My loneliness gives me an opportunity to learn to trust myself.

JANUARY 7

When nothing is sure, everything is possible.
—Margaret Drabble

Life is not like it was, that's for sure. When we start over after a separation, it feels like nothing is sure. That's the bad news. We simply can't go back to the way things were. And, in most cases, we probably don't want to. When nothing is sure, the good news is that anything is possible.

If we give up having to be sure of ourselves, having to be sure that we'll act or react in the same way we used to, new things are possible. When our lives are thrown into an uproar, the good news is that we don't have to be the way we were. We can try out new things—from hairstyles to relationships. We can give ourselves the freedom of trying without being sure *because* we're in a state where things aren't sure.

When things seem to be sure in our lives, we tend to immediately discard possibilities for adventure and exploration. Taking off in a new direction might upset the applecart of surety. Well, now it's upset and we don't have to worry. We can relax and explore the possibilities.

Giving up my old sureties is a sure way of finding new possibilities.

JANUARY 8

The maxim "Nothing avails but perfection" may be spelled "Paralysis." —Winston Churchill

If we can't accept that we'll do things imperfectly, we run the risk of not doing anything. When we try to be perfect we become, if anything, more imperfect. To rewrite another time-honored maxim, "If at first you don't succeed perfectly, look at your effort and your result to see if it's good enough." It might be.

When our marriages fail, many of us react by striving for perfection in other parts of our lives. Clearly we weren't perfect in our marriages, we tell ourselves. They wouldn't have failed otherwise. (Do we ever consider that they might have failed because we were trying to be perfect?) So, in an effort to demonstrate our worth to ourselves, we set out to be the perfect mother, sister, friend, professional woman.

And we try and we try and we try and we try, until we're so tired we can't try anymore. We're paralyzed. We have to stop, and when we stop trying to be perfect we'll be able to get something done.

I can cure my self-enforced paralysis, but not perfectly.

JANUARY 9

Nothing is so good as it seems beforehand.

—George Eliot

Or as bad. It might be better. It might be worse. And it might be that we'll never know which because we're too busy trying to figure out what will be and how it will be. When what will be gets here we often don't recognize it because it doesn't look or feel like we expected it to.

When our marriages end, our lives are changing dramatically. Things aren't turning out like we expected they would, so we think we have to make adjustments. The bad news is that we feel like we don't know what to expect. The good news is that this is a perfect opportunity to give up our expectations. Instead of adjusting our expectations and acting accordingly, we can begin to act according to what's going on in the here and now.

Our capacity to fantasize or imagine how good or how bad things will be always exceeds our ability to control how things will turn out. If we give up the fantasy of how things will be, we can, in turn, give up trying to control the outcome.

Life is simpler since I gave up expecting how my hand will play out.

JANUARY 10

Then give the world the best you have, / And the best will come back to you.   —Madeline Bridges

When trying to give the world our best, there are a few things we might remember. The first is that we're part of the world. Making an effort to give the world our best means making an effort to give ourselves our best. The second is that best doesn't mean perfect. If we wait until we can give the perfect effort, we never will. The third is that best doesn't necessarily mean lots.

When we're recovering ourselves after ending our marriages, our best may not seem like very much to us. We may feel as though we don't even know who we are, let alone what we have to give to the world. When we make an effort, put ourselves out, one of the best things that can come back to us is some new sense of who we are.

The little things we do for ourselves and for others make us feel good because we do them. In the doing, we find that we make connections with ourselves and other people, and we appreciate what the world is giving back to us.

Making a little effort to give the world my best can go a long way toward helping me discover what my best is.

JANUARY 11

Intimacy is not static. It is always moving to a new level. It is an energy flow with no barriers. Intimacy cannot be controlled. Like a feeling, it cannot be reproduced at will. We notice intimacy. We do not produce it.

—Anne Wilson Schaef

We cannot manufacture intimacy. Having ended a marriage relationship, one would think we'd know that. Whatever our intimacy issues—and every marriage that ends has them—we probably found out that we couldn't make intimacy and we couldn't control it.

That is, we did if we were paying attention. We can only notice whether something is or is not there if we're paying attention. To pay attention we need to know what to look for. We need to know where to look. And the first place to look is at ourselves. Do I feel intimate with myself? Am I willing to let myself grow, to notice who I am? To notice my energy when I'm feeling good about myself—and when I'm not?

When we notice our intimacy with ourselves, we can't help noticing our intimacy with others. We're now paying attention. And to keep the energy flowing we need only to keep paying attention.

Paying attention doesn't create intimacy, but it sure lets me know whether or not I see and feel it.

JANUARY 12

As a singer you're a great dancer.   —Amy Leslie

As an ex-wife, I'm a great mother or worker or friend or enemy. But who am I really? In order to feel connected to myself and again to others, I need to know who it is who wants to feel connected. I pay attention to myself, and I begin to know who I am.

When I pay attention and know who I am, I can know if I want to sing or dance, change jobs or find a new relationship. Maybe I want to travel or take up a new hobby. Maybe I want to simply go on living the way I am for a time while I get used to this single life.

We can all be great singers and dancers. We can be single again, and we can then be married again. We can be the same person we were yet with different things to do or different ways of doing them. We can do all that when we pay attention to who it is who is singing and dancing, who it is who is living our lives.

I can be a great me by knowing who I am and doing what I do.

JANUARY 13

A young woman once said to an old woman, What is life's heaviest burden? And the old woman said, To have nothing to carry. —A Jewish tale

It is natural and healthy to try to avoid pain. We do not put our hands into an open flame. It is not natural or healthy to try to deny pain. If we are accidentally burned at the stove, we cry out. Yet, in the midst of a life crisis, when the pain of loss and change seems unbearable, we sometimes try to bury our pain and deny ourselves any feeling of it.

In time, we find ourselves in the position of the woman who is carrying life's heaviest burden. We have nothing to carry because we care about nothing. To become so deadened to our own pain and to that of others that we care about nothing is to be in isolation.

If we are not to live in isolation, without feeling and without the possibility of connecting with our own and others' feelings, we inevitably must acknowledge and carry our burdens. We acknowledge the truth of the old woman's wisdom, knowing that we cannot live for long under the yoke of life's heaviest burden—caring about nothing at all.

As long as I care, I can carry on.

JANUARY 14

"I'm late, I'm late for a very important date."
        —The White Rabbit in *Alice in Wonderland*

Who set up the schedule I run to anyway? I *must* work hard, take care of others, pick up the dry cleaning, keep in touch with my parents, finish the projects I start, spend time with my friends, get everything on my list done—*now*! Get it? This is a virtually endless list.

And when I get everything done, I have permission to get some well-earned rest as soon as I answer one last question. Who am I? Chances are if we spend our days running about, we're late for an important date with ourselves.

It's time to give ourselves a break, to find a small, cozy room, with a soft cushion to rest on. I sit there, close my eyes, and let myself be. I release all the tasks I've done. I release all the tasks I haven't done. Now I release all those adjectives I *have* to be: good, loving, smart, wonderful. And I just be. If I repeat this daily, chances are I won't be late for my own life.

I can stop running long enough to find my center.

JANUARY 15

There are all those early memories; one cannot get another set; one has only those. —Willa Cather

When we're getting divorced, we might reinvent ours as a perfect marriage and wallow in regret that we'll never have it again. Or we might remember only the terrible things—the betrayals, the losses—until we wonder how we could have been so stupid as to marry that so-and-so in the first place. But we did. And now, if we're truthful with ourselves, we have what memories we have. Both the good and the bad.

Even if we could get rid of our memories, we couldn't get another set. So we might as well use these for all they're worth. We can use our memories to help us accept and nurture ourselves now.

To do that we start by remembering everything we can and accepting it for what it was. That means not judging it, not second guessing, not trying to make it something it wasn't. We can use a happy memory to create new circumstances that might make us happy. Remembering a time when someone took care of us, or we took care of ourselves, can teach us how to do it now.

When I accept my memories, I accept myself. When I accept myself, I can nurture myself.

JANUARY 16

Some people think it's holding on that makes one strong.
Sometimes it's letting go.   —Sylvia Robinson

Letting go can mean deciding to end a marriage in the face of pressure from others, i.e., family or church, not to. Letting go can mean beginning to accept that a marriage is over even if we don't wish it to be. As a relationship ends we find ourselves faced with letting go in a variety of ways— of our marriage, of the way we were in it, of the small habits of a life together, of the arguments, of the good times and the bad times.

Power struggles over who's right and who's wrong in regard to joint possessions, a previously shared house, children, or simply principles are among the hardest things to let go of. Holding on to power struggles with our ex-spouse won't make our lives easier. Holding on or holding out won't solve any of the problems and will sap our strength to resolve our differences.

Letting go is giving up our old ways of being. Letting go is not giving up ourselves. By giving up our old ways of being, we are, in fact, apt to discover new things about ourselves, including new reserves of strength.

Letting go lets me find my own true strength.

JANUARY 17

*It is the vast, formless, unknown and unknowable things
we fear. Anything which can be brought to a common
point—a focus within our understanding—can be dealt
with.*   —Lara Jefferson

When we face dramatic changes in our lives we
may fear the future like a child fears the dark—
because we don't know what's there. Asking ourselves questions we can't know the answers to is
not dealing effectively with our fears: How will I
go on for the next ten, twenty, thirty years? Will I
be able to support myself, my children? Will anyone ever love me again?

We can't know the future. We can, however, focus on what we're really asking when we ask a
question like: Will anyone ever love me again?
Does it mean I'm afraid to live my life alone?
Does it mean that I have specific wants and
needs? How can I get them met?

Dealing with our specific fears is to alleviate
and, in some cases, eradicate that specific fear. It
can also give us confidence to bring our other
fears into focus and deal with them, one by one.
Knowledge and understanding can help us con-
duct our lives despite our fear or use our fear to
understand our lives.

*Finding a frame of reference for my fear allows me to
hang it in proper perspective.*

JANUARY 18

> *With him for a sire and her for a dam,*
> *What should I be but just who I am?*
> —Edna St. Vincent Millay

We all are who we are, having all got here basically the same way. Like all the animals and human beings with whom we share this planet, we have two birth parents. With that biological fact we begin to be who we are. We get or don't get what we need in our growing-up years. And then the show is ours.

Whether we had the world's best parents or the world's worst, we are who we are. Whether we had the world's best marriage or its worst, it's over now and the show must go on. We can, in large part, determine who we are and how much that pleases us by what we do, by how we live in the world. And it is so much easier to live in the world if we can say, "I am who I am, with my strengths and my weaknesses."

I may want to change some of who I am, some of how I act in the world, and it will be much easier to do if first I accept myself just as I am. Once I accept myself I can appreciate myself. This time of transition is a perfect opportunity for me to find out and acknowledge who I am.

Who else would I be but who I am? And how can I be the me I want to be?

JANUARY 19

*There is only one history of importance, and it is the
history of what you once believed in and the history of
what you came to believe in.* —Kay Boyle

The old saw that those who don't remember history are condemned to repeat it applies to our
personal histories as well. And in our personal
history of belief we can, if we remember to look,
find a thread of truth that will serve us well in the
present.

When we end a marriage, we begin to believe
new things about ourselves. Often, at first, those
beliefs are negative: I am not lovable. I am not a
worthwhile person. I am powerless to accomplish
anything. I am trapped by my circumstances. If
we believe any or all of those things we are likely
to want to change them, but to what? and how?

If we remember a time when we didn't believe
those things about ourselves, our memories of
how we felt and acted then can guide us to
change now. Even if we never basically changed
our belief that we were capable, creditable people,
perhaps our recent circumstances and our reaction to them has led us to act otherwise. In that
case, reminding ourselves what we believe about
ourselves can help us through our present crisis.

*My history of who I believe I am can help me be who
I want to be.*

JANUARY 20

If we could sell our experiences for what they cost us, we'd all be millionaires. —Abigail Van Buren

And if wishes were horses, then beggars would ride. Dwelling on how valuable our experiences might be if only the world valued experience is a way of regretting. To think of our experience in terms of what it cost us is usually to regret that we paid such a high price.

Our past experiences are really only valuable to us as they are applied to our present. We can't appreciate that value if we bemoan the high cost and our current state of poverty. We can't appreciate that value if we continue to throw good money after bad by refusing to learn from our experience and repeating it. And we surely can't value our experience if most of our energy goes into wishing we'd spent our time and money gaining different experience.

Using our past experiences to live in the present, without regret, is undertaking a sort of balancing of our emotional bank accounts. We can pay off debts, make amends to ourselves and others, figure the value of our current assets.

I can reconcile my past experience with my present circumstances.

JANUARY 21

Being oneself is always an acquired taste.
—Patricia Hampl

The self I get to know may be the self I get to like and value. If I don't get to know her there's no chance I'll get to like her. Acquiring a taste for myself is a process. Self-esteem is not something we simply have—or don't. Our self-esteem depends on only one person—ourselves.

Many of us depended on our partners for our self-esteem. If they felt good about us, we felt good about us. If we had to do or be things we didn't like, that was a small price to pay to have our self-esteem reinforced. Having depended on someone else for our self-esteem—or tried to—when we get divorced our first inclination is to blame that person for destroying our self-esteem.

Getting divorced offers us choices to learn about and to esteem ourselves. We can go on blaming the past and live with shattered self-esteem. We can continue looking outside ourselves for someone to give us self-esteem. Or we can begin to acquire a taste for ourselves by discovering what ingredients we have. And by relishing what we make of them.

I can't acquire a taste for someone I don't know.

JANUARY 22

> *It is brave to be involved,*
> *To be fearful to be unresolved.*
>   —Gwendolyn Brooks

Paradoxes like finding our strength in our weakness are hard enough to understand and harder still to live by. If we can take the plunge to be involved in life even though we are afraid, we're apt to find reservoirs of strength we didn't know we had. Being brave doesn't mean being unafraid. Nor does it mean being absolutely sure.

The very act of admitting our fears to ourselves is an act of bravery. To admit we're unresolved is often to find the strength to discover a new direction. To be involved in life when we're afraid and ambivalent requires bravery and strength. Yet another paradox: The very involvement that requires bravery and strength also fosters it.

To name and acknowledge our fear is to name and acknowledge our bravery. We can say, "I am afraid of losing anything else, having lost a relationship that was part of my identity." We can also say, "I am a brave person for continuing to try to connect with people in my life even though I'm afraid of losing them."

My fears and indecisions are not signs of my weakness; they're seeds of my strength.

JANUARY 23

Women like to sit down with trouble as if it were knitting.
—Ellen Glasgow

Knitting is one of those repetitive acts that allow our minds to wander, resting on small details or discovering large insights. Knitting can be comforting and satisfying. We first untangle a skein of yarn, rolling it into a soft, yet substantial, ball that unrolls smoothly as we create, through repetition and pattern, something new.

Sitting down to solve trouble as if it were knitting is not such a bad idea either. Imagine a heap of yarn lying in a box or bag over the years, becoming hopelessly tangled. Imagine beginning to unravel that yarn and to roll it into usable balls. Imagine your life after separation as being that yarn. You don't know where one part of you begins and another ends. You want to move on, to create your life, and first you must untangle the yarn, untie knots, make things smooth.

We can't untangle a mess of yarn or life hastily, at one sitting. Both knitting and recovering from grief and going on from there require time, patience, and involvement in a repetitive process that eventually produces something new.

I am open to tending to the process and the metaphor of knitting my life together again.

JANUARY 24

It is easier to understand a nation by listening to its music than by learning its language.   —Anonymous

In the countries of our hearts, our feelings are the music, and our rational language often serves as a barrier to truly understanding them. As we seek to make sense of a traumatic experience, we can become obsessed with finding just the right words to describe how we feel. We think that if we can only search around in our psyches and figure out why our lives are the way they are, then we will understand and accept.

When we take time to listen to the inner music of our hearts—whether it's the banging, clanging, cymbal-clashing climax of rage or the peaceful and pensive flute of calm—we begin to know and understand ourselves differently. We begin to really feel what we are feeling, to take the time to sit through each movement.

Sometimes we need to study all the parts, articulating them with words as if we were the conductor, who must know each and every note, its tone, length, and volume—its purpose for being there. And sometimes it's time to simply sit and listen to the music, letting it wash over us.

Sonata or rock and roll, I'll listen to whatever comes from my heart.

Don't compromise yourself. You are all you've got.
—Janis Joplin

I'm all I've got and I've got all of me. Independence thrust on us by becoming single again can make us feel like all isn't nearly enough. We may feel as though we've got too much independence and not enough resources. It's scary to be responsible for making all our own money decisions, for doing all the household chores.

We often compromise ourselves, sell ourselves short about our own powers to take care of business and take care of ourselves. As we begin to take care of ourselves, something happens. Often we begin to see that we weren't living up to our fullest, we weren't making choices based on what we needed and wanted. If I don't compromise myself, if I begin to accept my full potential and exercise it, being all I've got becomes something great.

Have you ever watched a small child accomplish some new task for the first time—perhaps climbing the stairs? Often a child who has climbed the stairs for the first time will literally crow with the pride and pleasure of independence. What can I crow about in my life?

I've got all of me, and I can rely on her.

JANUARY 26

See, the human mind is kind of like . . . a piñata. When it breaks open, there's a lot of surprises inside. Once you get the piñata perspective, you see that losing your mind can be a peak experience.   —Jane Wagner

When the piñata is broken open the piñata no longer exists. When our minds are broken open, they *do* still exist, which, if we can only believe it, is a big relief. We expect to find good surprises inside a piñata; we don't know what we'll find when we lose our minds. We're usually afraid we won't find anything or we won't like what we find.

Breaking a mind open, particularly one that has been fastened to old ideas and feelings about ourselves and closed to new ones for a long time, can be a painful experience. When we're in the identity crisis of being single again, we don't know who we are anymore. Being broken open to find all kinds of surprises can be a relief and a delight, if we take the piñata perspective.

When we open our minds with the piñata perspective we're allowing ourselves to be amused, pleased, informed, and amazed at what's inside. What's inside can point us in new directions; it can nurture and transform us.

Breaking into myself can be a breakthrough to a new me.

JANUARY 27

Never go to bed mad. Stay up and fight.

—Phyllis Diller

We've all read stories about people, mostly famous, that make us want to scream. Their marriages are *so* successful because they never go to bed angry. They always work things out between each other. They talk, they kiss, they make up. Do those people ever sleep?

Getting rid of our anger is probably not what we really want to do anyway. We may think we want to avoid feeling angry and end up trying to bury anger in food, alcohol, busyness, sleep, or anything else. We may feel that we want to lash out in our anger, hurting those who have hurt us. What we *do* want is to avoid turning our anger in on ourselves so that it diminishes us and our capacity to feel anything but anger. So we probably don't want to go to bed in the height of anger.

I can laugh. Or cry. Or scream. Or experience my anger, letting myself feel it, express it. I can pound on a piano or a pillow. Or talk to a trusted friend. Who am I angry at? My friends, my family, my ex-spouse? Myself? What am I angry at? What can my anger teach me? What do I want to do about it?

It's my anger, and I can do something constructive with it.

JANUARY 28

*. . . a series of failures may culminate in the best possible
result.* —Gisela Richter

As surely as necessity is the mother of invention,
failure is often the mother of success. We've all
heard stories of scientists who set out to discover
one thing, failed at it, and ended up discovering
something altogether different. And most of us
were raised with the maxim If at first you don't
succeed—to wit: you fail—try, try again.

The good thing about failing at something we
set out to do is that the process leads us somewhere else if we'll let it. In effect, our failures
make way for and room for our success. And
sometimes they even lead us to our success—a
different success than we set out for to be sure,
yet success nevertheless.

When a relationship ends, even one we're not
happy with, we call it a failure. It looks like a
failure and it feels like a failure. And failure, in
and of itself, neither looks nor feels good. Yet in
the process of accepting the failure and letting go
of this relationship, we make room for something
new in our lives.

*My failed relationship leaves an empty spot in my
life, one I can succeed at filling.*

Isolation has led me to reflection, reflection to doubt, doubt to a more sincere and intelligent love of God.
—Marie Lenéru

When we feel isolated, we sure hope it leads to something—anything—else and soon! When we're getting divorced, we are sure to feel isolated from our ex-spouses. And we're apt to feel isolated from friends, family, our work, our lives. Nothing is the way it was, and nobody seems to be able to understand that.

Living with our isolation leads to reflection. Alas, reflection in isolation doesn't lead to belief in anything or anybody. We are apt to reflect on how we're cut off, by being different and in pain, from everything we ever knew, loved, or enjoyed. At times we doubt that we'll ever feel anything but isolation again.

Yet, when we stay with ourselves in isolation, a shift occurs. We are with ourselves. We are not, maybe for the first time in years, isolated from ourselves. The very isolation that led us inward to reflection has reconnected us to ourselves.

Reflecting on my isolation helps me see that I'm not alone with it.

JANUARY 30

Make today something you'll want to remember tomorrow.
—Amity Buxton

The surest way to guarantee that we won't remember our todays in our tomorrows is not to be present in our todays. So when we're trying to live each day so that it counts, so that it will be worth remembering, the first thing we have to do is to live that day for that day. When we're feeling the pain and rage of the loss of our marriage, our inclination is to pay as little attention to today as is humanly possible.

Tomorrow will come whether we pay attention to today or not. Yet if we don't feel today, we won't remember it. Recovering from our pain depends on feeling it and remembering it.

Some days just are better than others. When the kids are sick, the bills overdue, and the toilet breaks, we might not think there's anything we'll want to remember. But while we're making chicken soup, writing checks, and waiting for the plumber, we might feel good about being able to take care of things. And tomorrow, when we remember the satisfaction of handling a bad day, we know we're on our way to recovery.

I can recover myself through my memories, one day at a time.

JANUARY 31

Never think you've seen the last of anything . . .
                                        —Eudora Welty

The more things change, the more they stay the same. The fact that we can't be sure we've seen the end of anything can be comforting or frightening, depending on the particulars. When we're in crisis or transition, everything seems different.

We might even get to the point that we're afraid we wouldn't recognize ourselves if we caught a glimpse of ourselves in a mirror. We think we've seen the last of that old self who was married. And so discovering that something, almost anything, is the same can be comforting. Perhaps an old friend calls expressing enduring affection. Perhaps we discover our favorite brand of jam for the first time in our local supermarket.

While we're discovering new things, we're apt to discover some things we'd just as soon see the last of. And telling ourselves that we have, perversely, may be the surest guarantee that we haven't. Promising ourselves that things are going to be perfect now simply won't work. We're still the same fallible people. We're bound to make some of the same mistakes. And we're bound to learn their lessons.

I haven't seen the last of me, and I can discover the best of me.

FEBRUARY 1

We hand folks over to God's mercy, and show none ourselves. —George Eliot

If we can't show compassion to ourselves, we can't show it to others. And vice versa. To lack compassion is to blind our eyes, plug our ears, harden our hearts to suffering. To have compassion is to see, hear, and feel the suffering of the world—including our own.

Compassion doesn't require that we solve or fix our own problems—or anybody else's. That's control and interference. It only requires that we be there. Maybe in small ways—offering a cup of tea, a smile, a chat on the phone, a shoulder to cry on, a hug. Maybe in bigger ways—volunteering at a shelter, giving money, getting involved in politics. And when we're compassionate, the first person we must shelter, feed, cry with, is ourselves.

Doing so many "good works" that we burn out is not showing compassion to ourselves. Yet compassion breeds compassion. If we have it and share it, we get it back—more of it—to have and to share. Once we start showing compassion for ourselves, we'll show it for others. And we're not going to run out of it.

I can hand myself over to the mercy of a Higher Power by showing compassion for myself.

FEBRUARY 2

Our entire life, with our fine moral code and our precious freedom, consists ultimately in accepting ourselves as we are. —Jean Anouilh

During times of change, we're tempted to set goals and resolutions for ourselves as if we might be perfect—and, by implication, easier to accept as ourselves—any day now. As soon as we arrange our lives "correctly"—get a different haircut, lose weight, get a job, quit a job, get into a new relationship, get happy alone—we'll be able to accept ourselves. In the meantime, we'll just work toward that elusive, perfect woman we know we can be. Bring on the superwoman costume, please.

It sounds sort of silly, doesn't it? But how many of us spend more time thinking about what's wrong with us, how we can change, improve, grow, than we spend reminding ourselves that there are some things about ourselves and our lives that we must just accept—not judge, accept? If we don't accept ourselves, our lives are ruled by our attempts to control them. We are, literally, bereft of our precious freedom to be ourselves.

I can accept me without even thinking about how I'd change myself if I could control everything.

Today is a good day to accept the way I am today.

FEBRUARY 3

Life is not perfect. It is an untidy process. And it is not a place to get to. It's uncertain, frustrating, and it's exciting. A process, rather than a product.
—Roberta Jean Bryant

Life is a process. Yet how many of us live our life as if it is a product? When we get or have what we want—a better job, a new place to live, thinner, smarter, older (younger?), serenity, peace—then we'll have something. Then our lives will be worth living. The only known destination in life is death, and even dying is a process. We go through the experience, and who knows what happens then?

And each of us, ultimately, lives only with ourself in our own process. We're who we've got to live with when we're born and when we die. Today, this moment, whatever we're doing, wherever we are, is the only part of the process we can be in right now. We can't live today's process if we're invested in tomorrow's product.

Just as we can only live one day at a time, we can only accept ourselves one day, today, where we are and who we are. Self-acceptance, too, is a process, not a product. I accept myself, in process, as I am, and then? Then I go on living.

Mirror, mirror, on the wall, what I see is what I am —today.

FEBRUARY 4

*Whatever those unacquainted with it may think, solitude
and utter loneliness are far from being devoid of charm.
Words cannot convey the almost voluptuous sweetness of
the feelings experienced. . . . Mind and senses develop
their sensibility in this contemplative life made up of
continual observations and reflections. Does one become a
visionary or, rather, is it not that one has been blind until
then?*   —Alexandra David-Neel

Now that we're single again, we face loneliness
under different circumstances than we did when
we were married. Some of us face what feels like
"too much" loneliness. Some of us fling ourselves
into frenetic activity so we won't be alone. Some
of us withdraw nearly completely from social life.

We don't have to live the life of a hermit to gain
insight, to become a visionary. We do have to allow ourselves time to be alone with ourselves.

Letting ourselves see and be is letting ourselves
feel the feeling of being lonely. It's also letting
ourselves notice and feel a wide range of emotions that we probably ignored in our previous
blindness. The insight we gain from solitude has
very little to do with the amount of time we
spend alone. It has a lot more to do with the quality of time we spend with ourselves.

*My loneliness can lead me from the despair of blind
isolation to the solitude of being able to see me.*

FEBRUARY 5

Well, being divorced is like being hit by a Mack truck. If you live through it, you start looking very carefully to the right and to the left. —Jean Kerr

Being divorced or being hit by a Mack truck gets our attention, all right. And it does tend to make us start looking very carefully to the right and to the left. The big question is, What are we looking for? After we look to the left and the right, are we going to look ahead or are we going to look back?

Suppose this truck hit me early one morning on a road I drive every day on my way to work. I could decide never to drive down that road again. I could decide that I was never leaving my house again. I could decide to come to a dead stop every time I see one. But what if I miss one?

Just as it's ridiculous to envision coming to a dead stop every time we see a Mack truck, it's equally unrealistic to think that we can live our lives after divorce never encountering another situation in which we might get hurt. The best way to not miss seeing the truck—or anything else in our lives—is to look to the left and the right, to be where we are, as awake and as aware as possible when we're there.

Being on the lookout for situations in which I can get hurt doesn't mean I avoid living.

FEBRUARY 6

. . . truth could never be wholly contained in words. All of us know it: At the same moment the mouth is speaking one thing, the heart is saying another . . .
—Catherine Marshall

To tell the truth, we must listen. To hear the truth, we must listen to the words we speak to ourselves and others. To hear the whole truth, we must listen to our hearts, our guts, our feelings. And listening to the words we won't let ourselves speak or even think is just as important.

How many times have we ignored a gut feeling? Perhaps our minds are telling us everything we're saying or hearing is true. And our hearts are busily occupied, fervently wishing it were so. Yet in the pit of our stomach is a sinking sensation saying "It isn't so."

Often during the time our relationships are ending, we try to tell and hear the truth in a flurry of words. Explanations, counter-explanations, accusations, defenses, apologies, regrets. There may well be something of the truth in all of them. And the only way to find that something is to listen to the words and beyond the words to the secrets of our hearts.

Telling the truth means listening to what I say and what I leave unsaid—even to myself.

FEBRUARY 7

Courage is the price life exacts for granting peace.
—Amelia Earhart

When we're making major changes in our lives, whether in the traumatic time soon after our separation or as, over time, we build our new lives, we often say we want peace. We want peace within our families, within ourselves. We are making the changes that will grant us that peace.

Those changes may not come easily and they surely will not come all at once. What do we do to change our lives? We take courage, take heart really, to do things we thought we couldn't do. And to do the things we always did a bit differently. It's surely a cliché to say that courage is not one big heroic act. Courage can be simply getting through the day.

When we make courage an everyday occurrence, peace enters our daily lives, too. If we act with courage today and things come out okay, we have the peace of knowing we did well. If we act with courage today and things don't turn out the way we wanted, we have the peace of knowing that we acted from our hearts and that tomorrow will come.

I can afford the price of peace when I live with courage from my heart.

FEBRUARY 8

Being physically attractive counts much more in a
woman's life than in a man's, but beauty identified as it is
with youthfulness, does not stand up well to age. . . .
—Susan Sontag

Despite the fact that the cultural perception that women lose their youth and attractiveness earlier than men may be changing, it remains by and large true. It's not just a figment of our imagination. This double standard is one of those unfair realities we have to live with as women.

And when we find ourselves single again and aging, we have options. Bemoaning statistics and unfair standards is one. That and $1.50 will get us a cheap new lipstick. Complaining bitterly is another. Or we can deny we're aging through extreme measures: addiction to exercise, altered birth certificates, plastic surgery.

Or we can begin to live to please ourselves, to be comfortable in our own bodies. This can include exercising reasonably because it makes us feel better, or dressing and doing our makeup and hair to please ourselves. It can be enjoying the luxury of a long bubble bath and pretty lingerie because it makes us feel good. We can affirm who we are by taking care of ourselves.

Is there anybody who notices and cares how I feel
more than I do?

FEBRUARY 9

*Do not use a hatchet to remove a fly from your friend's
forehead.*   —Chinese proverb

A fly is a small annoyance. Wielding a hatchet is
an extreme response—especially if our friend
never asked us to get rid of the fly in the first
place. Using a hatchet on a fly could easily lead to
bloodshed. At the least it's going to lead to misunderstanding. Coming at our friends with literal
or figurative hatchets in our hands hardly ever
leads to communication and connectedness.

Friendship, at any time in our lives, can provide us with opportunities to support and be sup-
ported, to understand and be understood, to help
and be helped, to share pain and to share pleasure. When we're in crisis our friends can be invaluable. And it's also when we're probably most
tempted to come at them with hatchets—over-
reacting because we're under a lot of stress.

Friendship is a back-and-forth endeavor. And if
we find that we have a hatchet of anger, resentment, frustration in our hands and are tempted to
use it on our friends, we can ask our friends to
help us find the nearest woodpile—the most appropriate way to use the hatchet.

*My friends can help me figure out the right tool for
the job.*

FEBRUARY 10

Dependency is probably a result of fear. I have found that most people who stay in destructive relationships are afraid of their mates and afraid of leaving.
—Anne Wilson Schaef

Fear is one of the most dependable things in life. As long as we're willing to live with our fear, we can depend on it to keep us dependent. Yet if we take one step outside the cycle of fear and dependence, we might be astonished at how fast our fear becomes unreliable.

Most of us probably continued our marriages long after things became pretty unpleasant because we were afraid of the unknown. When the marriage finally ends, we have an opportunity. Having faced one fear and lived to tell the tale, we can begin to face our other fears. We no longer have to depend on fear.

When all our energy is no longer tied up in fear, we can depend on feeling our whole range of emotions: relief, grief, sadness, anger, joy, pain, depression, happiness. As we live with our feelings, we begin to know that we can rely on them and on ourselves.

Facing my fear can be my declaration of independence.

FEBRUARY 11

Running around the boat does nothing to ensure progress through the water.   —Anonymous

Running around in circles anywhere never does anything to ensure progress or growth. Running around a boat can, in fact, ensure that we sink the boat. Just as it's not a good idea to run around in boats, it's not a good idea to run around inside our heads. We can sink ourselves, too.

It's easy to imagine catastrophes that might befall us if we ran around in a boat. Falling overboard, slipping and hitting our head, getting tangled in the rigging, bouncing the boat up and down until we get seasick. When we run around inside our heads we can get so absorbed in the running that we lose sight of where we were trying to go. We use up time and energy that could be better spent. And we tend to live as if we're literally unconscious of our own lives.

The good thing about running around in circles is that we can't do it for too long—we get dizzy or exhausted or both. Then we have to sit down. Sitting quietly gives us a chance to look at where we're going and to figure out how to get there.

Sometimes I progress best by sitting and pondering.

FEBRUARY 12

The forest will answer you in the way you call to it.
—Finnish proverb

You will reap what you sow. Do unto others as you would have them do unto you. The world will treat you how you ask to be treated. Proverbs that tell us what we'll get back from the world and the people in it abound.

When we reach out, perhaps to make a new friend, to find a new job, to learn a new skill, to ask for help with a problem, to ask for someone to simply be with us in times of trouble, we will get a response. If we call out in anger, the response will be different than if we call out in need. If we call out in desperation, the response will be different than if we call out in joy. If we demand, the response will be different than if we ask.

It is true that if we reach out and ask for things we might get them and not want them; we might get something slightly different from what we had in mind and not want that. We might get what we wanted and still want it, or we might get something slightly different and want that. *And* if we don't reach out and ask for things, we are less than likely to get them.

The opportunity for the world to respond to me is only there if I call out to it.

FEBRUARY 13

*Make enthusiasm your daily exercise. People whose lives
are out of control because they indulge their addictions are
sad and fearful. An essential part of turning things around
is becoming converted to enthusiasm.*   —Eileen P. Flynn

People recovering from addictions to substances
like alcohol or drugs know that the only way to
stay in recovery is to practice it daily. They know
they leave fear and sadness behind overnight
only one day at a time. We don't have to be addicted to alcohol or drugs to have our lives be out
of control, to be sad and fearful people. We might
simply be unwilling to give up our pain and sadness—to be, in short, addicted to it.

We do not wake up one morning enthusiastic
and satisfied with our life. To be satisfied requires
enthusiasm. To move from sad and fearful to
enthusiastic requires transformation. Transformation can't happen through willpower. Transformation *can* happen through daily practice.

Beginning a daily program of enthusiasm exercise is like beginning a physical exercise program.
If we're sitting still we can't be exercising; if we're
holding on to our fear we have no room for enthusiasm. We'll have better results if we can start
with small exercises.

I can transform my life by exercising my enthusiasm.

FEBRUARY 14

I realize that when one no longer loves, one no longer lives. —George Sand

We celebrate Valentine's Day as a day to remember love, to greet those we love. When we're recently divorced, this can be a difficult holiday. We may not feel very loved or very loving. And that's okay. There's no rule that says we have to show our love for ourselves or others on any given day. Yet we are alive.

So we might as well take this opportunity to reach out to ourselves with whatever love we can muster. Maybe nobody's going to give us a Valentine's gift or card this year. But, if we were to get a valentine from ourselves, what would it be? Maybe we'd give ourselves the gift of a little time to be alone with our feelings, to cry, to remember a time when we felt more lovable. Maybe we'd write ourselves a little note acknowledging the things we love about ourselves.

Maybe we'll discover what we love about ourselves if we reach out to others. Being alive depends on loving ourselves and others. When we reach out to ourselves or someone else with love, we might be surprised at what we get back.

I can be alive to the possibility of loving myself today.

FEBRUARY 15

I didn't know what to do about life—so I did a nervous breakdown that lasted many months.

—Margaret Anderson

Okay, and then what? Being overwhelmed is feeling that our lives are so crazy and out of control that we can't possibly keep up. We have so much to do we can't possibly do it. We don't know what to do next. Because we can't possibly keep up and we don't know what to do, we feel inadequate.

Feeling inadequate and overwhelmed is thinking we have to do something about life. We have to rearrange ourselves and the world so they're perfect. Then we can start to live in the present with our feelings of inadequacy and being overwhelmed—instead of trying to conquer them.

We start looking at living as a process instead of doing something about life as an end or a goal. If we listen to ourselves when we feel overwhelmed, what might we hear? Maybe our self tells us that the thing to do when we have too much to do is nothing. To wait and listen some more. Maybe our self tells us that we don't have to be perfect to be adequate.

If I give up feeling I must do something about life, I might feel adequate to do some living.

FEBRUARY 16

Mine is not that species of weak or abject affection which can exist under the sense of ill-treatment and injustice . . . —Maria Edgeworth

Affection unimpeded flows *and* grows—in strength and amount—as it flows. Affection impeded weakens and dies, leaving in its place room for abuse and injustice to flow and grow, as a parody of true possibility.

We all encounter impediments to affection for ourselves and others. We send out messages that say: I care for you; I want to spend time with you; I want the best for you. And the object of our affection returns ridicule, rejection, and blame. When we respond to those impediments in kind or with abject apologies, scraping and bowing, promising to do better, the affection cannot grow.

When affection for others withers and dies, we grieve the loss of that person from our lives. When affection for ourselves dies and we lose *our selves* from our lives, we're in big trouble. We may not be legally or biologically dead. But if we continue to impede our affection for ourselves with unfair abuse, we surely and rapidly are on our way to anybody's definition of dying.

I can show my affection for myself by treating myself well.

FEBRUARY 17

The best antidepressants are expression and action. That way our depression is not an end but a meaningful beginning. —Marilyn Ferguson

Depression feels like it will go on forever, no matter how hard we work at alleviating it. When our marriages end we are almost certain to feel depression. And often the feeling spreads to our work, our lost youth, our future prospects for intimacy, our physical condition, our homes.

We may throw ourselves into a literal frenzy of activity in an attempt to have so much to do that we have no time to feel depressed. Action undertaken solely to make us forget our depression is not the action that can be an antidepressant.

It is only when we begin to allow ourselves to feel our losses, to experience and articulate what we're feeling, that we can begin to see what openings there are for making a new way of life. By expressing our feelings and then acting on them, we're using our depression. Articulating the scope of our depression lets us see how we want our lives to be. Acting on the articulation moves us from depression into a new beginning.

I can use my depression as a springboard to a new way of living.

Despair

FEBRUARY 18

And my faith cannot be restored by any sort of reasoning or logic. Now, I am in another world and I am deaf to singing. —Susan Griffin

Deaf to music, blind to color, touching with hands enclosed in heavy mittens, smelling stale air, tasting ashes, and dead to any feeling except the depths of despair. When we're in despair our senses seem to desert us. Our whole lives seem to be shrouded in black cloth.

Despair is irrational and illogical. We can't talk ourselves out of despair with pep talks or stern lectures. Doing things and seeing people doesn't work either. Reminding ourselves that we haven't lost everything—I may have lost my shoes but I still have my feet—doesn't alleviate despair. Nor does counting our blessings.

Despair seems to last a long time; time goes so slowly. And only with the passing of time will our despair lift. We're in despair now. We're not in the past or in the future. Giving up, letting go to our Higher Power is the first step to getting out of despair. Then, as we go on about life, doing things that we remember used to give us pleasure can encourage our senses to feel again.

I am the only self I have to be with, even in the dark winter of despair, and I can be with her.

FEBRUARY 19

Clapping with the right hand only will not produce a noise. —Malay proverb

We often think of cooperation as happening between or among two or more people. Yet all of us face times when parts of ourselves have more than one agenda, and we need to figure out a way to "work together" to get our needs met.

There's nothing quite like going through the process of separation and divorce to bring to our attention that we've been trying to march to the beat of the sound made by one hand clapping. We haven't been listening to our inner self because we haven't been engendering cooperation with our bodies, our minds, our hearts, our spirits. If we neglect one part of ourselves, we create inner silence.

In order to make a noise—a beat we can now live by or enthusiastic clapping to urge us on—we gotta get both hands clapping. Or get in tune with body, mind, heart, and spirit—our own "all of me." We begin by listening to ourselves carefully in the present moment. Listening tells us what we need right now.

Knowing what I need makes it possible to cooperate with myself to get it.

FEBRUARY 20

Children are likely to live up to what you believe of them.
                              —Lady Bird Johnson

Sometimes children act as we would expect. And sometimes they act in reaction. Divorce, with the specters of separation, loss, change, is one of the scariest things that can happen to children. It's scary and it's confusing.

When we're unclear about our expectations of our children, our children can only react accordingly. Without clarity, they act on clues. Some children will try out "good" behavior to see if they can get the family back together, or at least make Mommy less sad. Some children try out "bad" behavior to see if they can reclaim attention they feel they've lost. Some act as if everything has changed and so anything goes. Some act as if nothing has changed and try to live as if that's true.

When we can't be entirely clear about what our expectations of our children are, we can be honest. We can let them know that some things are changing and that some aren't. We can reassure them that we believe that they are lovable, capable people who can cope with the change. We can state our known expectations clearly and simply.

Changing expectations don't have to muddy the waters as long as we're clear that they're changing.

FEBRUARY 21

*Something of vengeance I had tasted for the first time; as
aromatic wine it seemed, on swallowing, warm and racy:
its after-flavour, metallic and corroding, gave me a
sensation as if I had been poisoned.*   —Charlotte Brontë

We think it's going to be sweet. And it ends up
poisoning us. And if we're truthful with ourselves, when our marriages break up there are numerous occasions when we'd like to take revenge.
Those times afford us an opportunity.

One way to take advantage of the opportunity
is to fantasize and turn our fantasies into something useful. We might fantasize that we can rattle
off the perfect French put-down to our ex. And
forget the put-down but decide to study French
anyway. Or we might fantasize that our svelte
new body would drive our ex-husband mad with
jealousy. And forget the mad with jealousy part
but decide to start a new exercise program anyway.

The most useful opportunity revenge offers us
is to look at ourselves. What is it about me that
makes me feel like I want to get even? Am I allowing myself to feel and articulate my feelings of
rejection, my pain, my grief?

*When I feel like taking revenge, I know it's a good
time to take a look at myself.*

FEBRUARY 22

*May you have a lawsuit in which you know you are in the
right.*   —Gypsy curse

In working out conflict with our ex-spouses being right doesn't count for much. In fact, it often
obscures and complicates things. So what if we
are right and they are wrong? Is badgering and
beleaguering the other person going to get us
what we want? Is knowing that I'm right ever
going to resolve the conflict? Am I looking for an
admission that I'm right—and good? And the
other person is wrong and bad?

Starting a conflict resolution from the point of
"I am right and you are wrong" works mightily
against resolution. If we can get past the idea that
the issue is seeing which of us is right and which
is wrong, then perhaps we can begin to resolve
the conflict so that each of us gets some of what
we need in the resolution.

In a dispute, even if we are 100 percent sure
that we are right, the point is to settle the dispute
so that we get whatever it is we need from that
person—from an admission that we are right to
money, changed behavior, better future commu-
nications.

*I can resolve conflicts to get what I need, even if I'm
right.*

FEBRUARY 23

I can only go once again to . . . the planet on which all sentient life was sightless. If nobody could see, other senses would take over, and everybody would get along perfectly well. But if you tried to explain the joy of sight to anybody on that planet you couldn't do it. —Madeleine L'Engle

We can perceive only what our experience has taught us to perceive and with whatever faculties we possess. If we have lived our married life "blind"—to what has gone on around us, to our feelings, to the lack of communication, to the effect of conflict, to the death of commitment—we will not wake up on our first single morning with the ability to see.

If we can't "see" who we are, we will have to rely on other senses. Perhaps we can hear ourselves as we begin to think and talk about what we want our life to be like. We can also perceive through our feelings, the feelings of grief and sorrow, and the first fleeting feelings of joy at being ourselves.

The "blindness" that comes from not paying attention to our perceptions need not be a permanent condition. As we use our other senses to perceive, our sense of sight will likely return to us.

Seeing is perceiving; so is touching, feeling, hearing, and smelling, and I can use one to cultivate the others.

FEBRUARY 24

To want to forget something is to think of it.
                                    —French proverb

When we think we want to forget, think that we would be happier if we could somehow erase all memory of our past, particularly as it relates to our marriage, things pop unbidden into our minds. Sometimes at the oddest time.

Why can't we watch a movie or read a book without having it remind us of a time we were contented and happy with our spouses? Or without contemplating murdering them? Why can't we just forget they ever existed in the first place? The harder we work at destroying our memories —sometimes with the help of drugs, alcohol, spending money, etc.—the more persistent they're likely to become. We'll keep remembering but we won't learn anything.

Or we can work with our memory. Perhaps we will remember what it felt like to have an intimate to share with when we're making a new friend. Memories can entertain us and comfort us. We can learn from our memories or be controlled by them. Whatever we do, they are part of us.

I can't get a divorce from my memories, so I might as well use them constructively.

FEBRUARY 25

*This became a credo of mine . . . attempt the impossible
in order to improve your work.* —Bette Davis

Inspiration makes the impossible possible only
when it is attempted. To attempt what seems impossible
is sometimes indeed to turn it into the
possible. And if the impossible proves truly to be
impossible, the inspiration has, at the least, improved
the possible.

We set out to establish a new household with
our new family configuration, to find a plumber
on Sunday when we've never even called a
plumber before, to endure and perhaps even fleetingly
enjoy our first holiday season without our
ex-spouse. From somewhere, and somehow, the
steps we need to take in order to accomplish the
impossible become clear to us. Once we begin
the attempt, solutions occur to us as if out of the
blue. Ideas crop up faster than spring flowers,
some of them dying as fast as they grow, others
bearing fruit. And suddenly, we have achieved
the impossible.

Accomplishment, the old saying has it, is 1 percent
inspiration and 99 percent perspiration. Yet
without the 1 percent, the voice telling us it might
be done if only we'd try it, the impossible never
does become the possible.

I aspire to be inspired every day.

FEBRUARY 26

One gives people in grief their own way.
—Elizabeth Gaskell

Giving people in grief their own way is not giving *in* to them. It's not letting them harm themselves. It is not giving them advice about what they should do so they'll feel better soon. And it's not a sign of weakness. It is giving them time and space to grieve however they must. It is, in short, nurturing them in their grief.

And when we are grieving the end of our marriage, we ourselves are the people in grief to whom we can give our own way. We can indulge ourselves a little—treating ourselves to a new outfit, a hot bath in the middle of a hard afternoon, a day off work because we need time just to be with ourselves in our grief.

We can give ourselves the time and the space to grieve. And we can give ourselves the gift of finding people who will support and nurture us. We can find people who will be honest enough with us to question us. We can find people who will pamper us, perhaps bring us food or help us clean our linen closet.

When I give myself my grief, I give myself my life.

FEBRUARY 27

There is a shame in naked pain. —Anne Truitt

Do we feel ashamed because we can't alleviate our own naked pain or that of others? Who put us in charge of doing that? Are we ashamed because others might see our pain and turn away from it because they can't alleviate it? Who put them in charge? Are we ashamed of our own pain because it makes us different? Because everybody else seems able to cloak their pain.

We may feel so ashamed about feeling pain because we're single that we try to hide our pain and shame. Maybe we stay in bed all day, refuse to socialize, or even lie about being married. And then we feel more shame. And we tell ourselves to buck up, other people have gotten over this. And then we feel ashamed that we can't hide our pain.

We can break this cycle of pain and shame when we begin to acknowledge it and ourselves. We can acknowledge which of our own actions contributed to our pain and which things are beyond our control. Letting ourselves feel pain lets us begin to release our shame. We begin to feel that we are not bad people because we feel pain or shame.

My pain and my shame are mine to acknowledge and to release.

FEBRUARY 28

Destruction is the first step in conscious change. The old dies so that the new might be born. —Gloria Karpinski

Plants, animals, people, all experience this rule of nature, dying and being reborn, either literally or figuratively. In most climates it's far easier to accept and appreciate this aspect of living in spring than it is in winter.

When we decide to make a conscious change—say, to stop smoking, get out of a bad marriage, move to a new house, take a new job, begin a new friendship—we make that change because we expect new "spring" growth to result from it. And we are almost always surprised that the first thing we feel is negative—the destruction and death of an old way of being. What was present in our lives becomes past.

Losing the familiar is hard, no matter how pleasant the contemplated change may be. Sometimes it's enough to simply remind ourselves to persist, the change will be worth it. And sometimes we get stuck in "winter." We stay there, not being able to let go of the old and dying, not being able to embrace the new and living. At these times, the best thing we can do is to accept this uncomfortable "dying" process.

When I let go of winter in my life, I begin to feel spring.

FEBRUARY 29

We have a choice: to rebel or to recognize our
powerlessness while maintaining our faith.

—Anne Truitt

We are always going to be frustrated in our attempts to make decisions if we don't realize our powerlessness. We are powerless to change the fact that our marriages have ended. We can rebel by denying, scheming, plotting, obsessing in a futile attempt to change reality. We can rebel by attempting to bury the fact under mounds of food, gallons of alcohol, piles of work.

Admitting our powerlessness is the first step to acknowledging our power. When we admit our powerlessness, we take away our need to react in rebellion. We open the way to accepting that there *are* things in our life we *do* have choices about. We open the way to make and implement decisions.

When we're not in control we can give up our fear of making a decision because we might make a bad one. That gives us a lot of power to make decisions about how we want our lives to be, what we want to do next, with whom we want to share our lives.

Realizing my powerlessness to change reality gives
me power and permission to make decisions.

MARCH 1

Women will starve in silence until new stories are created which confer on them the power of naming themselves.
—Sandra Gilbert and Susan Gubar

To suffer in silence, figuratively if not literally to starve, has too often been considered a womanly virtue. We all know women about whom it has been said, "She's a saint. She suffered so much and never complained." No doubt she is and she did. But do we want to suffer in silence? Do we want the stories of our lives forgotten by everyone—including ourselves?

Especially, do we want to be known as poorthing, divorcée, ex-wife of so-and-so? Or do we want to tell the world who we are? Do we want to take charge, claim the power of saying that we are more than someone's ex-something? Do we want to tell the world our story by our thoughts, our actions, our lives?

Power, in its best sense, is taking charge of those things we can take charge of. There are many different ways of telling a story and living a life, different aspects to accent, details to put in, new information to incorporate, events to leave out. Shaping a story, or shaping a life, is an ongoing process that needs to go on every day.

What's my story today?

MARCH 2

*Rosiness is not a worse windowpane than gloomy gray
when viewing the world.*   —Grace Paley

Truth be told, when we're viewing the world, looking out to see what's happening, and how it affects us, clear glass gives the clearest view. Yet to try to look at the world through clear, clean glass all the time is to strive for an objectivity and a perfection that doesn't exist. Besides, nobody wants to spend all her time washing windows.

The realistic thing is to look through clear glass when we can and the rest of the time to make sure we know what color glass we're looking through. We can't force ourselves to look through rose-colored glass when things feel grim and gray. Yet when the glass is rose-colored, when things look prettier, softer, easier than we expected, we don't have to paint the glass gray out of fear things won't stay pretty, soft, or easy.

Through a glass clearly, darkly, or rosily. None of these is intrinsically the best or worst way to view the world. Each reflects an attitude about what we're seeing. The best thing we can do for ourselves is to be aware of our attitude, to accept its current color, and to know the color can change.

*I can wash my windows to the world or paint them
different colors.*

MARCH 3

All serious daring starts from within.   —Eudora Welty

For many of us, *dare* is a word that conjures up childhood power struggles that didn't end well. "I dare you to climb the tree, jump the river, try to hit me in the mouth . . ." If we met the challenge, we ended up doing things we didn't really want to do and often got hurt in the process. If we didn't meet the challenge, we were probably taunted for being stupid or cowardly. And we probably felt ourselves to be both.

Childhood dares give way to their adult counterparts, often couched in terms of somebody else's "shoulds." Trying something new—making new friends, getting out, learning a new skill, finding a new job or a new love interest—because *somebody else* thinks it would be good for us, is likely to get the same result as our childhood dares.

Our self-confidence, if we really listen to it, won't lie to us. It will tell us when we're ready to take on new risks. That doesn't mean the new things won't feel daunting. It means that we'll have an internal conviction that this is the time to try. We'll know we're daring to do something that we really want to do.

I dare myself to be myself.

MARCH 4

A moral choice in its basic terms appears to be a choice that favors survival: a choice made in favor of life.
—Ursula K. Le Guin

We face making a number of choices as we reconstruct our lives after a divorce. Many of them are *big* choices: where to live, who will have custody of the children, how to get a job, how to handle the possibility of new intimate relationships. And we must make these choices at a time when our lives are in upheaval. We're not sure what our lives are, so we're not sure if we're making a choice in favor of life.

And who ever knows that anyway? Choices affect our future, but they're made in the present. No one has yet invented a litmus test that would turn a piece of paper green for a life-affirming choice or red for a life-damaging choice. We can seek advice, consult oracles, or flip coins.

In the end, we've all got to make choices and to rely on our trust in ourselves as we make them. We can make them based on only what we know today, and, if our circumstances change in the future, we can remake them then. We can ask ourselves: Will doing this or that thing enhance my life? Will I feel better if I choose it?

I can make choices that make me feel more alive to my life in the present.

MARCH 5

Protest long enough that you are right, and you will be wrong. —Yiddish proverb

When a relationship ends it often seems important to us to "prove" that we are right. We are the ones wearing the white hats. Our ex-spouses are in the black hats and in the wrong. We may go about telling at great length the world, ourselves, and anyone who will listen that we are right and have been wronged.

Yet by virtue of being human, no one of us is right all the time. When we feel the need to protest that we are right, to defend ourselves as being right, we do well to listen to ourselves. Are we trying to convince ourselves? Are we defending past actions or stances? Are we, indeed, deceiving ourselves, remaking the history of our relationships, so that we can be right?

And why is it so important to be right anyway? What investment do we have in *protesting* that we are right? If we are right, will that make our lives any different? Will it make us happier? Will it make us adjust more easily to no longer being married? Will it change the fact that our relationship ended?

Protesting "I'm right" won't make it true if I'm lying to myself.

MARCH 6

A family unity which is only bound together with a table-cloth is of questionable value.
　　　　　　　　　　　　—Charlotte Perkins Gilman

Eating dinner together has long been high on the list of family self-help hints. The idea seems to be that eating together—or doing anything together —makes for a healthy family. Healthy and happy families *do* do things together. Yet they are not healthy and happy *because* they do.

Divorce changes family unity. And if our family unity couldn't stand some changes, we probably wouldn't be getting a divorce. When we're upset or worried about what's happening to our families, we might ask ourselves what it is we're concerned about.

Divorce gives us the opportunity to look at what our family has been and at where our perceptions didn't meet reality. It also gives us the opportunity to build a family unity based on open, shared communication. We can begin being together in ways that we value, even if they're not ways that magazine experts say build family unity.

If family unity around the dinner table gives me indigestion, it's time to look at what I mean by family unity.

MARCH 7

The efforts which we make to escape from our destiny only serve to lead us into it.   —Ralph Waldo Emerson

Running away almost always leads to running in circles. Running in circles, sooner or later, leads us to running into what we were running away from. We almost always expend more effort trying to escape ourselves and our situations than we would in accepting them.

Sometimes we're so busy running that we don't even know that we're trying to escape or what we're trying to escape. We're separated or divorced. That hurts, sure. But we haven't got time to dwell on that. We have to make new friends, take classes, get involved.

I'm not running to anything when I do all that stuff. I'm running away—or trying to—from my feelings. Essentially I'm trying to run away from myself. Sooner or later, I'm going to get so tired I have to stop running. I may be exhausted, burned out, hitting bottom. I'm here in my destiny anyway, so I might as well take this opportunity to see what it is. I can quit running. I can start feeling.

If I run into the same problems over and over again, I'm probably running around in circles.

MARCH 8

The pain is the aversion. The healing magic is attention.
Properly attended to, pain can answer our most crucial
questions, even those we did not consciously frame.
—Marilyn Ferguson

Healing the pain we feel when our relationships end—the pain of loss, grief, anger—requires that we pay attention to ourselves; nothing less and nothing more. Paying attention means letting ourselves feel the pain, allowing ourselves to have questions without knowing answers, and allowing ourselves to hear answers to questions we did not know we had asked.

The longer we avoid or try to avoid feeling our pain, the longer our healing will take. Healing might mean uncovering pain we've kept secret from ourselves for a long time. Uncovering our pain leads to recovering our capacity to feel. Recovering our capacity to feel leads to discovering new things about our healing selves.

Paying attention to ourselves can be like playing the guessing game of twenty questions. Answers to the first questions in the game lead us to the next questions. Just so, asking ourselves questions about our pain can lead us to discover who we are and what our healing might be.

To know my pain is to know my healing.

MARCH 9

We see the same colors; we hear the same sounds, but not in the same way. —Simone Weil

Today the same sights, sounds, people, work, hurts, and problems are out there. I cannot change them all, and God knows I've tried. Perhaps I've tried to make my ex-spouse see "reason" about any number of things. Perhaps I've tried to change people at work or tried moving to different surroundings so that things will be better. Maybe that only made things worse.

Pain will always be with us. The child within me, my own children, the children of the world will cry. When I accept that I cannot stop all the crying in this world, I begin to hear it differently. I begin to distinguish between cries. It becomes easier to make the changes that will soothe and still some of the cries.

I see my life with new eyes. I do not see a different life. I may, however, when I'm looking at my life with these new eyes which are accepting things I cannot change, see things I never saw before. They probably were there all along. My vision is not perfect. But it is, indeed, different.

Serenity is seeing and hearing things differently with the eyes and ears I've always had.

MARCH 10

. . . it is easy to starve, but it is difficult to stoop.
—Mary Elizabeth Braddon

Getting down to business and getting our needs met is hard work. It often seems easier to let our needs for affection and affirmation go unmet—to starve ourselves—than to get to the bottom of what we need and to figure out how we're going to get it. Starving ourselves this way doesn't require any effort. We just sit back and wait for nature to take its course.

Imagine a hungry worker in a field of potatoes who refuses to stoop. There's no way she's going to get those potatoes without bending over to pick them up. If we're starved for attention, affection, connection with others in our lives, there's no way we're going to get them without reaching out.

Reaching out means figuring out *what* we need and *where* or from whom we can get it. If we don't figure out what we need to nourish ourselves, we'll continue to go hungry. Figuring out where to get our emotional needs met is just as important as knowing that we can't buy bread at the hardware store. Saying "I need . . ." doesn't diminish us. Emotional starvation does.

Picking up what I need to nourish myself is not beneath me.

MARCH 11

> *For my omniscience paid I toll*
> *In infinite remorse of soul.*
> —Edna St. Vincent Millay

Which came first, the attempt to be perfect or the remorse we felt because we weren't perfect? Go back, how many years? To before I was married? To before I left my parents' home? If only I knew then everything that I know now about how my life would unfold, then surely I could figure out a way to avoid doing anything that I would later regret. If I were omniscient, I'd be perfect, and I wouldn't have any regrets. Right?

The time when we try to control the outcome of events, to manipulate the will and action of ourselves and others—because we know what's best —is the time when things are most likely to go wrong, wronger, and wrongest. The harder we try, the wronger they go. Until we hit the bottom and live with profound remorse.

Sometimes our lives get so crowded full of control and remorse that there's little room for anything else. Giving up the need to control, to be omniscient, means we also let go of regret.

When I give up remorse and my attempt to be perfect, I can get on with my life.

MARCH 12

Sometimes I go about pitying myself, and all the time I am being carried on great winds across the sky.
—Ojibway saying

Self-pity is not intrinsically bad. And life goes on while we are pitying ourselves. Meanwhile, we can decide whether we will continue to feel sorry for ourselves or look around us to see where we are being carried.

And we can dress for windy weather. Sometimes the winds of life are cold and cruel. It's time to wrap our faces in a woolen scarf of feeling sorry for ourselves, to wait out the storm. It's just as important, though, to know when to lighten up. If we wrap the heavy scarf too tightly around our eyes, our ears, our hearts, we're likely to miss the change of season.

The winds will carry us through our lives, whether we want to go or not. We'll inevitably be blown through good times and bad. As we are blown, we can curl up tight into a little ball of self-pity, trying to protect ourselves from seeing, hearing, feeling what's going on around us. Or we can face the wind, throwing our arms open to embrace it.

When I'm wrapped up in myself, I can let the wind blow me open.

MARCH 13

*Healthy relationships imply supporting each other, yet
there is no focus on "fixing" the other person.*
—Anne Wilson Schaef

To give support is to lend a shoulder, a hand, an ear, even a word of confrontation, to someone when they want support and ask for it. To try to fix someone is to tell them when they need support, what support they need, and what they should be doing—courtesy of your "support." In short, it is trying to control who they are and what they do. Small wonder that someone we're trying to fix with that kind of support might tell us what to do with it.

When we see someone we love—including ourselves—fall into destructive, unhealthy behavior or make a mistake we've made before, it's tempting to try to fix them and/or their situation. Our reasoning is that we know best. We've either been there or can see better from our outside vantage point. We could save them so much grief.

A person who's being fixed (besides resenting the intrusion) has no opportunity to learn from his or her own experience. They get a fix from us, almost as if they were getting a drug, so they don't have to deal with their lives.

When I feel the need to fix someone, including myself, I can offer support instead.

MARCH 14

Living in the modern world, clothed and muffled, forced to convey our sense of our bodies in terms of remote symbols like walking sticks and umbrellas and handbags, it is easy to lose sight of the immediacy of the human body plan.
—Margaret Mead

The symbols we use to convey our bodies, or what we wish they might be, are so pervasive that they *mean* body to us. These symbols define who we are: rich/poor, young/old, fat/thin, adorned/plain. We all must, of course, go clothed and symboled into the world. We could get locked up for appearing naked at board meetings.

It is the attitude with which we dress that is telling. So many of us have lost sight of what our bodies are. We tend to treat them as if they exist separately from us to present a facade to the world. When we are disconnected from our own bodies, we're disconnected from a major part of ourselves.

To connect ourselves to our bodies we can do things with our bodies. We can dress, exercise, make love. We can let ourselves feel how that feels. We can practice affirming that our bodies are ours and that we have choices about what we do with them.

Who would I be without my body?

MARCH 15

Buried garbage has a way of rising to the surface—and stinking. —Anonymous

Resentment smolders, burns, putrefies. We often use disgusting and/or destructive words to describe what resentment does. When our relationships end we feel very real insult and injury. We resent that our lives are changing. What are we to do with our very real resentments? Cover them up, pretend they don't exist, say it doesn't matter?

Sometimes it feels like the only other choice is to dwell on them, to feed them until they are so big they burst. And that is the only other choice if we perceive that we must react to our hurts. Either we put them behind us prematurely, bury them, and hope they don't stink too much in the future. Or we hold on to them.

When we bury our hurts too soon or cling to them too long, we don't take our resentments apart. We don't find the need that went unmet and caused us to feel this deep injury. We don't look for the truth we might learn about ourselves. When we reflect on our resentments, we can give them up without giving up the lessons they would teach us.

I can recycle my "garbage" and use a lot of it in the creation of something new.

MARCH 16

To make a new world you start with an old one, certainly.
To find a world, maybe you have to lose one.
—Ursula K. Le Guin

*L*ife could well be substituted for *world* in this
quotation. Here I am—the same body, the same
mind, the same me—yet profoundly different.
When we are single again we must make a new
life, beginning with the old one. And, in many
ways, how we make this new life all depends on
what we choose to keep of the old one—what
parts of ourselves and our relationships we'd like
to retain, what we'd like to change. A lot depends
on the beginning.

As we begin to make a new life, do we dwell on
what the past one was? Are we so obsessed with
the lost life that we can't imagine anything new?
Are we so enraptured with the new that we willy-
nilly cast off the old? That we don't stop to take
stock of the parts of ourselves and our old lives
that have served us well? Or do we grieve for it in
such a way that a new beginning emerges out of
the old?

We have all lost something. Yet we can hold it
in our memory if we want, waiting for what it
will show us about our new life.

What in the world will be new for me?

MARCH 17

Sometimes all we can do when the challenge comes and we feel our parts flying to their edges is hold on and wait.
—Gloria Karpinski

When our lives are stable, we're confident that we can name the parts, that we know them, and that they somehow add up to who we are. When we're thrown into a crisis, as we are when we divorce, we lose part of our lives and suddenly we don't know who we are at all. The challenge is to redefine ourselves. But we feel like we're falling or flying apart.

Overnight, it seems we can't rely on our minds, our hearts, our bodies. We may no longer take pleasure in our work, our friends, our children. We may try to work harder and get nothing done; try to make decisions and feel like we're only making mistakes. We may feel stupid and powerless. We may reach the point where we can't do anything but stop and wait.

And as we wait, we begin to get used to our new self. We begin to realize that waiting is not doing nothing. We begin to see a new vision of who we are and to act accordingly. And we begin to realize that underneath and beyond all the changes in our lives, we are becoming ourselves.

When I am powerless to avoid a crisis, I have the power to wait it out.

MARCH 18

*Never doubt that a small group of thoughtful, committed
citizens can change the world: indeed, it's the only thing
that ever has.*   —Margaret Mead

Most of us find it easier to give support than to
accept it. We may know from experience that a
small group of committed people can change
something—build a day-care center, reroute a
freeway, help an elderly person. We freely give
our support—money, time, and effort. Yet when
our lives need to be a better place, we somehow
fail to believe that there might be support for us.

Perhaps our support system was divided and
conquered in that messy, but mostly inevitable,
splitting of friends and family. Perhaps, having
"learned" that we can't rely on the support we
thought we had, we've decided to go it alone.
Perhaps we've concluded that because our relationship failed, we are no longer worthy of support.

It's time to look for a small group of committed
people, among which I can count myself. I can
support myself. And part of the way I can do that
is to look for help among my friends and family,
to ask for it, and to believe that it will make a
difference. Together we can make a difference in
my life as well as in the world.

Regarding support, both a lender and a borrower be.

MARCH 19

Love can't be pinned down by a definition, and it certainly can't be proved, any more than anything else important in life can be proved. —Madeleine L'Engle

We tend to want love to be pinned down, defined, and most of all proved. We tend to make love a struggle. We may know with our heads that love can't be defined or proved, yet we continue to try to live our lives as if it might not be so.

Loving me means that you will—fill in the blank—not spend time with others, make me feel good, put my needs first, mow the lawn and empty the garbage, etc., etc. If you truly loved me, then you would—fill in the blank—not leave me, make love more often, do what I want you to, etc., etc. One way to approach understanding love, which can't be defined or proven, is to turn from "you, if/then" statements to "I, and" statements.

I love myself and I will—fill in the blank—take care of myself by exercising more, let myself have some time to just be. I love you and I hope—fill in the blank—to wash your socks, to live with you in conflict and in harmony, that you love me. None of these "I, and" statements attempts to limit love by defining it or proving it.

I love myself and others, and though I can't define it or prove it, I can do it.

MARCH 20

> *And all the loveliest things there be*
> *Come simply, so, it seems to me.*
> —Edna St. Vincent Millay

Simplicity is simply lovely, if only we can achieve it. Getting divorced never seems simple. There are things to take care of: Who's going to live where? Who gets what? There are legal issues, papers to file, custody arrangements. There are countless and seemingly endless explanations to make to friends, families, coworkers, not to mention bankers, doctors, and utility companies.

And then there are feelings—guilt, recrimination, anger, sorrow, pain, joy, relief, grief—to sort out. How could we see any of this as simple? In sum total, if we try to deal with everything at once, it's not simple. It's overwhelming.

It's time to let simplicity simply come to us. Maybe the simple pleasure of putting our feet up for fifteen minutes while we drink a cup of tea and nurse our wounds. Maybe the simple pleasure of seeing a ray of sunshine break through a gray, rainy afternoon. Maybe feeling the relief of knowing we can deal with complexity by not trying to do everything at once.

Keeping my life simple means doing one thing at a time.

MARCH 21

> *Can I hope, though I am burnt,*
> *That spring will come again?*
>
> —Lady Ise

Spring, the season of the year, of course, comes again, inexorably, whether we hurt or not, and whether we notice it or not. It is the impulse to hope, perhaps vague and surely elusive, that allows us to know in the midst of our darkest winter that we might again feel an internal spring as well as notice an external one.

After we suffer a major loss, it's natural for life to seem hopeless for a time. And hope often first comes to us as a question: Won't my pain ever diminish? After what I've been through, how can I ever be happy again? And finally, we may be able to ask, can I hope that spring will come again for me? Just as the world might not look spring-like when the calendar announces the first day of spring, we might not notice the first signs of hope in our life.

We can't manufacture hope through an effort of will. What we *can* do, when we hear our inner voice asking the questions, is to pay attention, to nurture the seedling hope, and to let it grow within us.

Hope can move me from question to conviction that spring will come into my life again.

MARCH 22

> *Futile the winds*
> *To a heart in port.*
>
> —Emily Dickinson

How do we recognize that our hearts are in port, that we're at home with ourselves, when the winds of our lives have been blowing everything topsy-turvy? Whether we were happily or unhappily coupled for two years or twenty, we felt àt home in our lives, safe from the upsetting winds of change, used to the good and the bad.

Visualize your heart—your truest, strongest, most vulnerable self and the beautiful lump of muscle that nestles in your chest, working nonstop to keep you alive—safe inside the port of your body. If my heart is safe, beating away, making me alive and making me who I am, what can hurt it? Can anything if I keep it safe in my own home port?

Now visualize the port. Where is it? What does it look like? How is it different from a port that might have kept me safe yesterday? last year? when I was a child? What do I want my home port to be? What home do I want to create for my heart?

I trust that I can create a safe home for my heart, my truest, most vulnerable self.

MARCH 23

It appears that even the different parts of the same person do not converse among themselves, do not succeed in learning from each other what are their desires and their intentions. . . . —Rebecca West

"And, so," I said to myself, "when's the last time you and I sat down over a cup of tea for a catch-up chat? What have we been doing lately? Learned anything new? How's it going?" Yes, we can talk with ourselves without being taken away by the people in white jackets.

The stereotype is that people who talk to themselves have no one else to talk to. Yet if we can't talk with ourselves—make clear our own goals or aspirations, just check in—how can we expect to be able to make anything clear to anyone else? Communication with ourselves—or with others—is give and take, talk *and* listen. Without the talk part, we can't express what we want, need, feel, think. And without the listen part, we won't have feedback—from ourselves or others—to know whether we're making ourselves clear.

Listening may well be the hardest part of communicating. And listening to ourselves may be the most important part.

I can do myself the courtesy of talking and listening to me.

MARCH 24

A lot of what appear to be feelings are really just programmed emotional reactions. I might deeply feel that forgiveness is what I want to give, but when an old injury is stimulated, I might have a spontaneous reaction of anger and self-justification.   —Gloria Karpinski

In order to feel what we're feeling and to learn to trust our feelings to guide us, we need to figure out what it is we are truly feeling. After the breakup of a relationship hurts can accumulate faster than we can count them. And our tendency often is to react to them swiftly and with blind fury.

Getting beyond that fury to the "real" emotion gets us beyond a programmed reaction. Discovering what's under the anger is *not* enumerating what he did to me. It *is* looking at what I'm really feeling—hurt, sad, threatened.

We may know in our heads that we want to forgive past hurts. However, forgiveness is not something we can will, particularly while we're using anger to mask our other feelings. To feel forgiveness we have to make room in our hearts to feel what we are truly feeling.

I am not a computer that reacts the same way every time a button is pushed, and I can get beyond reaction to feeling.

MARCH 25

If you're never scared or embarrassed or hurt, it means you never take chances. —Julia Sorel

By the time we reach adulthood, most of us have accepted that we can do certain things even if we risk getting hurt or are afraid of the result. Some of us even know that when we face our fears and risk vulnerability, the result is positive, even when we're embarrassed. Yet many of us are afraid to risk it. We'd rather be dead than mortified.

And it feels silly to admit that we're afraid of being embarrassed. So instead we pretend. We pretend that we know things we don't know. We pretend we never make silly mistakes. We exhort ourselves (and maybe our children): "Don't be embarrassed to be who you are. There's nothing to be embarrassed about." If there's nothing to be embarrassed about, why are we so all-fired eager to avoid embarrassment?

When we take chances and new action, we will make mistakes. And when we make mistakes, we will feel embarrassed, scared, and hurt. If we wish to avoid those feelings entirely, the net result will be that we do nothing.

I'm embarrassed to admit I don't remember the last time I did something silly and allowed myself to feel embarrassed.

MARCH 26

In contrast to revenge . . . the act of forgiving can never be predicted; it is the only reaction that acts in an unexpected way and thus retains, though being a reaction, something of the original character of action.
—Hannah Arendt

When we react, we often feel victimized and without control. When we act, we feel that we have some control over the circumstances of our lives. If we constantly react to others' demands, whether they're actual or imagined, we can get ourselves into a place in which we literally have no energy left to act. All we can do is to react some more. We have set up a reactionary cycle for our lives that produces anger and resentment.

At the end of a relationship there is often a lot to forgive—others' actions or attitudes *and* our own. If we are in a reactionary cycle, we need to break out of it before we can forgive anything.

And forgiveness, truly sought, can be the thing that helps us break the cycle. Forgiveness is both reaction and creative act, which allows us to move beyond what we're forgiving.

I can forgo the cycle of revenge for giving myself and others a chance at living.

MARCH 27

Custom controls the sexual impulse as it controls no other.
—Margaret Sanger

With the conflicting messages of right/wrong, free/repressed, responsible/irresponsible, and with the added risk of unwanted pregnancies and sexually transmitted diseases, it seems impossible to figure out what we might do about sexual relationships beyond our marriages. And we threaten our own lives and well-being if we do not make the attempt.

When we become single again, we must face the question of sex. No one can face it for us. And in that respect, facing the question squarely can become for us an aid to facing our own ultimate responsibility for all our decisions and actions.

Whether we decide to begin a new sexual relationship or not, we will also, no matter what our age or body type, face the issue of our own perceived attractiveness to others. Facing that question offers an opportunity to ask: Am I depending on a sexual relationship to prove I'm attractive? Am I looking for a sexual relationship to affirm me in ways not related to sex?

Sex is a complicated question, informed by complicated custom. I can figure out what's right for me, and I don't have to do it all at once.

MARCH 28

I love my past. I love my present. I'm not ashamed of what I've had, and I'm not sad because I no longer have it.
—Colette

If I love my past and my present, by definition, I accept myself. We cannot accept ourselves without accepting our past and our present and without reconciling ourselves to our losses. When we're grieving the end of our marriages, especially the good times, it's hard to see how we might ever say, "I'm not sad because I no longer have it."

Saying that we're not sad because we no longer have it doesn't mean we don't remember having it. It doesn't even mean that we don't remember being sad that we don't have it. It means accepting that we no longer have it. Acceptance takes time. It takes experiencing the sorrow. It takes letting go of any shame we have of losing what we had.

There's no right or wrong way to experience our sorrow and let it go. Letting go of the sorrow makes room for us to love our present. We can't hold on to past sorrow and truly love our present. When we can say that we love our present, we know that we've let go of our sorrow.

Losing my sorrow can mean finding my self.

MARCH 29

Every wish is like a prayer to God.
                    —Elizabeth Barrett Browning

Wishing our lives would change, we know, won't make it so. Particularly if our wishing is all about wanting things to go back to the way they were. Or fantasizing about what would have happened if we had done things differently. Yet when we're in the throes of pain and grief over the end of our relationship, we do wish our lives would change and we do wish we would feel better.

When we make a wish or a prayer to God, we release it. We say out loud what we want. And we let go of our expectation of controlling when and how we might get it. A wish or a prayer like this is not a wish to go back in time. It's not a wish to take back things done and said or left undone and unsaid. It's not a wish to control other people. It's a cry from our hearts.

When we make a wish from our hearts that things will be different, that we will feel different, that we will get over our grief, we can listen to it at the same time we release it. In truly listening to it, we begin to know our heart's desire. In releasing it to God, we give ourselves the chance to gain our heart's desire.

Wishing is a way of listening to my heart's desire.

MARCH 30

Paddle with and not against the current.

—Amity Buxton

When we paddle against the current of our lives, we try to exercise our willpower to control where we are and where we're going. We're certainly not open to where the current might take us. We may, for instance, make a list with a timetable attached. We're not so naive as to think we can feel better on schedule. But we tell ourselves if we get our legal work all done, get this divorce behind us on a time schedule, then we can begin to live with the current.

And things go wrong: our ex-spouse doesn't cooperate, our lawyer doesn't call us back, our settlement gets backed up in court. And we get a sore back from paddling against the current to our specific destination.

We don't want to change destinations. We want to get this taken care of. But we can give up going against the current of time and trying to control other people; we can go with the flow of getting it done when it gets done. In the meantime, we can continue to live out each day going with the flow, and seeing where the flow takes us.

Paddling with the current can take me where I want to go and to some new, unexpected places as well.

MARCH 31

When Sleeping Beauty wakes up she's almost 50 years old.
—Maxine Kumin

And, finally, she gets to live her life. Of course, in the story, Sleeping Beauty is nowhere near fifty years old. Time has stopped while she slept her enchanted sleep. When we get divorced, we may feel like we're waking up to ourselves. We may have been sleeping somehow, but the world and time didn't stop while we were asleep.

Now that we know we can be awake to life, let's do it. Let's not dwell on what might have been if we'd not been asleep in a marriage all those years, if we had put our time and energy into being who we wanted to be. Fifty—or forty or thirty or sixty—or any age I am is a fine time to start my life.

Did Sleeping Beauty know all that time had passed? What did she think about? Why did she choose to go off with a prince rather than looking about at the world around her, seeing what was going on, grieving, maybe, for the time she lost? That's the beauty of not being Sleeping Beauty. We aren't limited, at any age, to sleeping until the prince comes. Nor do we have to go with him if we don't want to.

Let me wake up at my age to the possibilities in my life now.

APRIL 1

Humor is tragedy revisited. —Phyllis Diller

The end of a marriage always has its tragic aspects. For some of us it feels like our life is over—the ultimate tragedy. Being able to laugh at ourselves and some of our mistakes or misfortunes doesn't make them less real or less tragic.

Yet when we can laugh, even a little bit, at the rotten turns our life takes, we begin to see things from a new perspective. As time goes by, we can look back at the high drama of our tragedy. Now it seems funny that our utilities were cut off because our ex-spouse signed up for service at his new place. It becomes a bureaucratic joke rather than a patriarchal plot against us.

Sometimes we have to go looking for the humor in our lives. And sometimes we just trip over it in the darkness of our tragedy. We might feel like Laurel and Hardy trying to do a simple household repair for the first time by ourselves. Later, in the recounting, it's funny how the bookcase we worked so hard to put up fell down just as we put the last book in it. What was infuriating at the time becomes a silent movie pratfall, and we can't help laughing at ourselves.

Today is a good day to look for the humor in a situation I thought I wouldn't live through.

APRIL 2

Speaking of life . . . when the cards are stacked against you, reshuffle. —Katherine Schoen

We only get dealt one hand at a time in this life. If we're sitting at the table with cards that don't work for us anymore—with old ways of communicating, with feelings of bitterness, resentment, or being trapped—we have to turn them in or throw them away before we can go on.

Letting go is the first part of starting over. One way to begin this is to visualize the things we want to let go of in our new life. We might even write them down on cards. Then, one by one, when we're ready, we can tear them up in little pieces and throw them away. Literally or figuratively, anytime we need to let go, we can make a card and throw it away.

As we throw away the cards we don't want to play with anymore, we can create new ones. Each new card can help us start over in an aspect of our lives. If the old card said, "I'm trapped in a relationship that doesn't let me grow," the new one might say, "I can leave this relationship behind me and begin to have a growing relationship with myself." One by one, I can replace the old cards with new ones that suit me now.

Letting go lets me start over.

APRIL 3

*When anger spreads through thy breast, guard thy tongue
from barking idly.* —Sappho

When my tongue barks like a dog in anger, I'm
likely to hurt others—*and sure to hurt myself*—
which seems a good reason for not barking like a
dog, screaming like a banshee, or kicking like a
mule. It doesn't, however, seem like a good reason for not finding a way to express my anger.

We've all heard lots of *don't* messages about anger: "Don't blow off steam idly." "Don't make
threats unless you intend to follow through."
"Don't shout, hit, kick, bite, scream."

Anger is a normal, human, and understandable
emotion. Traditional sayings about anger aren't
designed to stop us from feeling anger. They're
designed to keep our expression of anger within
bounds. They fall short, though, in helping us figure out how to express anger, since they only tell
us what not to do. Perhaps it's time to invent
some *do* messages about anger: Get mad and get
what you need. Anger is nothing to be afraid of.
Anger creates energy I can focus. Anger is a great
motivator.

*Feeling my anger won't hurt me, and it might just
help me focus my angry energy on positive changes.*

APRIL 4

The word crisis *originates in the Greek word* krines,
*meaning "the parting of the ways." In the wake of a major
crisis we nearly always part ways with our past view of
reality—whether we do it willingly or kicking and
screaming.* —Gloria Karpinski

Divorce or separation is a literal parting of the
ways and a real crisis. Living with someone, happily or unhappily, is a concrete and intimate reality. When that reality changes, we are suddenly
experiencing a different reality.

Whether we welcome or resist our new reality,
it is a major shift in our lives. And it appears to us
in numerous ways. We are surprised when we
wake up in the morning—alone. We may grieve
when we have news—good or bad—and no one
at home to share it with. Or maybe we rejoice in
being able to lie in bed all day on a Saturday reading a novel.

Once the "parting of the ways" has sunk in, we
begin to make a new "connecting of the ways."
We might say we're beginning to feel like ourselves again. What we are beginning to do is to
live in our new reality.

*Parting with yesterday's reality lets me connect with
today's.*

APRIL 5

> *Let us not burden our remembrance with*
> *A heaviness that's gone.*
>
> —William Shakespeare

Remembering and regretting are not twin sisters. We can have one without the other. In fact, our regret can burden our memory to the extent that we don't remember. We can spend so much time and energy regretting how things turned out that we don't remember how things really were.

After our marriage ends we all have regrets. We might spend a lot of time living over certain times and scenes in our heads, regretting that we didn't do something—anything—to make the outcome different. We might get stuck regretting that our marriage ended. We might get stuck regretting that we ever got married in the first place.

As part of recovering ourselves after our marriage ends, we can meet face-to-face with our regrets. Facing our regrets and naming them leads to accepting them. We can give up the burden of regret and give in to remembering, without judging, what our marriage was really like.

Regretting what might have been dooms me to repeat it. Remembering what was allows me to go on.

APRIL 6

Isolation means separating an idea from its emotional content so that, while the memory of the unwanted impulse remains, all of the feelings connected with it are pushed out of consciousness. —Judith Viorst

It's not very far from isolation to desolation. Both words mean separated from others, alone. Isolation's root is *island*. To live in isolation is to live on an island, separated from others because we're separated from our feelings. To be separated from our feelings is to be alone in desolation.

When we separate from our partners, we don't have to separate from our feelings. Separation makes us feel sad, angry, depressed. We feel grief and loss. Nobody likes to feel these things, so maybe we try to get rid of our feelings—deny them, rationalize them, separate ourselves from them. Eventually, even though we remember the event that made us feel the way we do, we have no feelings about it.

If we try to live by isolating ourselves from feelings of pain and loss, we soon lose our feeling blueprint. We don't feel pain, but we don't feel anything else either. If we try to bury our feelings, isolate ourselves from them, instead of feeling better, we feel desolate.

Separation from my partner doesn't have to mean isolation from myself.

APRIL 7

Intimacy is a process; this process is the same whether we are talking about a paired permanent relationship or a garden of intimate friendships . . . At times it is important to value our "insignificant others" and recognize that we do have intimacy even if it is not sexual-genital intimacy. —Marilyn Mason

One of the biggest losses we face as our marriages end is the loss of intimacy: nobody to talk with about the dog's latest escapades, the boss's unreal behavior, the absurdity of the daily news. No one to share breakfast with, to watch TV with, or to complain to about the garbage not being taken out.

As the relationship ends we need to find new ways of fulfilling our needs for intimacy, for sharing the details of our lives with others. No one person is going to fulfill all our needs.

One way to make intimate connections is to inventory who lives in our garden of intimate friendships—who we can call for what. And then to call them, because intimacy doesn't just happen. We must tend the garden. That means connecting with others, sharing conversation and activities that reveal ourselves to others and allow them the opportunity to do the same.

I can reach out and recognize the people I have intimate connections with.

APRIL 8

To jealousy, nothing is more frightful than laughter.
—Françoise Sagan

We know in our heart of hearts that jealous people are not nice people. We know that feeling jealous isn't going to get us anything. We also know that jealous people are mean-spirited and small-minded. There's no way we're going to own up to being mean and small.

And we're afraid that we'll be consumed with jealousy for somebody else's relationships, possessions, job, life. How many of us have wished our best friend ill because she has a new boyfriend? How many of us would admit that feeling? As far as we're concerned, jealousy is no laughing matter.

It's not easy to see the humor in our jealousy. To do that we have to spend enough time feeling our jealousy to get to know what it's about. We can't laugh at a joke we don't understand. We can't laugh at our jealousy if we're denying or repressing it. When we can see humor in wishing that our friend with the good skin would wake up with green splotches or our tall, thin sister would get squashed into a shorter, wider person, we can see what our jealousy is really about—like maybe how we feel about our skin and size.

I jealously guard my ability to laugh at my jealousy.

APRIL 9

Can you do this? Lose control and let wild mind take over? It is the best way to write. To live too.
—Natalie Goldberg

Sometimes the only way to gain control is to lose control. The way to lose control is to begin with three little words that generally take a bad rap: I give up. I can't make things turn out the way I want them to—or think I want them to. So I'll just let go and see what happens next.

What generally happens next is that our inner resources take over. Whatever we name as the source and the power of these resources—God, the universe, our unconscious selves—we all have them. Giving up is simple; it is not easy. It takes practice. And it is a practice to live by. The more we do it, the easier it becomes, and the more we want to do it.

Giving up is not quitting. It's not saying, "I can't concentrate on my work and get anything done since my divorce. So I just won't do this work anymore." It's saying, "I give up. I can't do my work the way I used to. So I'm open to finding a new way of doing my work." Giving up can be done once a day or twenty times a day.

Giving up is simply giving in to whatever might open up.

APRIL 10

*The tears . . . streamed down, and I let them flow as
freely as they would, making of them a pillow for my
heart. On them it rested.*   —Saint Augustine

Tears are undervalued. We think they don't accomplish anything, and we don't tend to like
things that are "useless." Or we think they accomplish things through subterfuge and coercion,
as in "she cried until she got what she wanted."
So many of us, when we're inclined to cry about
something, think we ought to do something—almost anything—instead.

Yet sometimes there's nothing to do but cry.
And if we let ourselves cry enough tears we will
begin to feel the comforting effect of tears. A pillow for our heart wouldn't really need to be very
big. Yet it takes a lot of feathers to fill even a small
pillow. And it takes a lot of tears to take up the
space of even one feather.

It may take a lot of tears to support a tired
heart. And it makes our hearts even more weary
to try to stem the flow of tears. Crying relieves us.
To cry freely, without expecting ourselves or anyone else to stop the flow of tears, is a gift we'd do
well to accept.

Crying can make my heart grow freer.

APRIL 11

The universe is made up of stories, not atoms.
—Muriel Rukeyser

Ultimately and literally, the universe is not made up exclusively of either. Every atom has its component parts, as does every story. Our stories are made up of relationships and their changing nature. We understand our lives through the stories (hopefully true ones) we tell about them.

There are stories and there are interpretations. Consider the story of Eve. Told from different perspectives, that story becomes the rationale for thinking women are weaker than men, the story of a woman who made a mistake trying to achieve her full potential, the story of a man who listened to a woman and lived to regret it, the story of what happens to people who try to be perfect. And that's just a bare beginning.

When we tell our story, we are making sense of what happened in our marriage. The perspective we have on that story is likely to change as we move through grieving the relationship, relief that it's over, regret that it didn't end sooner—or that it ended at all. Looking at our own story from differing perspectives gives us a perspective on who we are now in our lives.

Telling my story helps me write my life.

APRIL 12

. . . In rejecting secrecy I had also rejected the road to cynicism. —Catherine Marshall

Cynics don't believe what they see or hear on the surface and do believe that other people, motivated by base self-interest, manipulate the truth by telling lies *and* by keeping secrets. Keeping secrets from ourselves and others can easily lead to cynicism.

A secretive and cynical life is complicated. It takes a lot of time and energy to second-, third-, and fourth-guess everything and everybody—especially ourselves. The cynic's life is a bumpy road. Cynics need to constantly stop to lift up this rock or that cobblestone to try to figure out what's underneath it. Cynics dig deeply into lots of holes, trying to find out what's *really* there. Cynics go off on circuitous routes on their way to uncovering secrets.

Revealing secrets to ourselves and others takes courage and belief that we or they can handle it. People who don't keep secrets engender trust and honesty. If we don't keep secrets, people in our lives are less inclined to keep secrets from us.

I believe in myself enough not to keep secrets.

APRIL 13

> *There is so much good in the worst of us,*
> *And so much bad in the best of us,*
> *That it ill behooves any of us*
> *To find fault with the rest of us.*

—Anonymous

Surely we've known this from our cradles. No one is all good—perfect—or all bad. Finding fault is finding the bad, pointing it out, laying the blame. Finding fault by laying blame is expecting perfection. Expecting perfection, whether from ourselves or others, is a fault.

And what if "us" is me? There is so much good in me and so much bad in me, when I'm at my worst and when I'm at my best, that there's really no benefit to me in blaming myself. When we acknowledge that we are good and that we can do things that are bad, things that hurt ourselves and others, we are acknowledging that we're human. Ditto when we do bad things or when we do things that don't turn out the way we hoped.

I and me, we and us. We can acknowledge what is bad in me and in us. We can acknowledge what is good in me and in us. We can point out, without laying blame, what is bad.

If I lay aside blame, I can find the good—in myself and others.

APRIL 14

The real voyage of discovery consists not in seeking new landscapes but in having new eyes.   —Marcel Proust

Discovery depends on seeing what's in front of our eyes. Sometimes a change of scenery helps us see something new. A change of scenery can be large—moving across the country, taking a new job. Or it can be small—moving to a different chair in the same room of our lives, for instance.

The problem with moving across country to make new discoveries is that very often we find ourselves seeing or discovering the very same things. If we saw ourselves as dependent victims in our original circumstances, and if all we do is change the circumstances, we're likely, after a while, to see ourselves that same way.

If we can move to a different vantage point in our current circumstances, we might indeed discover something. Perhaps we'll discover that what we have seen as dependent behavior is what makes us a good friend because it lets us really connect with others. By simply looking at the room of our life now from a different angle, we might see a whole new way to arrange it.

Looking in the mirror at who I am and where I am today may lead to some surprising discoveries.

APRIL 15

In this world nothing is certain but death and taxes.
                                    —Benjamin Franklin

Filing a tax return as a single person is a mile-stone. Here we are, maybe for the first time in years, checking "single" in the appropriate box on that ubiquitous statement. It's a small thing. And no matter how messy or painless our divorce, it took a lot of adapting on our part to get to this day. That's certain.

Here we are alive, on tax day, having survived a divorce and who knows what else—one day at a time. Adaptability on a daily basis, perhaps more than anything else, is what's required of us as we go through a separation and divorce. Every single part of our lives is affected—from the legal work we must attend to, to how we feel when we go out socially as a single person.

We've lived until tax day. That's also certain. We're still breathing, aren't we? This might be a good day to spend some time with ourselves re-counting some of the particular adaptations we've made, to go ahead and pat ourselves on the back for making our own uncertain way into a new life with precious few certainties.

I hold with certainty my ability to adapt to an uncertain life one day at a time.

APRIL 16

A nation is not conquered until the hearts of its women are on the ground. Then it is done, no matter how brave its warriors or how strong their weapons.

—Cheyenne proverb

A heart lying exposed on the ground is a heart in despair. If our hearts sink to that point, it is likely that nothing short of a miracle can bring them back, no matter how strong our internal warriors are and with what weapons of intellect, reason, and emotion we fight. Yet, truly, our hearts are strong and resilient. Bringing a heart down is at least as difficult as raising a heart up.

When we face grief, sadness, loss of our identity and self-worth at the end of our marriages, we may well feel as if our hearts are falling to the ground. We can't reason ourselves out of our feelings. We can make sure that we aren't our own worst enemies, that we don't contribute to our own heart's demise by denying our own self-worth.

Even though we feel our hearts falling, they are unlikely to hit the ground as long as we stay with our feelings and use our resources to build ourselves up, and as long as we trust in our hearts' strength and resilience.

I have resources to prevent my heart from falling.

APRIL 17

*There is a vitality, a life force, an energy, a quickening,
that is translated through you into action, and because
there is only one of you in all time, this expression is
unique. And if you block it, it will never exist through any
other medium and will be lost.* —Martha Graham

We don't have to be creative artists to express
our true selves in action. All we have to do is be
true to ourselves. Every day we're alive we have
hundreds of opportunities to take self-expressive
action. Many or most of them are what we call
"small"—fixing dinner, arranging flowers, working on a report, comforting a child, taking a walk.

Blocking self-expressive action is not doing the
things we want and need to do. Or it is doing
them without investing anything of ourselves in
them. Or it is doing them without being present
to ourselves and the activity we're engaged in. Or
it is not knowing who this "I" is who is doing
them, looking over our shoulders to see if we are
doing them right.

To act with self-expression is to be alive to the
present moment—nothing more, nothing less. It's
knowing who we are. It's knowing what we're
doing. It's knowing that no one else could be doing it just this way. It's doing what we're doing to
the best of our knowledge and ability.

I'm the only one who can act like myself.

APRIL 18

You leave me much against my will.
                                    —Edna St. Vincent Millay

If willing or not willing had much to do with the endings of marriages, they'd probably never end. (Or more likely, they'd never begin.) Acts of will-power are attempts to control and have little to do with the weaving and connecting or the tearing and unraveling that make or end a marriage.

However, if we look at will as "willing," as in: I am willing to consider, to be open to the possibility of, to explore, we may discover two things. First, what we "will" in that way will begin to come true for us. And second, we will discover our true will. When we are willing, we don't force things to happen (or not happen). We create a climate in which things might happen in our lives. We are open to exploring.

When we are willing ourselves to create what we want in life, we are more likely to be unwilling to create situations that put us in a position contrary to our heart's desire. And when those "bad" things do happen to us, we can use our process of willing or unwilling to take what comes and make what we will out of it.

I am unwilling to give up my will to arrange my life the way I want it to be.

APRIL 19

The more we fight resistance, the tighter the knots get. But we can also choose to see it as a necessary and meaningful part of the process of change. —Gloria Karpinski

Suppose you've decided to make a change—to move to a new house, for example. You want to do it. But you must do some things first—clean the garage, contact a realtor, find a new place. You may begin this change with enthusiasm. Then days, weeks, maybe even months go by. You are meeting resistance.

Do you tough it out? Try to force yourself to get everything done? Decide to move to a place that isn't what you wanted? Become a trapped victim of circumstances? Fight and wrangle with your resistance as it becomes a tighter and stronger knot no matter how hard you pull?

We have all encountered our own deep resistance to change. Resistance is part of change. Instead of seeing resistance as our enemy, we can start to look for what our resistance is teaching us. Maybe this truly isn't the right time to move. Maybe the resistance forces us to consider creative options. Or maybe our resistance is just asking us to slow down and allow ourselves time.

I can use my resistance to make change when I acknowledge that resistance is part of change.

APRIL 20

*You need only claim the events of your life to make
yourself yours.* —Florida Scott-Maxwell

To recover one's self is to make one's self one's
own—an especially apt definition for recovering
after a divorce. We may have spent years trying to
be someone we weren't in order to live in a relationship. It may have gotten to the point that
we couldn't get what we wanted out of it because
we no longer knew who we were and what we
wanted.

One common way of not claiming the events in
our lives is to keep them secret—from others, yes,
and from ourselves. If every time something bad
happened in our marriage we wrote it off to bad
luck, bad behavior on our spouse's part, bad tim-
ing, bad anything, we were not claiming the
events in our lives. If we were not admitting what
we were doing and what our spouse was doing,
we were keeping secrets—from each other and
from ourselves.

Claiming events is saying, "Yes, this happened
to me." It's owning up to what happened without
trying to assess blame. It's refusing to keep secrets
about ourselves from ourselves and others.

*When I refuse to keep myself secret, I begin to know
who I am.*

APRIL 21

*If we can let go of asking—just for the moment, and as
soon as we realize we're doing it—"Why is this happening
to me?" we can save ourselves a great deal of anxiety.*
                                        —Gloria Karpinski

Worrying about why something is happening to
me is a good antidote to feeling and discovering
what really is happening in the present moment.
When I ask "Why?" I'm reaching into the past for
answers. "What's going to happen next?" often
follows hot on the heels of "Why?" Asking
"next" questions is another way of worrying.

We can be Ms. Why What-Else driving down
the freeway. Worried that we might not be able to
change lanes quickly enough to keep up with the
flow, we ask why and conclude. . . . If we don't
change lanes soon we'll miss our exit. Here we
are, in this freeway moment, worrying about the
past and future. And we don't see the truck bearing down on us.

Or we can ask present-tense questions: Where
am I? What am I doing now? How do I feel about
it? We can do what we are doing when we are
doing it, without worrying about why or what
next. If we do, we'll probably see the truck.

*Living in each present moment relieves my anxiety
and might save my life.*

A P R I L   2 2

Certain gestures made in childhood seem to have eternal repercussions. —Anaïs Nin

Things learned in childhood stay with us to help or hinder us as we make our way in the world. Generosity, independence, friendship learned in childhood can inform the adult as equally and as profoundly as withdrawal, denial, and withholding love. As adults, we can choose how the repercussions will echo.

We can, for example, use memories of our childhood accomplishments to choose how we work now to get maximum satisfaction. Or maybe we learned: If you work hard, people will love you. In that case, we may want to change the message. We can remind our inner child that she doesn't have to please others by taking on projects.

Looking within can help us discover the woman we are and the woman we are becoming. This is a process of remembering, choosing, and transforming. It involves giving ourselves permission to remember as much as we can; it involves listening carefully to ourselves; and it involves choosing what we will do.

I will always possess what I learned in childhood, and I can choose what to do with my possessions.

APRIL 23

The only thing that makes life possible is permanent,
intolerable uncertainty: not knowing what comes next.
—Ursula K. Le Guin

There seem to be two kinds of people: those who
are sure the future is going to be a lot better than
the present and those who are sure that it's going
to be a lot worse. The truth is, of course, that it's
going to be both better and worse. And we're not
going to know which it is until the future becomes the present.

Not knowing what's coming next keeps us
around to see what it might be or keeps us from
running because of what it might be. Worrying
about the future won't change it. Waiting for the
future won't bring it on any faster. Neither makes
us any surer of what the future will bring.

So we might as well do what's possible—which
is to live in the present. And we might find after
all, when we're living only because things will be
perfect soon or living in the fear that they'll only
get worse, that we are better off living with what
happens as it happens.

Paying attention to the present allows me to live
with the knowledge of an uncertain future—
especially if I think I'm certain about it.

APRIL 24

The ability to simplify means to eliminate the unnecessary so the necessary may speak.   —Hans Hoffman

What can we get rid of? The berating voice that tells us we'd probably still be married if we were prettier, smarter, more tolerant? The adult voice that tells us life is too serious to waste time having fun? The scared voice that tells us if we don't take risks we don't get hurt? These unnecessary messages are brought to us by ourselves.

We don't want to hear these messages. Yet we don't want to get rid of or deny a part of ourselves. Simplicity is not denial. And, presumably, we can find the value in these messages. We can assure ourselves that we *will* honor anything we have to say to ourselves, but that we can't do it all at once. One voice at a time, please.

Perhaps the voice that says we'll never get everything done perfectly is cautioning us that we have unreal expectations of ourselves. Hearing that message could simplify our lives. So could hearing that we know there's a time to be serious and a time to have fun. So could acknowledging that we care enough about ourselves to care whether or not we get hurt.

Living simply is listening to what I say and how I say it.

APRIL 25

Now that this growth and expansion has started I am
unable to stop it. I feel no boundaries within myself, no
walls, no fears. Nothing holds me back from adventure. I
feel mobile, fluid. . . .   —Anaïs Nin

By the end of April, early flowers are blooming,
or at least poking green sprouts through the soil.
Ice has melted and rivers flow in their fullness.
Leaves burst forth overnight. The world is grow-
ing, pushing against the boundaries of winter.
Adventure is in the air.

If we are in the throes of despair over our marriage ending, this bursting forth can seem like a
cruel joke. Everywhere we look we see new
growth, new beginnings. Everywhere, that is, but
in our mirrors. Yet we can take comfort in the fact
that after winter, spring comes—at different times
in different climates and at different times and in
different ways to each of us.

Perhaps we've already seen glimpses of our
own personal spring. Maybe we're just at the
point of bursting forth, of crossing boundaries,
leaping over walls, casting aside fears. Once
we've let ourselves begin to grow, we can't stop
the process, any more than we can stop the sea-
sons.

I can look for and celebrate signs of my own internal
spring.

APRIL 26

Prophecy is the most gratuitous form of error.
—George Eliot

When we try to prophesy the future, we run the risk of setting up self-fulfilling prophecies. We fantasize about what it will be like—what we'll do if it happens, what we'll feel like, what we'll do next and after that and after that. Consciously or unconsciously, we set out to control our lives so that what we prophesy comes true.

When a relationship is ending, we can fall into the control trap: Everything will be terrible and I won't be able to cope. Everything will be wonderful now that I'm out of that mess. And we get a promotion, have a wonderful day, meet a new friend, look great. It doesn't matter because everything is going to be terrible. Or we go on drinking or eating binges, fall behind at work, begin a new relationship with an unsavory character. But everything is going to be wonderful.

Reality pales in comparison to our prophecy. We make all our decisions based on the prophecy. We haven't got a clue about what our true feelings are. Our lives are controlled by our prophecy. Our lives are out of control.

Giving up my crystal ball is the first step to getting my life back under control.

APRIL 27

*From a timid, shy girl I had become a woman of resolute
character, who could no longer be frightened by the
struggle with troubles.* —Anna Dostoyevski

When we feel timid, shy, and fearful—no matter
what our age—our tendency is to want to avoid
the process of finding our resolution and independence; we want to *be* there. Of course, it's only in
struggling that we learn that the struggle will not
overpower us.

Being independent is a process, not a goal.
We're not going to wake up independent one
morning, with our struggles, fears, and obstacles
all behind us. The girl we were can help us live
the process of being independent. If we'll listen to
her, she can share a wealth of information. If we
don't remember and own that we've faced struggles in the past, we'll continually live in fear of
facing them in the present.

Being independent means integrating our past
and our present. What the child remembers of
how it felt to be free and resolute in childhood as
well as what it felt to be timid, shy, and afraid
allows us to struggle with our troubles. Being independent means not being afraid to face our
fears.

*I can't be independent without owning all of me—
the girl I was and the woman I'm becoming.*

APRIL 28

*I think that knowing what you can not do is more
important than knowing what you can do. In fact, that's
good taste.*   —Lucille Ball

It's good to know ourselves well enough to know
what we can do and what we can't. Yet how do
we know until we try? Trying is one thing, and
putting ourselves and others through the agony
of repeated efforts to do and be who we aren't is
where the good taste part comes in.

Rebuilding our lives as single women is likely
to be a process of being challenged to figure out
what we can do. And we're quite likely to find
that we can do things we never expected we
could—from taking a vacation alone to taking on
household repairs to learning to deal with our
feelings. And one of the most important parts of
learning to know what we can do is accepting
that there are things we *can't* do.

Yet when we find ourselves alone and virtually
forced to do and be a new way, the temptation to
berate ourselves for not being able to do everything is great. In a time when we should be gentle
with ourselves, we're less likely to admit and accept that there are things we can't do.

*It is in bad taste for me to beat up on myself for not
being able to do what I can't.*

APRIL 29

I've got more confidence than I do talent, I think. I think confidence is the main achiever of success.

—Dolly Parton

If we trust that we might be able to succeed, we have a chance of succeeding. If we don't have the confidence that we can do what we set out to, we will always fail. Even when we reach a goal we set for ourselves, without self-confidence, the goal won't have meaning. It won't feel like success.

Having self-confidence is a process. We can't find it or buy it. We can't keep a spare set of it in our closets. We can't dress the lack of it up in expensive clothes, give it a fancy title, and take it out into the world. Even if nobody else sees, we'll know we lack confidence.

Having self-confidence means trusting ourselves to make mistakes as well as to achieve goals. It means acknowledging that we did achieve our goals. When we're self-confident we can choose a path, and when it ends or is blocked, we can move to another. Having self-confidence means trusting ourselves when things aren't going how we planned as well as when they are.

When I trust myself, I trust my failures and my successes.

APRIL 30

> *I bless you*
> *I release you*
> *I set you*
> *FREE*
> *I let you be*
> *I let me be*
>
> —Alla Bozarth

Loving others means wanting the best for them, wanting them to be free to be their best selves. Sometimes that means letting them go.

Once we're separated, our ex-spouses aren't any longer in our lives in the same way. But even though they're no longer around, we may not have released them from our lives. We may wish we could make our marriages work again. We may rely overly on them for emotional support. We may try to control them through money. Or they may try to control us, and we let them.

Releasing our spouses from our lives is a process. It takes time. It takes practice at letting them be and at letting ourselves be who we are and who we're becoming. In setting them free, we also set ourselves free. And in letting go of the old, we make room for the new.

As I let go of who I've been and who I've been married to, I can be me.

MAY 1

*I would like to live . . . open to time and death
painlessly, noticing everything, remembering nothing,
choosing the given with a fierce and pointed will.*
—Annie Dillard

Our "fierce and pointed wills" can be weapons of destruction, aimed at ourselves or others. We may use our will to try to destroy our ex-spouses, choosing to take them for all they're worth. Or we may use it to poke out our own eyes, refusing to see that we can live open to the possibilities of our new lives.

Or we can use our "fierce and pointed wills" to point the way to those choices that allow us to live fully in the present, neither regretting what has been nor worrying about what will be. We can use the pointed end to poke holes in our illusion that everything was fine the way it was.

We can cut away the blindfold that prevents us from seeing the possibilities in our present givens. We see things we didn't see before. We give up the illusion that we can't make choices and decisions.

*The only thing I need to remember today is that
today is the day I'm living.*

MAY 2

We look out and see the goodness in other people, but we don't see it in ourselves. The act of turning around and catching the goodness in ourselves is to wake up. Our consciousness, that lost, scared soldier, finally meets itself.
—Natalie Goldberg

We can't accept the goodness in ourselves if we don't see it. When we're ending a relationship, it's easy to see only misery and self-doubt. We need to catch ourselves unaware: the scared soldier, the brave hero, the girl who's afraid to live alone, and the woman who thrives on her independence . . . all our parts.

Imagine for a moment walking down a city street lined with storefronts with plate glass windows. As I walk I catch fleeting glimpses of women who look attractive, smart, good, kind, interesting, and strong. After walking a block or so, I am puzzled. There is something familiar about all these women. These women I'm meeting along the street are reflections of me.

In order to accept ourselves as a lost child, we also need to accept ourselves as a guide through the wilderness. We can't accept part of ourselves without accepting our whole true self.

Today I'm going to polish up my inner mirror and take a good look.

MAY 3

Well, people change and forget to tell each other. Too bad— causes so many mistakes.

— Anna, in *Toys in the Attic* by Lillian Hellman

Oops! The mistakes we make when we change and forget to tell ourselves or others can be trivial or they can be fatal. Suppose I forget to tell my hostess that I can no longer eat chocolate? She serves a homemade chocolate cake for dessert. When I announce that I can't eat it, her feelings will probably be hurt. Suppose, on the other hand, I forget to tell myself that I can't eat the chocolate, eat it, and have a full-blown allergic reaction.

When we're in the throes of major changes, it's sometimes hard to figure out who to tell what and to whom we told what—especially what we forget to tell ourselves. If we forget to remind ourselves that we've made a change, we may find ourselves falling back into old patterns.

Sharing changes we've made not only avoids the mistakes of misunderstanding, miscommunication, missed learning in our lives. When we share how we've changed with ourselves or others we reinforce the change in our lives.

I've changed. Would I recognize myself if I met me walking down the street?

MAY 4

When one has been threatened with a great injustice, one accepts a smaller as a favour. —Jane Welsh Carlyle

Any kind of abuse—from sexual and physical violence to emotional self-abuse—is an injustice to our selves. Nobody is justly abused; nobody deserves to be abused. Yet one of the dynamics of being abused is that we feel like that's what we deserve. Or it's all that we can expect.

If I'm being beaten, I may well (and rightly and temporarily) choose the lesser abuse of going on welfare so I can leave my spouse. If I'm *only* being verbally put down, emotionally abused, I may decide to stay in a relationship that at least offers financial security. If I have a history of abuse (of almost any kind), I may find that it's less hurtful to abuse myself than it is to wait for someone else to do it.

To stop abuse requires that we stop seeing the lesser injustice as a good thing and that we stop the threat of both the greater and the lesser injustices. That means removing ourselves from the abusive situation. It means never calling a "small" injustice or abuse a favor and refusing to accept it.

I do myself an injustice when I remain in an abusive relationship—with myself or anyone else.

MAY 5

But life's changes are nothing to a sage's heart.
— Yü Hsüan-chi

Our heart is our own true sage. What wisdom we know, we know in our hearts. The most fundamental thing we know in our wise hearts is that life does not happen despite change. Rather, life is change.

When we accept that life is change we can incorporate changes into our lives—in our feelings and our behavior—without being thrown into a tizzy. The countless changes that happen when our marriages end become a part of our lives rather than the end of our lives or something to get over before we can get on with living. A new house, new ways of doing things, changed economic circumstances, new relationships, are changes that may cause stress and tension.

We must get used to new and different, and not always pleasant, external circumstances in our lives. And that's a lot easier to do if we're not trying to create a life without changes, if we accept that life is change and expend our energy to live our lives rather than to prevent change.

Wisdom is knowing that life is change.

MAY 6

A secret at home is like rocks under tide.
—Dinah Mulock Craik

A secret is something hidden that changes things. Navigating through tidal waters with hidden rocks can be tricky. It's also tricky to negotiate a life that depends on keeping secrets. Often the breakup of a marriage is preceded by and processed with secrets under the surface.

It doesn't take a master sailor to recognize the obvious danger of rocks under water. Not knowing they're there can be life threatening. The rocks and the secrets are there, whether we acknowledge them or not.

Life, like tides, ebbs and flows. And sooner or later the rocky secrets underneath are going to be revealed. Rocks we can see aren't nearly as dangerous as those we can't. Secrets we speak out loud, even to ourselves, are no longer secrets and are no longer as dangerous.

I have clearer sailing when I don't keep secrets from myself.

MAY 7

I'll not listen to reason. . . . Reason always means what someone else has got to say. —Elizabeth Gaskell

Reason often means rationalizing. A friend may try to make us see reason when she thinks we can't. Or a part of ourselves that is afraid or belligerent is bound and determined to make us see "objective reality." We're not apt to discover reality by listening to reason.

When we are planning to do something— maybe something big like beginning a new relationship, moving to a new home, taking a new job —we reason with ourselves. Maybe we make a list of pros and cons. Maybe we ask others to reason with us. And, if we rely entirely on rational reasoning, we often find that we cannot make a decision.

Beyond reason comes trust. I can learn to trust myself, so that my reasoning, the "whats" and "whys," makes sense to me. They may not make sense to others. They might not have made sense to me six months ago, last week, yesterday—and they may not make sense tomorrow. When I trust my own reality, my life makes sense to me, and I can listen.

I'll not listen to reason when it's in my best interests to trust my reality.

MAY 8

> *Hope is the thing with feathers,*
> *That perches in the soul,*
> *And sings the tune without the words,*
> *And never stops at all.*
> —Emily Dickinson

How can we find the hope inside us when things are going wrong at every turn? Ending a relationship, whether by our own choosing or not, can make us feel pretty hopeless. Maybe it feels like we can never hope again. Maybe it feels like our ex-spouse stole our hope. But hope, living as it does perched on our souls, can't be taken away from us by others. And it can't be given by others.

Hope is always there—whether we're listening or not. Our hope may grow fainter and weaker if we don't acknowledge it. We need to nourish hope. Hungry and thirsty birds don't sing as sweetly or as truly.

Especially in times that seem hopeless, it may be best just to listen for the wisp of a melody line, our inner music. Hope isn't the false song that everything will be all right, that all our wishes will come true. Hope is the tune that says today is the only day I have in my life right now.

Let me sit and listen for the hope in my life.

MAY 9

Courage ought to have eyes as well as arms.

—English proverb

Usually when we think of courage, we think of it as that quality which will impel us into action. A courage with eyes as well as arms will impel us into action, seeing the possible courses we could steer, being aware of the effect of the changes we are proposing to make. Or it may be a courage that allows us to do nothing but accept things as they are for the time being.

Blind courage may well lead to blind, or un-aware, action. If we go rushing in willy-nilly to try to change our lives without considering the effect of those changes on ourselves or others, are we being courageous or are we being foolish? Of course, courage, even courage with eyes, doesn't come with a crystal ball. And to avoid action in the name of not being able to see the result is probably as uncourageous as impetuous action is.

Courage with eyes is courage that is open to the present moment. What's going on with me and around me right now? Can I see things for what they are? And see what it is that I can change? Once I see, can I use the courage with arms to change them?

Grant me the courage to see, to change, to be.

MAY 10

*For loneliness is but cutting adrift from our moorings and
floating out to the open sea; an opportunity for finding
ourselves, our real selves, what we are about, where we are
heading during our little time on this beautiful earth.*
—Anne Shannon Monroe

Marriage is a mooring to which we're no longer
attached, no matter how stable or rotten that
mooring was. We're lonely and adrift. What happens now is that we get to figure out where we're
going and who it is who's going there.

When we float in our loneliness, we're likely to
get water in our face. We might feel like we're
drowning in our loneliness. We might attempt to
fight the current, to exhaust ourselves trying to
swim away from our loneliness. Our last instinct
is to lay back, let the water support us, and look
around us at our loneliness.

And we'd better do it or we really are going to
drown. We can feel ourselves flailing and failing,
sinking. Or we can lay back and discover what it
feels like to float. Feel our bodies, get to know
what and who the water of our loneliness is supporting. Feel our hearts still beating in the loneliness. Feel our emotions. They're our guides.

*Adrift in my loneliness I discover the boundaries and
shores of me.*

MAY 11

*Far away there in the sunshine are my highest aspirations.
I may not reach them, but I can look up and see their
beauty, believe in them, and try to follow where they lead.*
—Louisa May Alcott

Many of us have given up our own higher aspirations in the face of fear, frustration, and set-
backs. Maybe we can point to a time when we
aspired to a career or family goal, when our hope
of reaching that goal inspired us to work toward
it no matter what obstacles lay in our way.

If I aspired to make my marriage work and it
ends, I may well feel like every other thing I
wanted will end badly. I may feel like it's useless
and frustrating to aspire to a successful career, to
being a good mom, or to live with purpose at all.
It may seem as if inspiration disappears altogether from my life.

Living with inspiration takes time, time to visit
with our aspirations, to nurture them, perhaps to
let them lie fallow, and time to work toward
them. When we get divorced, our aspirations
change. My aspiration for right now may simply
be to take care of myself, to reassure myself that
I'm okay.

*When I look for what I want, I find the inspiration
to aspire to it.*

MAY 12

*Let us rejoice in our sufferings, knowing them to be
symptoms of our potential health. Pain is a script, and as
we learn to read it, we grow in self-knowledge.*
                                              —M. C. Richards

Pain is the most basic of diagnostic tools. If we
don't know what part of our selves—body, mind,
soul—hurts, we can't discover the source of the
pain or what might be done to relieve the pain
and cure the ailment.

Relieving our pain without knowing the source
can lead to worse pain and dire consequences. It
is not uncommon, for instance, for someone to
take medication to relieve indigestion while an ulcer grows virtually unchecked. Many of us try to
alleviate our emotional pain by getting rid of the
symptoms, by distracting ourselves with food, alcohol, shopping, keeping too busy to notice the
clues in our pain that may lead to healing.

In order to use our pain constructively, we
need to face it. When we admit that we hurt and
work to discover what triggers our pain, we can
begin to make changes in our lives. We can begin
to make choices that make us feel good physically, emotionally, spiritually.

*Only when I know my pain can I prescribe my
health.*

MAY 13

Liberty is the mother of virtue. —Mary Wollstonecraft

Mothers nurture our abilities to grow in such virtues as responsibility, independence, caring, kindness, patience, and love. But if we are not free to think, act, and feel, we will never live out those virtues. Ergo, freedom becomes the mother, the nurturer, of any other virtues we want to cultivate.

In a sense, as adult women, we become our own mothers. We are the ones who can nurture our own freedom. It's up to us to provide the home atmosphere in our hearts and daily lives that will feed our freedom. If we're feeling trapped in a relationship, we may leave that relationship and begin to nourish our own independence.

Nurturing takes time and attention, which may well be in short supply when we are single again. Work, taking care of a house, of personal business, children, friends, family, all make demands on our time. By taking time to meet our own basic needs, to plan and do things we want to, to take care of ourselves, we can begin to see options for ourselves where we only saw ourselves trapped in situations that limited our freedom.

Every day is Mother's Day when I am at liberty to mother myself.

MAY 14

*In blocking off what hurts us, we think we are walling
ourselves off from pain. But in the long run, the wall,
which prevents growth, hurts us more than the pain
which, if we will only bear it, soon passes over us. . . .
Walls remain.*   —Alice Walker

Walling ourselves off from our own feelings prevents us from connecting to ourselves and others.
And if, by accident, some person gets through to
us, some feeling sneaks in, we tend to build more
confining, less breachable walls, until we find
ourselves living in a tower.

Then one day a crisis causes our carefully built
tower to come falling down around our ears. And
we find ourselves, if we're lucky, alive but
bruised, sitting in a pile of rubble. The higher the
wall, the more we're likely to be hurt when it
falls. That's the bad news.

The good news is that we can, if we choose, use
every one of those life-experience bricks to build a
road instead of a wall. We've got all those bricks
to build roads to lead us into new and unexplored
territory, to connect ourselves with our own inner
feelings, and to connect us in relationships with
others.

*I can use the building blocks of my disconnecting
wall to build a connecting road.*

MAY 15

> *Fear is a slinking cat I find*
> *Beneath the lilacs of my mind.*
> —Sophie Tunnell

This cat of fear is a cat with magical properties. It is fear and it feeds on fear. The longer we refuse to look under the lilac bush, the bigger she gets. As long as we refuse to look at her, she keeps right on growing—and threatening to get us.

Yet, truly, how dangerous can a little cat skulking about in our own minds be? Could it be that she's hungry, maybe looking for a tidbit to be thrown her way? Could it be that she's afraid to come out into the open? To be revealed for the truly small and lovable but frightened creature she is?

If we ignore our fears, trying to keep them tucked away in some corner of ourselves, they tend to grow out of proportion. If we bring them out into the light of day, facing them, we may find that they are still pretty powerful. They won't be more powerful simply because we know their names, what they look like, what they feel like. They are, in fact, likely to lose power over us when they're out in the light of day.

In facing my fears, I can face myself, in my full potential.

MAY 16

*Joy is what has made pain bearable and, in the end,
creative rather than destructive.* —Madeleine L'Engle

To create a life free from pain is humanly impossible. To create a good life while ignoring pain is
impossible. We all know of people who overcame
great obstacles, endured unimaginable pain, and
lived to say they are happy. Often their life stories
are the stuff of inspiration. What magic makes
this possible?

It *is* magic and it *is* available to all of us. It is the
magic of recognition, of being able to see beyond
the painful moments—into the joyful ones. And it
takes daily practice. Some days we settle for and
on the small joys that help us through the big
pains. Perhaps we see the rose of summer when
we are in the throes of mourning a relationship. If
we will notice, there are reminders that joy,
beauty, and happiness abound.

If we do not allow ourselves to feel great pain,
we can't allow ourselves to feel or imagine happiness. If we allow ourselves to feel joy, we can allow ourselves to feel pain. And in feeling that
pain, we can go around once again to feeling joy.

*Creating my life means creating my joy and creating
from my pain.*

MAY 17

When we uncouple, we must come to terms not only with
our loss, but with the possibility of our own contribution
to it. We are face-to-face with our own shortcomings.
                                        —Diane Vaughan

There are many losses to grieve at the end of a
relationship. The loss of companionship, sex, income, a house, mutual friends, building our
shared history. Grieving is natural and grieving
takes time. One aspect of grieving is to name our
losses, to acknowledge them, to feel them, to explore them.

As we explore our losses, being human, we are
pretty sure to run into ways we have contributed
to them. Those too must be acknowledged and
explored. Acknowledging our contribution to the
end of the relationship is not playing "if
only . . ." If only we had done this, that, or the
other thing—if only we had been perfect, then the
relationship might not have ended.

Acknowledging our contribution to our losses
is making an honest assessment of ourselves, our
own shortcomings, and choosing what we want
to do about them. As we do that we can proceed
to rebuild our lives.

Coming to terms with my losses, and my part in
them, can bring me face-to-face with myself.

MAY 18

An ideal, even if we intuitively sense it to be true, is not our belief until we live it from a molecular level. Then we become that belief. —Gloria Karpinski

To live a belief at a molecular level is to live out our belief rather than to live up to it. If we're trying to live up to something, it is by implication above or beyond us in some way. It's not necessarily unachievable, yet it's not within us—not as natural as breathing.

The opposite of belief is doubt. In times of extreme change, doubting our beliefs leads to doubting our very self. We no longer know what we believe, and therefore we no longer know how to act. When our worlds are turned upside down, we can look at what we're doing and how we're doing it to help ourselves figure out just what it is we still believe in. And our actions help us see what we're coming to believe in our new circumstances.

Sometimes we're acting out a belief we don't even consciously know we have. We may, in fact, be acting on a new ideal—for instance, "I believe that women are capable of taking care of themselves"—for quite a while before we know that we believe it.

To believe in myself is to be myself.

MAY 19

The body does not lie. —Martha Graham

Our bodies may be telling the truth, but are we listening? Every once in a while there will be a story in the newspaper about a woman who didn't know she was pregnant giving birth to a full-term baby. We've all heard stories about people who ignored early symptoms of diseases that might have been treated. Like anyone who isn't listened to over time, their bodies stop talking.

There are lots of ways not to hear what our bodies are saying to us. Our bodies tell us that eating certain foods will make us sick—and we eat them anyway. Our bodies tell us that regular exercise will make us feel better—and we find hundreds of ways to avoid doing it. Our bodies tell us they like to be pampered, perhaps with long hot baths—and we take quick cold showers.

The first step in listening to the truth of our bodies is to accept that they *are* our bodies— lumps, spots, bulges, imperfections, and all. Once we begin to listen, we find that we've got a good friend in our bodies, someone who will tell us the truth, and someone who—when listened to—will help us look and feel our best.

I can hear my body's truth when I listen.

MAY 20

One can never pay in gratitude; one can only pay "in kind" somewhere else in life.
—Anne Morrow Lindbergh

To be grateful is to be doubly gifted. The first gift is receiving something, from ourselves or others. The second is the feeling of gratitude that can brighten our day. Like other pleasant surprises in life, gratitude is hard to find when we seek it directly. It can't be bought with any currency.

Gratitude particularly can't be extracted from the emotional currency of guilt. Feeling guilty because we should be grateful for life's lessons or gifts is not going to make us grateful. Nor is feeling obligated to return the favor.

Gratitude has very little to do with give-and-take. We can't acquire a feeling of gratitude by giving and receiving, although that certainly may engender gratitude in our hearts. We can, especially when we're not feeling that there's much to be grateful for in our lives, open ourselves to small, good things that happen. Once we begin to recognize them, we begin to feel grateful; then we can pass it on by using the good feelings we have to do things for ourselves and others.

Gratitude is a gift that doesn't require anything from me.

MAY 21

If you attach yourself to one person, you ultimately end up having an unhealthy relationship. —Shirley MacLaine

Total and exclusive attachment to someone, even if that person is ourself, is a practically fail-safe guarantee for an unhealthy relationship. The pure and simple truth is that, in this world we live in, no one is an island. And no two are an island.

When we attempt to create an island of one or two, shutting out the rest of the world completely, the most likely result is that we'll drown in a flood of our own making. No one person, including ourselves, can be and do all for us. That seems patently obvious. Yet many of us, when we are (or were) involved with a person we think we can't live without, act as if it's not true. Others of us act as if we can live without others. Either way—we drown.

The alternative to drowning is to create a network of bridges between ourselves and others. We need both to reach out and to accept the support and connection we find when we do so. Building bridges takes learning, skill, practice, and patience. We have to trust that we can connect with others. We need to give ourselves time to build connections.

I can build my own bridges.

MAY 22

I tell you there is no such thing as creative hate.
                                        —Willa Cather

Hate does not create. Hate kills. Our hatred may hurt others. Our hate is most likely to kill us— and the creative spirit, the life force, within us. When our marriages end, we may be nearly consumed with hating—our ex-spouses for having got us into this situation; our lives for conspiring against us; our children, friends, jobs, ourselves, for trapping us in hatred.

If we continue to focus on what or who we hate, we'll continue to be held in a trap that can kill us. What we can come to see is that it is not our ex-spouse, our friends, our family, our work, that is trapping us. It is our hatred. Knowing that is the first step in being able to create something not with our hatred but *from* it.

Denying our hatred will only make us flail against the walls we feel trapped in. Suppressing it will only allow it to grow. Taking it out on others will send it out of control. Expressing the pain of being trapped and of feeling like we're being consumed by hatred is the only way to escape. By expressing our pain we allow ourselves to create a way out of our trap.

If I'm not creative about dealing with my hate, it is likely to kill me.

MAY 23

You'll never get me into one of those things!
—Caterpillar looking at butterfly

It's easy enough for us to see how the caterpillar becomes the butterfly. We can look at her from the outside. The caterpillar, on the other hand, is wrapped up in that cocoon and can't even look in the mirror to see if it looks as bad as it feels. One day she chafes and pushes to get out of the walls of her own making, and finally, she wakes up to find she's a new creature.

Transformation in our own lives is equally mysterious and magical. First, there's the "not me" stage. Here we are, our own old selves. Then one day, our present life doesn't seem to fit anymore. But we don't know how to make the change or even what it is. And so, confined in our old self, not knowing that it has already begun to change, we struggle against what's binding us and wait.

And finally, one day, we wake up to find we've shed the cocoon. It's gone, and we're different. It's a transformation based on accumulated changes. It's a process and it's an instant when we are somebody we never knew we could be.

May I recognize all the butterfly I can be.

MAY 24

There are two modes of criticism. One which . . . crushes to earth without mercy. . . . There is another mode which enters into the natural history of every thing that breathes and lives, which believes no impulse to be entirely in vain, which scrutinizes circumstances, motive and object before it condemns. . . . —Margaret Fuller

One kind of criticism kills and the other nourishes. For most of us, the first kind of criticism comes more easily. It takes little thought, less effort, and even less wisdom to kill with criticism. This criticism attacks our very selves. At its worst it says, "You are stupid," or "You are worthless."

When we find ourselves encountering this killing criticism—from ourselves or others—our best defense is to try to ignore the criticism and to take it as an article of faith that we are *not* stupid, worthless, without any virtue. We can remind ourselves that we do have a native beauty, talent, and intelligence, even though we make mistakes.

When our lives are changing rapidly and dramatically, the second sort of criticism, which is thoughtful and careful, from ourselves and others, can be invaluable. That sort of criticism actually recognizes and encourages the worth of the efforts we're making, even as it points out how we might grow differently.

I'd like to be my own best critic.

MAY 25

I am not one of those who say, "It is nothing; it is a woman drowning."   —Anonymous

Too often we say to ourselves and the world, "Never mind, just let me drown. It's nothing." We may feel that we are drowning in despair, in tears, in sadness. Yet we fervently and constantly say to ourselves, "It's not so bad. It will pass. Other people have survived this."

There's nothing intrinsically wrong with those messages to ourselves, and, at some level, they're true. However, feeling like we're drowning is *not* nothing; it is, in fact, literally and metaphorically life threatening. If we don't acknowledge the feeling of drowning, feel it, and ask for help, we will keep drowning.

What is it that prevents us from saying, "Help. This is terrible! Somebody throw me a lifeline until I learn how to swim." If we were literally drowning, would we think we were worth saving? Would we make the effort to figure out which way the shore was? Would we want somebody to rescue us? Would we think, after the crisis, that we were grateful to be alive? So too, when we're figuratively drowning in despair—we *can* scream for help and we *are* worth saving.

Acknowledging that I'm drowning can save my life.

MAY 26

In a culture where approval/disapproval has become the predominant regulator of effort and position, and often the substitute for love, our personal freedoms are dissipated.
—Viola Spolin

Earning approval makes us feel good. And sometimes we forget to count the cost. When we rely solely on the approval of others, we lose our freedom to do, be, think, and act to please ourselves. We run the risk of losing our very identity. It's as if we use approval as proof of our own worth, if not our very existence. So we seek out more approval, which we can scarcely credit, since we're not worthwhile anyway.

Living for the approval of others is like riding a merry-go-round. We go up, we go down, we go round and round. We get dizzy. At first it seems like we might grab the gold ring—ultimate and universal approval. Then we discover that we win approval from one and disapproval from another —for the very same things.

Will others only love me if they approve of me? Will I only love myself if I approve of everything I do? Are we really willing to give up all that for something as elusive as approval?

I am worthwhile and I don't have to prove it by getting approval.

MAY 27

Total commitment to family and total commitment to career is possible, but fatiguing. —Muriel Fox

Total commitment to anything outside ourselves is also a trap. Most of us have been taught that good girls are concerned about others. They spend their time, energy, and creativity taking care of their families, business, community obligations—giving, giving, giving. We've given and given until we find our store of time and energy totally depleted. We're tired—or sick—or worse.

The person we haven't given anything to, too often, is ourselves. Give time to our selves; good advice. We know, at least in our heads, that if we don't give time to ourselves, we won't be able to go on. But giving to our selves often comes at the bottom of a never-ending list. We never get to ourselves because we run out of time.

Another way to look at time spent on ourselves is to imagine that it's yeast. Time for ourselves can expand our energy for commitment to others. If we add the yeast of time for ourselves to our lives, we have that much more to give to others. Keep that yeast alive by feeding it regularly and we keep expanding. Stop and it doesn't work anymore.

Who am I not to take time for myself?

MAY 28

Oh, I wish that God had not given me what I prayed for!
It was not as good as I thought. —Johanna Spyri

As the proverb goes, "Be careful what you pray for, you might get it." When we live our lives by "what-iffing" and wishing, it's as if we're living on two sides of a record. There's the past and the future. The present is a narrow rim we barely notice as we hold it in our fingertips to flip the record from side to side.

First, we play a cut from the past. What if I had been more careful, attentive, open, honest? What if I'd never married in the first place? Then I wouldn't be in this state I'm in now. That's for sure. Then we slip to the future, whose songs have two basic themes: What if I can't get my life together? And I wish I were smarter, prettier, richer, in a new relationship, feeling somehow, anyhow, better than I do now.

When we spend our time wishing and what-iffing between the past and the future, we never get around to knowing what state we're in now. We hardly know what to pray for because we don't know who we are.

One way to get what I want is to pray that I see what is.

MAY 29

Now I am beginning to live a little, and feel less like a sick oyster at low tide. —Louisa May Alcott

We know we're on our way to recovery when we can say we're beginning to live a little. In fact, we may be on our way to recovery before we can articulate out loud that we're feeling a little more like living. There is no time frame for recovery from the pain and grief of a divorce. And it's a process.

Tides ebb and flow and so does recovery. Some days we feel better. Some days we don't. So it's important to check our internal temperature, our pulse rate, our vital signs, on a daily basis. To notice how we're feeling. To admit to ourselves that we're feeling better when we are, and to allow ourselves days in which the tide is low.

Checking our vital signs means noticing and acknowledging how we feel. It is not to discount the evidence in front of our eyes: Yes, I feel better today; I actually felt free and happy for a moment, but it won't last. It is not to punish ourselves for having a bad day: I thought I felt better and here I am crying; I'll never get better.

Recovery is going with the ebb and the flow of my daily life.

MAY 30

To keep a lamp burning we have to keep putting oil in it.
—Mother Teresa

Most of us have lived our whole lives with electric lights readily available. The reality of having light available only if we regularly put oil in the lamps is something we can only understand intellectually. We often fail to see that regular effort put into our lives lightens the burden of our problems, and simply makes us feel better.

We want to be thinner, better employed, in a new relationship, happier. Or, if we are in the pits of despair, we just know that we want things to be different. If we focus on the goal without putting in the daily effort to diet, exercise, look at options, meet people, or simply live our lives intentionally, chances are that we find ourselves in the dark and no closer to our goals.

The regular effort we put into meeting our goals can have an effect beyond helping us reach them. If I undertake an exercise program, I may end up feeling better, losing weight, and, during the contemplative time of my walks, figuring out what it is I *really* want for myself.

Regular effort keeps my lamps lit so I can see to achieve my goals.

MAY 31

Some memories are like friends in common; they can effect reconciliations. —Marcel Proust

Memorial Day can be an occasion for remembering what has died in our lives. Remembering what our marriages were like, acknowledging the good and the bad, the joy and the pain, serves to remind us that we have a past and that we are no longer in it.

The point of reconciliation with our memories is not to bring us back into our marriages. The point is to bring us together, first with ourselves, and then with others in our lives in a new way. And when we take time to remember without judging, without wishing we could go back and change our past, we can effect reconciliation.

When we reconcile ourselves with our memories, we give up feelings of hurt and resentment. We can remember the angry pain of past struggles without feeling it or reengaging in fruitless arguments. We can remember the joy of our wedding day without feeling the bitterness of what followed. We can remember our own mistakes without being engulfed in guilt and shame. We can remember the good times without lamenting.

My memory can help me reconcile myself to my life as it is now.

JUNE 1

Yesterday's errors let yesterday cover.

—Susan Coolidge

Letting yesterday's mistakes be covered by yesterday means leaving them there. That means not dragging them out to beat ourselves up with at the first possible opportunity. And it means not having to make them again.

They are, in the words of an old hymn, "gone but not forgotten." Leaving yesterday's mistakes behind doesn't mean we forget about them. Forgetting them is, in fact, one of the fastest ways to make them today's mistakes. Nor does it mean we don't make amends to ourselves and others for the damage we might have caused.

When we're going through a separation and divorce, the past can seem safer than the painful present. We often feel like we'd be willing to make the same mistakes over again. Or that we'd make amends, if only we had the chance to go back and do things over. We can't, of course. So rather than build up an overwhelming load of mistakes while trying to live in the past, we might as well let yesterday's mistakes lie there.

I can go into tomorrow overburdened by yesterday's mistakes, or I can let the past be past starting today.

Genius will live and thrive without training, but it does not the less reward the watering pot and pruning knife.
—Margaret Fuller

We don't have to be geniuses to value the effect of caring. And, if and as we take care, we may well discover a hidden genius, a talent or activity we can nurture much to our own satisfaction. Caring for plants with watering pot and pruning knife will, over time, make their blossoms more glorious, their fruit more abundant.

After a divorce or separation we may be feeling like no one really cares for us, including ourselves. Each day may be a struggle. The ground in which we're currently planted may be dry and cracked from neglect. If I nurture myself today, when I'm feeling low, I may feel or look a bit better. If I keep up the care, over time, I'm bound to surprise myself by blossoming.

Caring feeds on itself. When we take care of ourselves, we feel, look, act, are better. We have more energy to care for others. We can't really take care of others until we take care of ourselves. And feeling the rewards of caring, we're apt to widen our circle of caring.

I can enfold myself in the circle of my caring.

JUNE 3

> *When a pair of magpies fly together*
> *They do not envy a pair of phoenixes.*
> —Lady Ho

The magpies don't want to be phoenixes. They have, if you will, accepted themselves as magpies. They fly the way they fly, one presumes, quite contented to do so. We too fly the way we fly. Using up energy in envying the way others fly only leaves us less to use flying in our own best way, toward our own best self.

The magpie flying alone, however, may in her birdlike way envy the pair of magpies flying together. Even though she accepts that she's a magpie, she sees the lack in her life. Dwelling in envy can use up our energy, work against us accepting ourselves, make us less than we are.

Envy has another side. If we envy our coupled friends for the companionship, shared responsibilities, or whatever they enjoy, we may use that envy as new knowledge: I'd like to have companionship like that in my life. What can I do to find it? Noticing what we envy can help us discover what we want and find new directions—if we know and accept who we are.

I acknowledge my envy for what it has to teach me about who I might become.

JUNE 4

Revelation is always measured by capacity.
—Margaret Fairless Barber

We only discover what we have the capacity to discover. When we learn new things about ourselves, our capacity to do that increases. And when we're ready to learn even more new things about ourselves, we have the enhanced capacity to do so.

Nobody ever said that discovering new things about ourselves isn't hard or hard work. Yet, if we are willing, we have the capacity to do it. When we're going through a separation it may seem like we have nothing else to do but discover new things about ourselves. The thing to remember and accept is that we have whatever capacity we have at the moment. We don't have to learn everything at once. We can take our time and move on to new discoveries as we are ready.

When we measure discovery by capacity, we take on only what we can handle. We don't worry that we won't be able to stand the pain of what we must learn. Nor do we expect that what we're discovering will make us instantly and constantly happy. We only expect that in discovering ourselves we will recover ourselves.

My capacity for self-revelation is ever-increasing.

JUNE 5

If I could tell you what it meant, there would be no point in dancing it. —Isadora Duncan

If only I could understand what's going on with me, I could do something about it. Figuring out what it all means in the midst of life-changing events can be a frustrating and illogical process. We can sit and try to figure out what's going on until our heads ache and our eyes won't focus. And still we don't know who we are or where we're going in our newly single lives.

Sometimes the best way to figure things out is not to figure them out and to do something, almost anything, instead. The worst that can happen is that we still won't understand how we feel, why our lives have taken this turn, what we want next. The best thing that can happen is a truly alchemical reaction, the kind that happens when art is made.

We can be doing almost anything—a work assignment, a gardening project, a long-neglected hobby. As we become absorbed in the action, articulating meaning becomes a secondary concern. And what often happens next is that we can make some sense out of our lives. The action becomes like dancing out a scene from our lives.

What I do is apt to teach me a lot about who I am.

JUNE 6

. . . memory is a storm I can't repel. —Dilys Laing

Memory will out. Try as we might to submerge, subvert, or divert the storm of memories of our coupled lives, they will overtake us. Some days we may feel consumed in a flood of grief of memories of our wedding, the good times that followed. Or we may be caught in a raging fury of a storm remembering the bad times.

Rather than wasting our time and energy trying to repel the inevitable, we might feel the storms of memory and then look at them in the different, brighter light that always follows storms. Perhaps we will see something we've not seen before—a strength we used in a time of crisis without knowing we had it. A kernel of ourselves in the person we were before we married. A friendship we've let drop that we might nurture.

Once we accept our memories, welcome even the unpleasant ones, and begin gently to rummage around in them, we find we can give ourselves the gift of new insights, the comfort of old songs, stories, jokes. By accepting our memories, we're accepting ourselves.

The storm of my memories can clear the air of my present.

JUNE 7

> *Women and men in the crowd meet and mingle,*
> *Yet with itself every soul standeth single.*
> —Alice Carey

When our marriages end we might think we're going to die of loneliness as we sit at home and feel our loss, our emptiness. When we go out in a crowd, we are almost sure we will. It looks like everybody else in the world is a couple, ergo, not lonely. Our rational minds tell us that this isn't true. And they might as well save their breath.

Going to parties, particularly weddings, anniversaries, showers, can be excruciatingly painful. We might try the deceptive ploy of comparison— telling ourselves we're not as bad off as this or that one. Indulging in comparisons is a way of avoiding dealing with loneliness.

Loneliness is a fact. No matter how connected we are to someone else, our souls stand single. Everybody's. And the only one I have is mine. The great paradox is that it's because we stand single that we can connect with other people. Unless we know this and are willing to feel and know ourselves—warts and all—we aren't going to be able to connect—in a crowd or alone.

When I'm feeling lonely, the first person to get in touch with is me.

JUNE 8

I am; therefore, I think. —Katagiri Roshi

The quotation most of us are far more familiar with—Descartes's "I think, therefore I am"—puts the cart before the horse when we're trying to fully live in the present of our lives. When I'm in the throes of pain and grief at the end of a relationship, I may be tempted to try to think my way out of feeling. If only I could intellectually comprehend my despair I might be able to think my way to feeling hopeful.

It's difficult, if not impossible, to think ourselves into being grounded and centered so that we can approach daily challenges with equilibrium. Thinking wonderful and inspiring thoughts about some single woman with a thinner body, more interesting work, fewer money problems, a perfect daily single life won't make me that woman.

On the other hand, if I begin by accepting who I am, by letting myself be with me, I can think. I may even surprise myself at what I think of. I may think of an inexpensive way to get in shape; an idea that earns me praise and a promotion at work; an innovative way to meet new people.

When I accept that I am who I am, I can give myself permission to think and do new things.

JUNE 9

When we finally learn that we are not the center of the world and that self-inflicted pain produces nothing, then we are able to turn our eyes outward, toward the spiritual.
—Jean Kirkpatrick

Looking at ourselves as the center of the world is a bit like looking at ourselves as the bull's-eye in a target. Here we are, ready to be hit and hurt, over and over again, by the arrows the world has to sling at us. The only time the pain decreases is when someone doesn't score a direct hit. Yet even those arrows cause us pain. They were, after all, aimed at us.

And if everybody else is shooting at me, I might as well too, right? At least I'll know where the arrows of hurt are coming from. And I'll be better at hitting the target—I know it so well. I can increase my pain by shooting at myself and then there won't be as much room for others' arrows.

After all, no pain no gain, as the saying goes. It might be said, "There's no gain in pain we simply absorb." If I turn outward in my pain, if I refuse to collaborate with it, I can transform it. I can see that the world really is a great big interesting globe, not a flat surface with me at its center.

I can gain from my pain only by turning outward.

JUNE 10

*It is not enough for parents to understand children. They
must accord children the privilege of understanding them.*
—Milton R. Sapirstein

We learn to be who we are and who we can be
both by understanding and by being understood.
Those of us who were fortunate enough to grow
up in loving, caring families know this. Those of
us who didn't can stop the legacy of past generations and begin to practice understanding with
our own children, and with the child within us.

When we mark Father's Day, we can celebrate
the fathers we and our children have. And, as
part of our understanding work, we can take
some time to articulate what we wish our fathers
understood about us. And what we wish our inner child and/or our children to understand
about their fathers.

Children of divorce (again both our children
and our inner children) have a particular need to
understand both their parents. If it's at all possible, they need time with and access to both. And
they may need us, their mothers, to process their
being understood and their understanding.

*I can give myself and my children the gift of
understanding and being understood.*

JUNE 11

Much violence is based on the illusion that life is a property to be defended and not a gift to be shared.
—Henri Nouwen

Violence can be done with the best intentions. Perhaps the least obvious and most insidious violence we perpetrate is against ourselves when we are attempting to protect ourselves from being hurt by not sharing ourselves with others.

This self-violence can be physical if we eat or starve ourselves into a position that makes it difficult for us to share ourselves with others. It can be mental if we become so absorbed with protecting ourselves from outside violence that we can think of nothing else. And, if we continue to defend ourselves against sharing ourselves, we run the risk not only of hurting ourselves emotionally, but of actually killing our emotional life.

We might have "good reason" to be leery of sharing our lives. We did that in our marriages, and look what it came to. We can continue this violence to ourselves. Or we can practice sharing ourselves, little by little, taking small steps and then bigger ones as we feel safer.

Sharing my life with myself and others helps make the world a safer place.

JUNE 12

Now is the time for a word about expectations and control in relationships. Whenever we get into expectations, we are moving into our illusion of control. We need to be clear on what we want and then be willing to let it go.
                                        —Anne Wilson Schaef

We can't control the course of relationships if we don't know what we want *and* we can't control the course of our relationships if we do know what we want. In short, we can't control our relationships. So what's the point of trying to?

Perhaps my expectation is that someone will be honest with me. If I find myself snooping or repeatedly asking the person to "prove" honesty, I am trying to control that person and our relationship. I have to be willing to expect honesty without trying to control whether or not I get it.

I don't need to give up wanting honesty in relationships. But if I give up trying to control honesty and find the person I'm in a relationship with isn't being honest, I might have to give up the relationship (and my expectations for it) so I don't fall into the trap of trying to control it.

Being willing to give up my expectations means I give up trying to control when, where, how, and if I get what I want.

JUNE 13

We lie loudest when we lie to ourselves. —Eric Hoffer

We all have an internal honesty gauge. We know when we're lying to ourselves. When we're lying we tend to talk faster and louder to try to get ourselves to pay attention. Whenever we find ourselves insisting that something is true, against our instinct, we should probably stop and listen. Not to the lies but for the truth.

Perhaps I took a new job, having convinced everyone in my life and *almost* convincing myself that it was a great move. The pay was great; the prestige was better. My internal gauge kept beeping, but I drowned it out, enthusiastically telling myself and others how great things were until I got an ulcer and couldn't work at all. When we're not honest with ourselves, we threaten our very existence.

If we lie loud enough and long enough, we lose our hearing for honesty, in much the same way people who work with loud machinery for a lifetime go deaf. To regain our hearing we need to filter out the loud noises. Honesty doesn't engage in shouting matches. Honesty often whispers. We need to listen for the quiet.

I can live honestly only when I listen to myself.

JUNE 14

I do not believe that sheer suffering teaches. If suffering alone taught, then all the world would be wise, since everyone suffers. To suffering must be added mourning, understanding, patience, love, openness and the willingness to remain vulnerable. —Anne Morrow Lindbergh

If we suffer, mourn, strive to understand with patience, love with our whole hearts, and are not open and vulnerable to life, we might as well forget all the rest because we're never going to grow. No matter what the specific circumstances of our lives, we all have pain to suffer, losses to mourn, situations that can be endured only with patience.

So why not learn something in the process? How? By remaining vulnerable, by reclaiming vulnerability. To be vulnerable is not to be a victim. Being vulnerable doesn't mean letting people walk all over us. Being vulnerable doesn't mean putting ourselves into situations of love and loss that will repeatedly wear us down.

Being vulnerable is welcoming our pain and grief into our hearts and doing it the honor of listening to it and feeling it long enough to learn what it might teach us. Being vulnerable is simply being open to the possibilities of each new experience, each day, each moment of our lives.

By being vulnerable I make sense of my suffering.

JUNE 15

Quite a few women told me, one way or another, that they thought it was sex, not youth, that's wasted on the young.
—Janet Harris

Sex is a voyage of discovery, and, for many of us, it was a scary journey. There we were with little information, less confidence, and even less knowledge of how to communicate our needs and wants.

So here we are now, no matter what our chronological age, older in our sexual experience. We've experienced sex in our marriages and the end of sex in that particular relationship. It doesn't matter how old we are, how attractive or unattractive we think we might be. The end of sex in one relationship feels like the end of sex.

Yet sex isn't youth, despite our cultural mythology to the contrary. Nor does it belong to one relationship or one time in our lives. Our sexuality and what we choose to do with it belongs to us throughout our whole lives. We can choose to leave it shrouded, saying it belongs to the young, the married, to anybody but us. Or we can begin, at any age, to own our own sexual feelings, thoughts, and actions.

I can write my own owner's manual for sex in my life.

JUNE 16

*Indiscriminate guilt is also the failure to distinguish
between forbidden thoughts and forbidden deeds.*
—Judith Viorst

Often we're tempted to feel guilty because our marriages ended. It's all "our fault"—no matter what our rational self tells us. We can't distinguish between what we did or didn't do and what we thought of doing or not doing.

As we put our lives together after our separation, there are even more opportunities for feeling indiscriminate guilt. I can feel guilty that my grieving is taking time and energy away from my job. I can feel guilty because my kids no longer live in a two-parent family. I can feel guilty that I'm taking time for myself or I can paralyze myself with indiscriminate guilt.

Denying guilty feelings doesn't banish them. The only way to alleviate all that guilt is to begin to ask ourselves discriminating questions. Have I really done anything? Or am I feeling this way because I thought of doing something and didn't? Or because I thought I should do something and didn't? Once we ask the questions, we can stop feeling guilty and begin to act on the answers.

*When I'm discriminate about my guilt, I can stop
discriminating against myself.*

JUNE 17

Cooperation is doing with a smile what you have to do
anyhow.   —Quote Magazine

Divorce involves a fair number of unpleasant
tasks we'd rather not undertake. These can range
from meeting with lawyers to negotiate agree-
ments, to reestablishing credit as singles, to telling
our families about the breakdown of our marriage. Simply getting the phone company to understand what's going on can be a major
undertaking.

Cooperation on these tasks can mean dividing
them up with our ex-spouse, which may not be
easy. We may not feel like smiling at our ex-
spouses, yet if we can state our needs for their
cooperation politely and pleasantly, we're likely
to get more accomplished. And we'll waste less of
our diminished emotional energy. It can also
mean enlisting, with a smile, the help of others—
from lawyers to friends and family members.

Most of all, we can cooperate with ourselves.
This is a time to go easy on ourselves, to smile
whenever we can. It might mean striking bargains
—call the phone company and I get to call my
sister just to chat. It might mean looking at unpleasant tasks from a different perspective.

I can cooperate with myself and others to make
unpleasant tasks easier.

JUNE 18

*Love, the quest; marriage, the conquest; divorce, the
inquest.*   —Helen Rowland

When the quest of love, the search for knowing
one another, turns into the conquest of marriage,
the clash of wills in which one party (or both)
tries to control the other, the death called divorce
is nearly inevitable. Divorce is death by uncertain
means and often requires an inquest into its
causes.

An inquest that is retributive, angry, and seeks
to place blame may reveal the cause of death. But
it won't get us beyond the inquest. It won't put
the body of the marriage to rest in peace. It won't
help us get on with our living.

Looking at how we acted in our marriages and
remembering what happened to end them, without trying to place blame or feeling guilt, can
teach us things about how we want to continue
living. We might look back to the days before
quest became conquest. What was it about seeking with another in love that made us want to
marry? What strengths might we retrieve from
that time? What happened next when we tried to
control each other? How might we give that up?

*Having survived the inquest, what did I learn to take
with me in my continuing quest for life?*

JUNE 19

To get power over is to defile. To possess is to defile.
                                            —Simone Weil

How often we put the word "will" in front of
power to make a big club of a word. We can use
willpower to beat ourselves silly. If only I had
enough willpower, I could . . . The litany is
practically endless, from getting more exercise to
working harder. It's a list mostly comprised of
things that are "good" for us, too, not things we
necessarily want to do. We want to use our willpower to put things under our control.

Yet to own our own power is never to overpower ourselves or others. Willpower that attempts to get control over something, to reshape
it into something else by possessing it, is power
defiled. If we think of electric power, power that
flows through a set circuit to light whole cities
and run vast machinery, we are closer to knowing
how to use our power in our lives.

When we channel our energy to accomplish
changes and goals in our lives, we don't try to
accumulate enough power to subdue something.
Rather we keep energy moving through carefully
plotted circuits to reach an end. This is power in
motion, power we can use to light our way.

I can go with the flow of my own power.

JUNE 20

*. . . I looked forward to the return of some of my
strength, or rather some of my optimism—the two are
really one and the same.* —Colette

No matter how strong we are in theory (or even
practice), we're always weaker if we're pessi-
mistic about ourselves and our prospects for applying our strength. And it's difficult to feel
optimistic when we're suffering a loss and facing
an unknown future.

No amount of willing ourselves to be optimistic
about the future is, of course, going to make us
feel that way. Yet if we find ourselves thinking,
however fleetingly, that we just might look forward to the day when our strength returns, we
might take that thought as a harbinger of the return of optimism.

And what might we do with it? Surely not too
much—driving ourselves to feel too optimistic or
to take on new projects, relationships, improve-
ment programs, or plans before we are truly
ready is to set ourselves back. We can build our
strength by living fully present in these days of
the present.

My strength feeds my optimism, and vice versa.

JUNE 21

*We are making hay when we should be making whoopee;
we are raising tomatoes when we should be raising Cain,
or Lazarus. . . . Spend the afternoon. You can't take it
with you.*   —Annie Dillard

It might be time for a critical new reading of the
fable of the grasshopper and the ant. Our profligate friend grasshopper spends the summer afternoons hopping around, enjoying life, while
industrious ant is storing up for the winter. Traditionally, the moral of this tale is that we're supposed to work hard, storing up for adversity.

That grasshopper was having fun and letting
tomorrow take care of itself. Something we might
practice doing. We're told the grasshopper came
looking for food in the winter. The truth is that
she probably didn't live through the winter.

And therein lies another lesson. We don't live
today any more than once. Granted we've got to
spend some of our todays raising tomatoes or
money to buy food. The trick is to raise tomatoes,
trouble, and new beginnings in our lives by paying attention to what the moment demands.
Sometimes the moment demands celebration.

*I can make hay in the sunshine and joyfully walk in
the rain.*

JUNE 22

*Studies show that early childhood losses make us sensitive
to losses we encounter later on. And so, in mid-life, our
response to a death in the family, a divorce, a loss of a job,
may be a severe depression—the response of that helpless
and hopeless, and angry, child.* —Judith Viorst

As we become adults we may put away the
things of our childhood. Yet we can never completely put away the child in us. Every child is
quite sure that if she gives up her bottle or her
blanket, nothing else will ever replace them.

Whatever our childhood losses, they ride with
us to adulthood. When we experience a major
loss, such as the loss of a partner, we inevitably
remember the losses of our childhood. If we truly
grieved our childhood losses, it may be easier for
us to go through our current loss. If we did not,
we find ourselves depressed over the current loss,
and also reliving earlier losses.

Honoring and acknowledging our losses is ultimately the way through our depression. If we
can't feel depression over a loss, we're not likely
to be able to feel anything else either. Ultimately,
feeling nothing leads to not being alive. So, small
comfort though it may be, we can at least tell ourselves that we're alive enough to feel something.

I can't live without loss, I can learn to live with it.

JUNE 23

A mind not aware of itself is like a passenger strapped into an airplane seat, wearing blinders, ignorant of the nature of transportation, the dimensions of the craft, its range, the flight plan, and the proximity of other passengers. The mind aware of itself is a pilot. —Marilyn Ferguson

Imagine the horror of being on an airplane destined for a tropical vacation, only to have the pilot announce the destination is a northern wilderness. Getting divorced can feel a lot like that nightmare. We were going somewhere. We were pretty sure of the direction when we started. Then the plane changed directions. Now we've woken up, and we don't know where or who we are.

Even pilots with the best-laid flight plans find themselves blown off course occasionally. Airplanes suffer mechanical failure. Even people who work at knowing themselves can be surprised to find their lives taking them in unexpected directions.

Pilots can make adjustments for weather and mechanical failures. People who know who they are can figure out where they're going. And people who wake up from nightmares can figure out who they are.

Once I've woken up, I can figure out who I am and where I'm going.

JUNE 24

Anger and jealousy can no more bear to lose sight of their objects than love.   —George Eliot

By the time our marriages deteriorate to the point that we separate, we may well have reached the point where we wish never to see this person, once the object of our love, again. Yet we may find ourselves incapable of carrying out that wish.

In fact, we can hold on to our anger and jealousy even when our ex-spouse is not literally in our sight. We may be green with envy when our children tell us about their father's new love interest. Or, perhaps, a friend's passing comment about an argument with her spouse triggers our memory of our marital arguments. Suddenly we are seeing red, vividly angry all over again.

Denying that we're angry at our ex-spouses or jealous of their new lives won't help us let go of them. Nor will venting our spleen to them. Nor will "rationally" discussing our anger and jealousy with them. Owning our feelings helps: I am angry and/or jealous. He didn't make me so. And I can choose to acknowledge how I feel, to let myself experience my feelings, and to use my experiences to get on with my own life.

Letting go of anger and jealousy is something I do for myself.

JUNE 25

*You gain strength, courage, and confidence by every
experience in which you really stop to look fear in the face.*
                                                    —Eleanor Roosevelt

We can see how tough experiences give us
strength and courage. Well, we lived through getting separated, so that must mean we're strong.
We've gotten through every day since then, so we
must have some courage.

But confidence? In ourselves? Confidence in
ourselves is such an unusual feeling that we
barely recognize it. Many of us can't even credit
our own successes enough to feel confident that
we can repeat them. Okay, I handled that situation, but what if I can't repeat it? What if I appear
overly confident and no one will help me? What if
I can't face my fears next time? What if?

What if we really stop to look our pain and fear
in the face? What if we face the bad things that
have happened to us or could happen to us
squarely, with confidence? What if we were to
give ourselves credit for facing them with confidence? And, if good things happen to us, what if
we own the competency and confidence with
which we participated in the "happening"?

*I can face my life with the confidence that comes
with looking for the truth of each of my experiences.*

JUNE 26

> *Strange we never prize the music*
> *Till the sweet-voiced bird has flown . . .*
> —May Riley Smith

Appreciation and regret are two ends of the same stick we can use to beat ourselves silly. Like this: Woe is me. I didn't know what I had until I lost it. It was wonderful, marvelous, and why in the world didn't I appreciate it? If I ever have it again, I'll certainly cherish it. Or will I?

The attitude that we don't know what we had until we've lost it can be just so much revisionist thinking. Especially when we say to ourselves we really miss something we hated at the time we had it. That might be birds in the backyard or our ex-husband's underwear strewn across the bedroom floor. We're saying to ourselves we *should* have ignored the mess and appreciated the bird or the person.

When we feel regret for losses in our lives, we can explore those feelings to discover what we really prize. We can learn both how to add things we appreciate to our lives and to appreciate them while they're still with us. Practicing the art of appreciation makes us better at it.

Regret and appreciation can be the baton I lead my life with rather than the stick I beat myself with.

JUNE 27

I was searching for a piece of luggage that seemed to have been mislaid, as my own life had for some time seem[ed] slightly mislaid. —Anna Maria Ortese

There is a particular frantic frustration that goes with mislaying a favorite object. As we search, without success, our searching becomes frenzied. We cover the same ground, over and over, missing the object that rests in plain sight. Then the object often turns up when and where we least expect it, after we've given up the search.

If we find ourselves rushing about frantically, searching for people, work, food, alcohol, or other substances to fill our time, if we find ourselves increasingly frustrated that something is missing from our lives, if we're easily distracted, floating or charging from one interest to another, we know that what we've lost, at least temporarily, is our selves, our sense of who we are.

When we're getting used to who we are as single women, we might mislay and find our slightly different selves repeatedly. We can rush around frantically. Or we can sit back, reflect, and let the magic of finding something when we're not looking for it take over.

I can find myself if I know I'm lost and am willing to proceed with my life until I turn up again.

JUNE 28

Important. *When we begin to take our failures
nonseriously, it means we are ceasing to be afraid of them.
It is of immense importance to learn to laugh at ourselves.*
—Katherine Mansfield

"I'm afraid I fail to see the humor of my failure,
which isn't funny, it's frightening." This vicious
cycle begins and ends in fear. Fear begets failure
begets fear begets failure . . . a regular three-
ring circus, but missing the clowns.

So send in the clowns. A clown's traditional
role is both to make the audience laugh and to
distract its attention from frightening possibilities.
During a crisis in a bullfight, clowns attract the
attention of both the audience and the bull long
enough for the matador to escape.

Sending in our own clowns, laughing at ourselves and at our failures and our fears, isn't going to make them go away. It is going to distract
us from our own self-importance long enough to
be able to put our fear and our failure into perspective.

When all else fails, I can send in my clowns.

JUNE 29

*Just when life is heaviest with pain and anguish, that is
the time when we will dance and sing together to waken
the sleeping God of Hope.*   —Sheldon Kopp

We are never too heavy with pain nor too old
with anguish to kick up our heels and dance. Our
step may not be as sprightly as it was on our wedding day. We are older and wiser now. Our voices
may crack with age and memory as we sing.

Yet sing and dance we can, even or especially
when we don't feel like it. We may not want to
dance the night away, humming into someone's
ear. We may not want to participate in a pas de
deux. Yet none of this prevents us from gathering
with friends, family, any group, to figuratively
sing and dance hope back into our lives.

We find hope in sharing our pain and anguish.
Not in recounting endless details of it, but in saying it out loud to sympathetic ears. Others who
know a similar pain may be particularly comforting in ours. And so may those who have known
the pain and gone beyond it to waken the god of
hope. We can learn from them that, though we
will always have the memory of our anguish, we
can wake up to the reality of hope.

*I can get together with myself and others to dance to
the music of hope.*

JUNE 30

Too few is as many as too many. —Gertrude Stein

Too few opportunities, too many problems. Too little money, too much to spend it on. Too much to do, too little time to do it in. Too few friends, too many people depending on me. Too few is as many as too many, depending on what we're counting and how we're looking at it.

Life is full of contradictions, and there's nothing like a divorce to make us notice them. How can I be glad I have time to spend by myself when I spend most of it grieving that I no longer have the companionship of my ex-spouse? How can I count my lovable qualities if I've been rejected? How can I see myself as a nice person if I've ended my relationship?

Contradictions can teach us what we really value. They put us on the track of discovering what's too little and too much in our lives. If we have too few friends we can rely on and feel like too many people are relying on us, perhaps we need to look at how we can ask for reciprocal support. If we have too much to do and too little time to do it, we can look at whether we really want to do all that we're doing.

Counting too few and too many can help me reach the balance of just right.

JULY 1

In periods of transition we are challenging the premises of [our life's] structure—raising questions, exploring new possibilities. Each transition leads to termination of a previous structure. —Judith Viorst

Our lives might seem simpler if only we knew for sure where we were at any given time—where the period of stability ended and the period of transition began. By the time we know we're in transition, we're probably well into it. When we're making a major transition—like ending a marriage—it's crucial to take the time to raise the questions and explore the possibilities.

It's dangerous to look at transitions as apart *from* our lives, not as a part *of* our lives. We may tell ourselves that when I decide where to live, how to spend my time, and with whom, then I will be living. Until then I'm in *transition*.

Yet living with a transition is truly living on the cutting edge. It's admitting that we have new, real possibilities and that they'll only be realized if we give up something of the old and stable. It's being unembarrassed to explore the "who am I" and "where am I going" questions. It's fearlessly applying the wisdom of years to answer those questions in whole new ways.

I live through my transitions by living with them.

JULY 2

To get maximum attention, it's hard to beat a good, big mistake.   —Gazette

When I can't get my own attention any other way, mistakes of commission or omission *will* get it: falling down the stairs, forgetting my mother's birthday or a major business appointment, making three sets of arrangements all for the same evening.

Our mistakes are really about forgetting to pay attention to the details, and failing to pay attention to ourselves—to what we want, need, and feel. Forgetting breeds more mistakes, more forgetting, more mistakes. Pretty soon we've overdrawn our "success" accounts. And we keep paying for our mistakes by compounding them.

The alternative is to pay for our mistakes by paying attention to what they're telling us. If my mistake is constantly overcommitting my time and energy and I find myself flat on my back, I can use the time to plan everything I have to do when I'm allowed up. Or I can pay attention to how I feel—probably in pain. And the pain can lead me to a new, slower and less frantic place.

Paying attention to what I really feel is the best currency with which to pay for my mistakes.

JULY 3

*Anger or revolt that does not get into the muscles remains
a figment of the imagination.*   —Simone de Beauvoir

Anger in our muscles becomes anger in action.
When we act on our anger—as opposed to in anger—we can cause a revolution—a drastic and
dramatic change in our lives. When we let our
anger fester, it can become an obsession that
leaves room for little else—in our imagination or
in our actions.

Many of us have grown up with the dictum
that it's not nice to be angry. And if we must be
angry, then we should dissipate our angry energy
by doing something useful like cleaning out the
linen closet. If we attempt to get rid of our anger
by cleaning closets, we're likely someday to find a
big mess of anger buried on a back shelf of our
being—one that we can't clean up overnight.

Using our anger to turn things around in our
lives takes some effort and some imagination. It
takes acknowledging that we're angry, working
at expressing our anger, and working, constructively, at removing or changing the circumstances
that make us angry. To cause a revolution is not to
make war on ourselves or others. It is to move
from destructive reactions to constructive action.

I can use my anger to turn my life around.

JULY 4

*It has been my experience that freedom comes as the
temperate zone integrates sunside and nightside, thereby
making wholeness instead of brokenness.*

—Madeleine L'Engle

Some people protest they have everything they
ever wanted but they still don't feel free. Some
people bemoan that they never get anything they
want so they're not free. Everything and nothing
do not lead to freedom. Freedom is a middle
ground somewhere between having it all and
having nothing.

Commonly we say freedom must be earned,
that we must pay a price for it. When we talk
about paying a price for freedom, we often focus
on what we must give up to earn it. Or we talk
about what we will have when we have freedom.

What if we were to look at freedom as something to be learned instead of earned? We can figure out how to feel, be, and act free. We can make
compromises between everything and nothing.
We can choose. We can begin to see the freedom
in our lives. We experience feeling and knowing
that, despite achieving what we want or losing
what we had, we are free to live our lives.

*I choose freedom to live my life—in the dark times
and in the light.*

JULY 5

Silences have a climax, when you have got to speak.
                                                    —Elizabeth Bowen

Once there was a married woman who didn't speak. She said nothing about her needs, her wants, her aspirations. She never complained; she never praised. She never nagged; she never asked. She was silent for so long that one day she realized she couldn't hear her own feelings. She not only didn't say how her day was; she didn't know how her day was. She tried to speak to her spouse, but her spouse was no longer there. She tried to speak to herself, and she wasn't there either.

Speaking out—to ourselves and our spouses—might not have saved our marriage. Yet it's a cinch that silence never preserved a relationship worth having. The climax always comes, the time we have to speak up for ourselves and to ourselves. If we don't, we lose ourselves to silence.

When we reach this point, we reach the climax of our story, the time when we need to speak. We must, indeed, start speaking to ourselves—and listening—to discover what it is we lost in all that silence. If we speak out to ourselves and for ourselves, we end our silence with others.

I find my voice when I end my silence.

JULY 6

When the heart weeps for what it has lost, the spirit laughs for what it has found. —Sufi aphorism

Life is not a game of hide-and-seek. We do not always find what we lose. Weeping helps us know what we've really lost. And it helps us find things, too. We may weep for the loss of our relationships, and find that we're really crying for the loss of what they promised to be and never were.

The only sure way to comfort our hearts is to cry over a loss until we're done crying. There are no rules about how long we'll grieve. We grieve our losses while we carry on with our lives. We grieve our losses while we delight in new discoveries that lead to our growth. We cry until we have grieved all that we lost. Our hearts know when that time comes.

When we let our hearts cry, we can also let our spirited selves laugh. Our laughter introduces us to what we're finding out about ourselves. Perhaps that we like our own jokes or that we didn't know we could feel so footloose and free. Perhaps that we didn't know we could laugh and cry at the same time.

I cried until I laughed.

JULY 7

*Freedom is a very great reality. But it means, above all
things, freedom from lies.* —D. H. Lawrence

Honesty is freedom from lies. When we're free
from lies, we're free to find out the truth of our
lives. Honesty may not be the best policy if what
we're trying to do is to preserve the status quo at
any cost. When we're honest with ourselves we
discover new things about ourselves.

Honesty gives us the freedom to face the things
we discover as they come up. In fact, if we continue to live honestly with ourselves, we lose
our ability to repress, deny, and run away from
ourselves. We lose the false freedom of telling ourselves lies. As long as we are honest with
ourselves, we retain our freedom. As long as we
retain our freedom, we are free to be honest with
ourselves. Suppressing our honesty suppresses
our freedom, and vice versa.

A brief dialogue with myself about freedom
and honesty: So where do I get this honesty?
From myself. How do I find it? I listen, and it
finds me. So how do I know if I'm being honest?
If I feel free when I act on it, it's honest.

*I'm free to be me when I'm honest with myself about
who I am.*

JULY 8

Since my house burned down I now own a better view of the rising moon. —Masahide

What we see depends on where we look and on what's blocking our view. Perhaps we don't like what we see from the new vantage point of being single. Maybe our view is blocked by old behaviors, old habits, old addictions that are hard to break. Maybe the view is blocked by a mirror in front of us that shows an angry, depressed victim of our circumstances.

Sometimes in order to get a new view, a new perspective, major shifting is necessary. If the way our single lives have shifted doesn't leave us with a view we like, what are we going to do about it? We can shift ourselves, giving up old behaviors, habits, addictions.

Or we can shift the stuff and circumstances of our lives. We might not burn down our house to see the moon. But if the house had already burned down, we might build a new one in a place where we could have the house and see the moon. We might build a stairway to the roof so we can climb up to see the moon. All these changes in our external circumstances offer us a different perspective.

I can shift my perspective until I like the view.

JULY 9

*For the healthy, a monotonous environment eventually
produces discomfort, irritation and attempts to vary it.*
                                        —Susanna Millar

Boredom can be an agent for change in our lives.
When we get irritated enough with things as they
are, we set out to change them. Yet variety for
variety's sake doesn't lead to no longer being
bored. In fact, we can become bored with change.

There is no "cure" for boredom. Changing our
hairstyle, our house, our job, our relationships,
won't cure our boredom, although these things
might distract us for a while. If we persist in
change simply for change's sake, we'll never hear
what our boredom has to tell us.

Boredom is really the soft voice telling us to
slow down and pay attention. It hints at the need
for us to immerse ourselves in our lives as they
are as well as in the changes we want to make. As
we pay attention to who we are, we notice what is
and is not important and interesting in our monotonous environments. When we know that, we
can change the things that are important to
change.

My boredom can lead me back to myself.

JULY 10

*"Ah! If only there were two of me," she thought, "one
who spoke and the other who listened, one who lived and
the other who watched, how I would love myself!"*
—Simone de Beauvoir

In order to love myself, I have to know her, accept her, and hold her in esteem. If I can't communicate with myself, I can do none of these
things. If we don't listen to ourselves, who will
listen to us? If we don't watch and understand
ourselves, who will do it for us?

We can listen to ourselves in quiet meditation,
in time set aside perhaps to have a cup of tea with
ourselves, to jot down our feelings in a journal.
We can watch ourselves walking along the beach,
enjoying an afternoon in an art gallery, or basking
in the accomplishment of a hard job well done.

We can listen to and watch ourselves only if we
will take time to do it. Listening to myself means
that I tune out other voices—the demands of job,
home, family, as well as the inner voices who
may say: "This is silly. You have nothing important to say." Watching myself doesn't mean judging actions before they're even begun. It means
giving feedback and taking time to savor it.

I can tune in to myself.

JULY 11

Wanting a ball is not wanting a prince.
    —Cinderella, in Stephen Sondheim's *Into the Woods*

Everybody knows Cinderella wanted to go to the ball. She made that quite clear. Everybody assumes she wanted the prince. To think about a Cinderella who makes her wants and needs known beyond the intoxication of romance and magic is to wonder why no one ever bothered to ask her—even if the shoe fit—if she wanted to wear it. The next question is, Did Cinderella ask herself what she wanted next? And do we?

When we got married we might well have thought that having the prince was the next logical thing. As our relationships unravel, though, we ask, maybe for the first time, what it is we need and want in life.

We might wait for someone else to ask and provide—the modern-day fairy godmother or prince. And the modern-day wicked stepmother—our ex, our children, our own worst selves—might keep us figuratively or literally doing the drudge work. Until I realize that I'm the only person who can figure out and say what the Cinderella in me wants, I will remain bound in rags or tripping around in silly glass slippers.

Saying what I want is the first step to getting it.

JULY 12

*I have to stay "turned on" all the time, to keep my
receptivity to what is around me totally open.
Preconception is fatal to this process. Vulnerability is
implicit in it; pain inevitable.* —Anne Truitt

When we give up our preconceived notions
about what might or should happen, we give up
trying to control what will happen. Often we tell
ourselves that we're giving up control and then
expect things to come out a certain way. That is
an illusion of giving up control.

If I think that going on vacation will erase my
pain because I'll have so much fun, I may never
get to the fun part because I'm defining fun as not
feeling my pain. When I give up control and stay
receptive to what's going on in my life, I'm there
to feel the pain, and I'm there to feel the happiness.

When our marriages end, giving up control can
feel like giving up our power to put our lives back
together. In reality, giving up control frees up our
energy and power to change those things in our
lives that we can. It relieves us from the illusion
that our power is based on our ability to control
the people and events in our lives.

*When I give up controlling my future, I am open to
my present—pain and possibility.*

JULY 13

Somewhere in our lives, each of us needs a free place, a little psychic territory. Do you have yours?
—Gloria Steinem

Psychic territory can be all kinds of places—alone or with others. Maybe it's our best friend's kitchen, where we hang out for an afternoon drinking tea and talking. Maybe it's a weekend away from the world. Or a regular meeting with a support group, or fifteen minutes a day spent in meditation. A free place, psychic territory is whatever supports me and makes me feel good.

When we're going through dramatic changes in our lives, giving ourselves time and space is not just a luxury. It is a necessity. When we regularly go to a place which supports us, we replenish our energy. We empower ourselves to be who we are at our very center.

When we're not feeling very good about ourselves, it can seem overwhelming and impossible to think of things to do or places to go to support ourselves. This is a time to be intrepid. To continue the search. To say to myself, If I can't find the perfect time and place, I'll try the imperfect one. If nothing appeals, I'll try something anyway. I'll do it more than once.

Giving myself time and space to be with myself is, in time, its own reward.

JULY 14

No matter how cynical you get, it is impossible to keep up.
—Jane Wagner

Killing, maiming, starving, neglecting, cheating, lying, stealing—the human capacity for actions that belie a belief in anything good ever happening is larger than our capacity to keep up with it. We can't keep current with the possibilities for hurt and evil. And we can't overcome them or counteract them by becoming cynical.

Cynicism and inadequacy feed on each other. If we believe that we're incapable of finding or creating joy, beauty, goodness, and love in our lives, there's no point in looking for the good because all we'll find is bad. Once we find it, we'll find more of it. We're likely to become so cynical and feel so inadequate that our lives become a daily grind that eventually immobilizes us.

Knowing I'm caught in that grind is the first step to turning the wheels in the other direction. If I know that becoming more and more cynical won't let me keep up with my own—let alone others'—capacity to make mistakes, do hurtful things, or fail, I can give up using cynicism to deal with imperfection.

When I give up trying to keep up, I'll have a lot of energy to use for something else.

JULY 15

Play so that you may be serious.   —Anacharsis

Recreation time, leisure activities, quality time, renewal time, relaxation, down time: we have a variety of serious words for something hardly any of us do enough of—plain play. Social scientists study leisure. Time management experts offer a variety of systems for us to schedule recreation. Therapists advise us that we should take time for ourselves.

We may swim so we'll have more energy. Or we read the latest book so we can talk intelligently. Or we schedule play time to do business—a tennis date to win a new client, dinner to discuss a problem. Fun things done with an agenda are often worthwhile and rewarding.

But they aren't playing. Playing is fooling around. It's doing something or doing nothing just because we want to. We can play alone or with others. We can plan our play in advance or do it spontaneously. What makes it play is that the only agenda is having fun; this lets us be fully present to ourselves in that moment. When we practice being fully present to playing, we get better at being fully present for the rest of our lives.

When I'm serious about playing, I have more resources to be serious.

JULY 16

*Perhaps we perceive expression, particularly emotional
expression, as risky because it makes us vulnerable to
others, vulnerable to embarrassment or failure, and so we
resist it. Looking at it another way, we need to relearn
receptivity before we can become expressive again.*
—Gabrielle Rico

When we've been hurt, just about the last thing
we want is to be hurt again. Yet we can't heal our
hurt until we express it—to ourselves or others.
And we can't express it without opening up the
possibility that we'll feel it all over again.

If we express our feelings, we run the risk of
appearing stupid or vulnerable, or of being mis-
understood. If we resist expressing our feelings,
we run the risk of not feeling anything. We have
to feel feelings to be able to express them. We
have to express feelings in order to deal with
them.

We can risk receptivity. We can practice allowing ourselves to feel what we are feeling without attempting to explain, rationalize, justify. We
can become a TV with good reception. When the
colors are true and the audio comes clear, we can
see, hear, trust, and know what we're feeling.

*When I'm tuned in to my own feelings, I can risk
expressing them.*

JULY 17

*To mention a loved object, a person, or a place to someone
else is to invest that object with reality.*
                                —Anne Morrow Lindbergh

It's a common enough experience to find ourselves saying something that we didn't know we
knew or believed until we said it. Having said it,
we feel a sort of "aha!" Saying it didn't make it
real. Saying it made us aware that it's part of our
reality.

When we're recovering from a loss of love,
naming our desires and our loves out loud can
help bring them into reality focus. We might discover that, in reality, we love sleeping alone, eating fresh fruit, going for walks, museums, nature
—any number of things we have been out of
touch with.

Truthfully articulating what it is we love puts
us in touch with our reality. Knowing our reality,
we can make choices that support it. We can
choose to surround ourselves with things we
love, spend more time doing things we love,
spend more time with people we love. Making
choices that support ourselves leads us to know
more about our reality.

*In reality, saying what I love may lead to saying
that I love myself.*

JULY 18

The net of the sleeper catches fish. —Greek proverb

According to traditional lore, fish is brain food. When we're feeling "stupid"—feeling like we can't figure out who we are or what we want, a feeling we live with when we're going through a separation—we can use all the brain food we can get. Our dreams net the fish for us.

The fish might be feelings—sadness, anger, rage, contentment, happiness, excitement. The fish might be events from our recent or past lives, as they happened, as we wish they'd happened, and/or with a weird twist. Or they might be images, places, people we don't recognize from our conscious lives at all. Whatever they are, they are fish in nets, ready and waiting for us to bring them up into our waking, conscious lives.

Dreams are food for living. When we look at our dreams, we might ask: What nourishing message is this dream giving me? How do the parts fit together? Have I got spicy fish stew here or simple grilled fish? Is this dream suggesting I might add something to my life? Or leave behind something else?

The fish I net in my dreams makes me smarter.

JULY 19

Nothing is so burdensome as a secret.

—French proverb

Keeping secrets complicates our lives. We might begin by keeping secret that our marriage is in trouble. We don't tell our spouses what we see because we're afraid they will confirm it. We don't tell our friends or family because we're afraid that they'll see it too or judge us. We don't tell ourselves because it's too painful to face.

Once we're keeping a secret it seems easier not to tell anything related to it. Pretty soon we're covering up whole areas of our lives, telling lies to protect our secrets. We might have started out keeping secrets to try to preserve our marriages, and we end up with our marriages ended.

We can't change the fact that our marriages ended. We can face our lives and our selves as we are now, without secrets. Revealing secrets doesn't mean I have to tell everybody everything. It does mean that I have to tell myself. And sharing my fears, my failures, my shortcomings, *and* my secrets with someone I trust completely helps me put them in perspective and prevents them from growing out of proportion.

Telling my secrets lightens my load.

JULY 20

Risk! Risk anything! Care no more for the opinion of others, for those voices. Do the hardest thing on earth for you. Act for yourself. Face the truth.

—Katherine Mansfield

When we begin to risk, to act for ourselves, ugly questions follow close on the heels of I will, I can, I want. What about my children? my ex? my job? money? my friends? my parents? the greater good? What will happen to all of them if I don't care for their opinions?

Envision a scenario in which we try to please everybody: My boss wants me to work late, my children want me home, my parents want me to call them at seven Wednesday night, which happens to be the time of the meeting my friend wants me to attend, which also happens to be when my ex wants to meet to talk about money.

So maybe we can imagine another scenario in which we do what we want. Yes, it's hard. The boss, the children, the parents, the friend, the ex— somebody's bound to be disappointed. Yet only when I act courageously to meet my own needs, when I risk doing what I want, will I be able to act on the behalf of others as well.

When I act for myself, I can act for others.

JULY 21

It takes taste to account for taste. —Spanish proverb

Taste is so highly individual that the more familiar saying about it, of course, is that there's no accounting for some people's. Taste is like beauty —in the eye of the beholder. And in our lives, with regard to our own persons and our own surroundings, we are our own prime beholders. If we do not think we are attractive, interesting, and tasteful, who will?

Taste, attraction, and beauty go beyond skin deep. And they have to do with who we are— what we think, feel, do—the whole sum is greater than the parts of our selves. Conditioned as we are by the popular "culture," we often think that attraction or taste has to do with sex appeal. As in, his taste in women runs to young and slim. If we look at things that way, no matter who we are, we can't be young or slim enough.

We *can* cultivate a taste for ourselves. If that doesn't account for or attract that taste we want in an intimate relationship or even a friendship, it will let us enjoy our own company. Expressing our own tastes helps us get to know a person to whom we are attractive—ourselves.

There is some accounting for my taste for myself.

JULY 22

Life itself is the most effective help for our development.
—Karen Horney

My life is not happening to someone else. And I only get this life. I can spend my time trying to learn to be a better, smarter, saner, happier person by searching for a guru, taking on self-improvement projects for my mind, body, or spirit, or reading books about what should be happening to women my age. Or I can accept that this is my life, right now, today.

What does it mean to accept my life? Does it mean that I don't strive to change? Does it mean that I wallow in the pain of my divorce? Does it mean that if I accept my circumstances as they now are they will never change? No, no, and no! When I accept that I'm single again, I can stop expending needless energy wishing I weren't. I can use that energy to change and grow in ways I never before dreamed possible.

My life may not be what I expected. My life may be longer, shorter, happier, sadder, more interesting, more mundane than the lives of other women. The one sure thing is that my life is mine. When I accept that, I can begin to read my life like a book and to learn its lessons for me.

I accept my life; I become my own best teacher.

JULY 23

Stay with what is, and it will give you everything that isn't.   —Natalie Goldberg

When we're sad, angry, depressed, and disillusioned—feeling like nothing is right and never likely to be again—one common impulse is to fight our present circumstances. We try to will away whatever it is that we don't like. We might not have a clue about what we want that *isn't* for us now. And yet we try desperately to live in the future, to bring the *isn't* to the *is now*.

Now is a good time to patiently and thoroughly experience what is in our lives. Patience is a habit of bearing what is. When we live with patience, we live in the present moment. We're not apt to act hastily. We are apt to notice what's going on in our lives and to get in touch with our heart's desires.

Patience is a good practice when things begin to look brighter for us as well. Once we've started to make some changes in our lives, to define and find what *isn't*, whatever that is will only really become present in our lives if we let it sink in slowly, with patience.

When I have the patience to live in the present, the future will become the present someday.

JULY 24

When one is pretending the entire body revolts.
—Anaïs Nin

It is now common knowledge that stress contributes to illness—headaches, stomach problems, backaches, and more. When we pay attention to our bodies, our bodies will tell us when we're pretending, living a lie, or making decisions not in our best interest.

When our lives are full of change and stress, we need to stop, look, and listen. Our bodies and their revolts give us clues. Perhaps we think we're dealing with the tension of our newly single lives. And our eyes twitch constantly. When we're making a decision we can take into account how our bodies feel. Do our stomachs ache? Do our backs sag? Or do we throw our shoulders back and smile at the prospect?

Learning to listen to our bodies takes practice. We may be surprised by a tension headache in the midst of an experience that was supposed to be relaxing or happy. Or we may be equally surprised by a tingling in our fingertips or shiver down our spines that indicates we're on the right track. Each time we pay attention to our bodies' reactions we increase our ability to "read" ourselves.

My body is a barometer I can learn to follow.

JULY 25

And we also find that if we can acknowledge, reclaim and harness some of the untamed feelings of our childhood, we can become, in mid-life, more empathic, more lusty, more daring, more nuanced, more honest and more creative.
—Judith Viorst

As children many of us were encouraged not to wear our hearts on our shirtsleeves. Perhaps our parents didn't want to see us hurt, so they discouraged enthusiasms they thought would lead to disappointment. Perhaps they couldn't stand to see us hurting, so they urged us to show a happy face to the world.

Perhaps nobody actually told us to hide our emotions. As we grew we simply figured out that it seemed easier to do so. We wouldn't make others uncomfortable. Maybe we wouldn't have to deal with wild uncharted country of that scary feeling. As adults we may continue this habit of burying our feelings. Or some crisis may jolt us into emotion—rage, anger, sadness, depression—that we can't bury.

Such a crisis affords us an opportunity to remember and unearth our feelings. And we discover that our feelings don't have to be only scary. We have the potential to harness our wild feelings, to put them to use in our own service.

I can reclaim my own emotional territory.

JULY 26

It is not easy to find happiness in ourselves, and it is not possible to find it elsewhere.   —Agnes Repplier

True or false: We won't find happiness in a bottle or in a bag of potato chips. We won't find happiness in a better job, a different house. We won't find happiness in a self-help book or a self-improvement program. We won't find happiness in a new lover. We won't find constant happiness. We won't find happiness until we look. True!

Have we stopped looking around for happiness yet? Good, now we can get down to the business of finding it where and when we can. Who, me, be happy? What am I, nuts? I'm getting divorced, my life is falling apart. I'm too old, too fat, too set in my ways, too weak, too dependent, too sure I'll never be happy again to be happy.

We haven't found it yet, have we? Let's stop looking and let ourselves feel what we're feeling. Grief, anger, rage, dependence, weakness, whatever. And now let's go on living in the here and now of how we feel. Let's finish a project; take a long, hot bath; plan a vacation. Let's call an old friend. Let's flex our muscles and move furniture around. Oops! It snuck up on me. Just this minute, I'm feeling a little happy.

I find my happiness when I'm living my life.

JULY 27

You cannot shake hands with a closed fist.
                                        —Indira Gandhi

We can't shake hands and make up while our fists are still clenched in anger. That's obvious. It's less obvious how we might, given a desire to forgive or be forgiven, let go of our resentment and negative attitude, how we might unclench our fists and be ready to shake hands. A simple brain-to-hand directive won't do it. "Hello, fist. Listen up. This is your brain speaking. It's time to open up. Time to forgive and forget."

No way is mind-over-matter going to make us ready to shake hands. It takes naming and saying out loud what brought us to the clenched-fist point in the first place. And it takes movement.

A clenched fist, particularly if it is held in that position for a long time, is a hand under stress. It needs to be relaxed. And I can relax it, one finger at a time, one muscle at a time, by meeting my resentments, articulating what I need to let them go and reaching an agreement with myself or whoever else I want to shake hands with. Then I can reach out with an open hand.

If I open my heart, my hand will follow.

JULY 28

Those who do not complain are never pitied.

—Jane Austen

Good girls don't complain. Good girls don't want pity. Pity is bad. People who complain to get pity are victims. Victims are bad. Victims complain. Complaining is bad. This circular litany often prevents us from taking care of ourselves by talking with other people about our troubles when it might do us some good to do so.

Perhaps we've all known someone who complains endlessly. It's frustrating because we never know what to do for that person. And, perhaps most of all, we're afraid of seeing that person in our mirrors in the morning. Complaining and pity have a negative connotation in our lives, in which standing on our own two feet, taking care of ourselves, and being independent are valued above all.

Telling other people our troubles doesn't mean we expect them to solve them or to do something to make us feel better. Nor does it mean we need to complain. Telling isn't complaining and pity isn't compassion. And if we never share our troubles, we're never going to receive the compassion we deserve.

Let me graciously ask for and gratefully accept the sympathy I need.

JULY 29

People who fight fire with fire usually end up with ashes.
                                               —Abigail Van Buren

What makes us want to hurt those who hurt us?
Theories abound: Some say human nature, instinct, self-preservation, self-defense. Behavior
learned in the sandbox. A show of strength. Still
others say: Self-defeating behavior. Cutting off
my nose to spite my face. Two more schools of
thought: The best revenge is living well. Don't get
mad, get even.

   If our house is on fire, we want to put the fire
out. If we want to resolve a conflict, we can't fan
the flames of revenge. We've all heard stories of
campfires, supposedly put out, but with one tiny
piece left smoldering. Fires like that have burned
whole forests. Smoldering resentments have
turned whole lives to ashes.

   In considering past conflicts with our mates or
in resolving those that arise after we separate, the
only real question can be how to put the fire out.
How to resolve the conflict, without making
someone the winner and someone else the loser,
without seeking revenge. How to see our way
through the smoke to getting what we *really* want
and need.

*I douse the fires smoldering in my heart by giving
up my need for revenge.*

JULY 30

. . . the total deprivation of sex produces irritability.
—Elizabeth Blackwell

Sex and sexuality are part of being human. Sometimes they seem like the most complicated and disturbing parts. We all must make our own decisions about when, where, with whom, and in what sort of relationship to express our sexuality after we divorce. And our decisions are affected by our own personal and religious beliefs, our families, and our culture.

It is not the total deprivation of sexual activity with another person that makes us irritable. It is the negation of our bodies, of ourselves as sexual beings. We may even try to deny that we have sensual bodies.

We can be aware that we are sexual beings when we're not engaging in sexual relationships. When we're feeling irritable we can indulge ourselves in a long, hot bath. We can let a trusted friend hug us or give us a back rub. We can talk to ourselves or someone else about the complicated question of sex after divorce. And we can let ourselves be open to the possibility of someday being involved in a loving, caring relationship.

Trusting myself when it comes to questions of sexuality is apt to make me feel a lot less irritable.

JULY 31

A little sunburnt by the glare of life . . .
                    —Elizabeth Barrett Browning

Experience, they say, is the best teacher. We may be sunburned from the glare of life, stoop-shouldered from carrying its burdens, exhausted from working at it twenty-four hours a day. But when it comes to figuring out what we're learning from life, we may feel like we're blind, deaf, and dumb —as in mute *and* stupid.

It may be time to lighten up. To put on some sunscreen and get out into the sunshine. To put down our grocery sacks, briefcases, backpacks, shoulder bags, and excess luggage, and take an unencumbered stroll. To call it quits and take a nap. Getting divorced can feel like getting burned by life. And getting through each day, doing everything we have to do alone, *and* figuring out what it all means feels like too much.

We can take a break from our experience and from seeking the wisdom of its lessons. And begin to see that knowing when to take a break is one of the lessons. Once we're out of the glare and the hubbub we can begin to hear our hearts, to speak our minds, and to listen.

Part of my wisdom is knowing when to take a break from experience.

AUGUST 1

*Being does mean becoming, but we run so fast that it is
only when we seem to stop—as sitting on the rock at the
brook—that we are aware of our own* isness, *of being.*
                                    —Madeleine L'Engle

How often do we feel like a grown-up Alice in
Wonderland? We are inundated with experiences,
duties, demands on our time. Why do I have
twenty-five things on a one-day "to do" list? Am
I going to be late for the tea party? Do I know
how to play today's crazy croquet?

When I'm here, in the present moment, I'm doing what I'm doing. We miss things when we try
to be two places at once. If I take a child to the zoo
but spend my time obsessing about the undone
laundry, will the laundry get done? No, and I
might miss a child seeing a real-life giraffe for the
first time.

Being means becoming, even though we need
to do things, too. "Doing" is breathing in the air
of this present moment—the middle of a tricky
job negotiation, of creating a cake, of a crisis with
our children. And we all need to find our own
rock at the brook, that place in time and space
where we "do" the being part of becoming.

*The only way to be in the present moment is to be in
the present moment.*

AUGUST 2

*In hell, people have chopsticks a yard long so they cannot
reach their mouths. In heaven, the chopsticks are the same
length—but the people feed one another.*
                                        —Vietnamese folk wisdom

When the best tools aren't available to us, the best thing we can do is to make do with the tools we have. And sometimes the best way to make do is to enlist the help of others.

Everybody knows that the best way to get something done is to have the right tools for the job. Yet life's circumstances are what we have to work with—and the perfect tool for "fixing life" hasn't yet been invented. The person who can adapt tools for the job at hand is likely to get it done faster than the person who spends her life searching for the perfect tool. And the person who enlists the help and cooperation of others is likely to have her needs met *and* to have the satisfaction of helping meet the needs of others.

Reciprocity is crucial to using less-than-perfect tools. Everybody is hungry. And cooperation is the only difference between heaven and hell. She who refuses food from the chopsticks of others or who refuses to feed others will find herself going hungry alone.

I can use the tools I have—including others' help.

AUGUST 3

*Facing shame . . . is like using Drano; all the jammed
gunk has to come up before our drains (our spiritual
centers) can function properly.* —Marilyn Mason

Many of us have gunky old messages about
what we were supposed to do and be as married
women. Lots of those messages have to do with
staying married—no matter what. And most of us
feel ashamed that we didn't "make it work," even
if we acted positively to get ourselves out of relationships that were abusive or stunting.

I could have been more compliant, caring, loving, giving, understanding, forgiving, honest . . .
the list is nearly endless. We feel shame because
we weren't perfect. And we feel more shame because we haven't lived up to somebody else's—
our ex-spouse's, our children's, our families', our
church's, our society's—expectations for us.

Shame thrives on unmet expectations—our
own and others'—held in secrecy. Facing our
shame, naming it out loud, breaks the secrecy.
When we know this we can examine what shames
us. We can distinguish the things we did that we
wish we hadn't from the pervasive, clogging feeling of shame that we are bad people.

Naming my shame unclogs my spiritual drain.

AUGUST 4

I tore myself away from the safe comfort of certainties
through my love for truth; and truth rewarded me.
                                        —Simone de Beauvoir

Hundreds of reasons and thousands of circumstances bring about the end of a relationship. One
common thread is that the truth of our lives has
somehow become blurred, obscured, and damaged in the comfort of certainties that are no
longer true.

Our safe certainty may have been obliterated
through sudden betrayal. Or it may have been
buried over the years as layers of dust cover a
chandelier. The certainty may have been a pretty
good life or a pretty awful one, but it was comfortable and certain. And it is not until we are
torn away from the certainties that we can begin
to see the truth of our relationship and ourselves.

The truth may not be—indeed, probably is not
—comfortable. Yet it is almost inevitably a relief. I
no longer have to pretend to be amused by my
ex-spouse's boorish behavior at a party. I no
longer have to keep my hair long because he likes
it that way. I can feel relief at not having to cover
up the truth of who I am and who I want to be.

Giving up my safe comfort of certainty for the truth
can be revealing.

AUGUST 5

*Like begets like. We gather perfect fruit from perfect trees.
. . . Abused soil brings forth stunted growths.*
                                                    —Margaret Sanger

When someone we know and love is being abused, the very first thing we need to do is everything in our power to stop that abuse. Abuse cycles through generations, and that cycle can be broken by a courageous person or persons who are willing to change the soil.

Abuse can be inflicted emotionally and verbally. That sort of abuse may not be as immediately life threatening, but it does cause stunted development in us and/or our children. We abuse ourselves when we tell ourselves that we're useless, worthless, less than perfect, and when we let others say the same things. We abuse ourselves when we don't accept our mistakes and go on. In abusing ourselves or others, and in allowing ourselves to be abused, we ensure stunted growth.

The opposite of tearing down is, of course, building up. To break the cycle of abuse in ourselves and our families, we must create a new sense of self. We must not only stop the tearing down, we must begin the building up.

I can build myself up.

AUGUST 6

It's odd that you can get so anesthetized by your own pain or your own problem that you don't quite fully share the hell of someone close to you. —Lady Bird Johnson

Compassion for ourselves or others means suffering with them. It doesn't mean getting so lost in our suffering that we disallow other feelings and experiences. Letting our own suffering exclude all else is called self-absorption.

There once was a woman who had suffered much. People knew this and came to her with their own tales of woe. She was willing to listen and to share her story. No matter what happened to them, it reminded her of something that happened to make her suffer even more than the other person. As time passed fewer people shared their sorrows with her. She couldn't understand why. After all, she was a woman of great compassion and even greater suffering.

Having compassion doesn't mean we try to meddle and "fix" people's lives—our own or others. It means we are present to and for the suffering. We see with compassionate eyes, we speak with a compassionate voice. In doing so, we may help ourselves and others see beyond the pain.

Compassion is being there, for myself and others, on the way through suffering.

AUGUST 7

Experience is a good teacher, but she sends in terrific bills.
                                        —Minna Antrim

Truisms become truisms because they're very often true and nearly universal. Like "Experience is the best teacher," or "You get what you pay for." So if experience is the best teacher, maybe her bills are terrific—terrifically high and worth it.

Being heavily invested in our experiences, good or bad, it's up to us how to use our investment. We can use the pendulum approach to bad experiences: this relationship didn't work out, so we look for exactly the opposite kind of person to love. For our good experiences we might be tempted to use the instant replay approach, living to re-create as exactly as possible our good experiences, avoid anything new.

Or, when we're starting over as singles, we might use the archaeological approach. We dig around in our own past part of the time, looking for facts, hints, clues about what's happened to us, how the choices we've made affect us. And part of the time we live our present life, carefully testing assumptions or conclusions we have drawn from our past experience.

My experience is part gold mine and part garbage dump, and I might find useful things in all of it.

AUGUST 8

> *I smother in the house in the valley below,*
> *Let me out to the night, let me go, let me go!*
> —Anna Wickham

Whether we choose to leave a marriage or have that choice foisted on us, we all were smothering part of ourselves in the relationship. And if we did not initiate our separation, it may be hard to see that. Once we see it, our cry can only be let me go—into the night.

Going into the night means I don't know where I'm going. I don't know why. I don't know what I want, except the chance to be me. Even if I don't know who me is. I will go out into the night, where it's dark. Where the house in the valley won't smother me, and where whatever heat and light it gave me won't reach me either. In any event, ready or not, here I go, breathing the night air. Night air is cold and dark. It can be scary. It can also be refreshing and invigorating.

We're on the road, out of the house, off to make our way in the world, with few clues about how to do it or where we'll go. It may be all uphill from here, and the views are great along the way.

Breathing in uncertainty is better than smothering in familiarity.

AUGUST 9

A difference of taste in jokes is a great strain on the affections. —George Eliot

Part of recovering from a divorce is recovering our relationships. This means being in "old" relationships in new ways and forming new relationships. People who are in recovery from addictions often find that they choose not to stay in relationships with their old friends, who are still behaving in destructive ways and because their perspective has changed.

When we share a sense of humor with our friends, family, or lover, we share a way of looking at ourselves and the world around us. When we don't share humor, our perspectives are so different that we probably don't have much else in common either.

When we're making new attachments humor can be a good barometer. If we don't understand each other's humor, will we understand each other's pain? If we can't share zany moments, will we be able to share peaceful moments? Shared humor can ease the strain of our new relationships with others and with our new single self.

If I can laugh with myself, I can live with myself. Ditto for others in my life.

AUGUST 10

Jealousy is no more than feeling alone against smiling enemies. —Elizabeth Bowen

And no less. Just as we're all going to feel alone at times in our lives, we're all going to feel jealous. The point of recognizing our jealousy is not to expunge it from our lives, despite centuries of cultural and religious teachings to the contrary. Attempting to deny feelings by erasing them only brings them back with a vengeance.

Getting to know our jealousy means getting to know who those smiling enemies are. They can be inside us or they can be people who make us feel jealous. What do they have to teach us?

Jealousy just might be a clue that we're somehow not living up to what we want for ourselves. We're jealous of A's job, B's love interest, C's vacation plans. A's job would drive us nuts; we'd probably kill B's partner if we lived with him for a week; and C's going camping without the comforts of home. We don't really want what they have. What we do want is the feeling of having what we want, which is what we think they have.

My jealousy can help me get in touch with what I want.

AUGUST 11

No one has ever loved anyone the way everyone wants to be loved. —Mignon McLaughlin

Our expectations of love almost always exceed the reality, in part because our expectations are both unconscious and ill-defined. We may think we know what we want because we think our parents or others in our lives have it—or they don't and we want it. We may never consciously say to ourselves that this person whom we love is going to meet all our expectations. We may even consciously say the opposite.

And we often proceed to act as if he will be all to us. We act as if he is responsible for the way we feel, for making us happy, for letting us be vulnerable, for making us strong, for comforting us, nurturing us, and letting us be our own person. To expect all this is to expect perfection from another, which is as disappointing and unrealistic as expecting perfection from ourselves.

Perhaps the only person who can love us as we truly want to be loved is our self. If love is total affirmation, full acceptance of ourselves, warts and all, who better can we ask for such love than ourselves? And our unconditional love grows and attracts the love of others.

I can be my own best lover.

AUGUST 12

*I learned that true forgiveness includes total acceptance.
Out of acceptance wounds are healed and happiness is
possible again.* —Catherine Marshall

Forgiving ourselves or others consists of three
parts—acknowledging that there is something to
be forgiven, resolving to participate in making
amends (either making them or accepting them),
and letting go. If we don't tell the truth about
what is to be forgiven or try to manipulate the
amends or don't let go, we easily reopen our
wounds of anger, hurt, remorse, and sorrow.

Acceptance has no conditions. Acceptance is
not thinking, "I acknowledge that I must forgive
myself for hurting my spouse, except he made me
do it." Accepting amends is not saying, "I forgive
you, but you must prove your love." When we let
go, we don't forget that we were hurt. We acknowledge and remember it, and then we release
our anger and hurt as we heal.

When we're getting a divorce it may seem like
the pain of our wounds will never heal. We've
accumulated hundreds of holes in our hearts. We
don't need to forgive all at once, and as we begin
to forgive and to heal, we get stronger in our ability to accept and forgive.

Forgiving makes my heart grow stronger.

AUGUST 13

Intimacy is the co-creation of an experience of shared
closeness and connection in a variety of activities that are
deep and personal. —Marilyn Mason

As we face our marriage's end, the reality is that
other intimate relationships are affected. They inevitably change because we do. Perhaps some of
our closest friends have only known us as one of
a couple. Perhaps we lose part of our family. Even
if we don't lose relationships, we need to cocreate
new shared connections.

Rebuilding intimate connections and building
new ones takes time and energy. Nobody ever
said intimacy is easy. At this point, reaching out
to create connections may be the last thing we feel
like doing. Especially if we believe that building
deep and personal connections means being
bright, entertaining, and interesting—sharing
only the "positive" side of ourselves.

Deep personal connections aren't confined to
the good stuff. They are connections; we both talk
and listen. We find other people to be there for us
and we're there for them. Maybe to share a good
cry, explore a beach, talk through a problem, or
see a funny movie. In a variety of ways, with a
variety of people, we can create intimacy.

Intimacy is reciprocity that begins with reaching out.

AUGUST 14

*Concern should drive us into action and not into a
depression.* —Karen Horney

Action can be taking a walk, a bubble bath, two
aspirin, and to our beds. Action can also be working on a project we hold dear, getting the laundry
done, or spending time with our family. Action
can be anything we want it to be.

If I'm feeling depressed, the action might well
be to take time to discern and own my feelings.
Owning feelings is naming them, living with
them when they come to me, not pushing them
down with busywork, but leaning into them. If
we can learn to lean into our depressions, we can
learn to take the actions that will lead us out of
them.

Action that comes from the heart, whether it's
hitting a pillow or giving ourselves a present, is
healing action. Taking time to ensure our actions
are serving us well is also taking action.

My concern drives me to act for myself, day by day.

AUGUST 15

One cannot collect all the beautiful shells on the beach.
                    —Anne Morrow Lindbergh

We all have to choose—which people we'll become intimate with, which jobs we'll take, and what we'll eat for dinner. We make some of our choices from a plethora of good options, like choosing shells from a beautiful beach. In those cases, we choose for the beauty, the pleasure, the good that will last.

At other times, we must choose from bad options, or even from options that are so well hidden as to seem no options at all. A tragedy befalls us—an illness, the inevitable end of a relationship—and it feels more like choosing our poison. Our only choice in some cases is what we will do to mitigate the bad effects.

When we're faced with choices like these, it's tempting to "forget" or deny that we have choices. We may have to choose between staying in our house and moving to a smaller place. But, since we don't like either option, we tell ourselves we don't have a choice. Avoiding choices means avoiding ourselves. Making choices means living with ourselves.

Making choices makes me better at seeing which of the beautiful shells I want for my life.

AUGUST 16

However, one cannot put a quart in a pint cup.
— Charlotte Perkins Gilman

We can't make ourselves into something we aren't. We can't force ourselves into roles that no longer fit us. And we can't know who we are and what role suits us unless we give ourselves the space and opportunities to find out.

When we feel like there's not space or time enough for us in our current lives, we can create space and time for ourselves. We can use that time to experiment. We can try new roles and discard them if they don't fit. We can try containing our emotions in a place that's not big enough for them, or we can find new ways to express them.

When we're getting divorced we may feel a lot like a person who's trying to fit a quart's worth of something into a pint cup. We've got all this pain, all this anger. We've got more to do than we have time to do it. And we're trying to hold it all together, keep it contained. That's as impossible as putting a quart of milk in a pint container; we're bound to spill some.

There's not room for a quart of experience in a pint jar. There *is* room for it in two pint jars.

I can make a space for myself and I can choose how I will fill it.

AUGUST 17

Open your mouth—or your pocketbook.
—Mary Lou Flandrick

If we don't speak up for ourselves, it's going to cost us. It may cost time, money, or a piece of our hearts. The longer we wait to speak up, the more it's likely to cost. We all have reasons for not speaking out our true feelings and ideas to our families, our colleagues, the world at large. They may think we're stupid, dissatisfied, ungrateful. They may not like us anymore.

It may cost us friendships, jobs, money, or marriages to speak out. We may find that once we've spoken our feelings aloud, we can't go on the way we have been. We may need to change our lives, giving up what seemed comfortable.

Yet to keep our mouths and ourselves closed, to let things pass as if they were unnoticed, day after day and year after year, takes a toll. If we state clearly to ourselves and others what we need and want, we might not get it. If we are silent about what we need and want, we surely aren't going to get it. If we are quiet enough for long enough, we eventually get to the point where we don't know what we think and feel.

Silence is too expensive for me.

AUGUST 18

How quick come the reasons for approving what we like!
—Jane Austen

When we find ourselves liking something or someone, we often find ourselves rationalizing our approval. We might gloss over or excuse objectionable qualities in the person we like. Or we approve of an idea, concept, theory, object, except for this, that, or the other part of it. If we find ourselves rationalizing or yes-butting our approval, perhaps we need to look at whether we approve of that person, behavior, or idea after all.

If we don't approve of someone's behavior, are we afraid that person will stop liking us back? Are we saying that if we don't approve of some part of the person we like—ourselves or another—we're afraid that we won't like that person anymore?

Are we using approval as a bargaining chip? If I approve of you, then you will return the favor and approve of me. We all need approval—from ourselves and others. To truly approve—or be approved—we have to basically feel related to, feel the truth of a person, action, idea, concept. Manufactured or justified approval will never truly feel like approval.

Self-approval means liking myself, but not
necessarily everything I do.

AUGUST 19

Worry does not empty tomorrow's sorrow; it empties today of its strength.   —Corrie ten Boom

Worrying uses up energy we might expend to deal with today's problems and challenges. As if that weren't enough, worry lets us live on credit until we're so far beyond our means we've used up all our reserves.

It works something like this: I'm worried. My life is changing. Who knows what tomorrow will bring? Surely, given today and yesterday, it can't be good. Besides, I might lose what good things I have; I've lost so much already. And even if tomorrow is okay, there's next week to worry about, next month, next year, after I retire.

Suddenly worrying has got me from today into a faraway tomorrow that I don't even know exists. It's taken me from morning to bedtime. I haven't done a lot, but I sure am tired. And since I spent today worrying about what might happen, I didn't accomplish any of my goals or solve any of my problems. So I go to sleep worrying about what I didn't get done and wake up worrying that there's so much to do.

If I gave up worrying, I'd have the energy to prevent some of what I worry about.

AUGUST 20

When I think of the incredible, incomprehensible sweep of creation above me, I have the strange reaction of feeling fully alive. Rather than feeling lost and unimportant and meaningless, set against galaxies which go beyond the reach of furthest telescopes, I feel that my life has meaning.
—Madeleine L'Engle

When we feel overwhelmed, it is usually at the prospect of all we have to do. We feel overwhelmed at the prospect of living up to our own unrealistic expectations, or those we think others have of us. Feeling overwhelmed is looking inside ourselves, seeing only chaos, and being sure that we are powerless to create order.

We are powerless to control chaos in order to create order. And if we're caught up in the whirl of feeling overwhelmed, sometimes it's best to take a stroll under the stars. Looking up and looking out can help us put ourselves in perspective.

There is order even if we can't see all of it. Not being able to see all of it means we don't have to control all of it. Not having to control all of it means we can probably manage our part of it.

I can get over feeling overwhelmed by giving up my attempt to control the world and letting myself find my place in it.

AUGUST 21

> *and I*
> *grow younger as I leave*
> *my me behind.*
> —Dilys Lang

Letting go of the past is neither trying to forget it nor clinging wishfully to it. Letting go liberates us from ourselves and from those parts of our past that we don't want to keep reenacting. The parts that we leave behind make way for the new.

Letting go of parts of our lives is not the same as leaving luggage in a locker at the airport and throwing away the key. Nor is it like burying garbage and hoping it won't rise to the surface. We'll never find anything new to feel younger and freer about if we try these ways to get rid of the past. We'll always remember what's buried where. We'll still be carrying it.

Letting go is more like taking the old clothes inside the luggage to a consignment store, one item at a time, and being surprised at what we can trade in exchange for our old stuff. Or it's like planting a piece of potato or an apple seed, nurturing the soil, and waiting to see what comes up.

As I let go of heavy old baggage I feel younger and freer to begin new adventures.

AUGUST 22

Inside the fallen brown apple, the seed is alive.

—Marge Piercy

When we get divorced, we may well feel like the rotten, brown apple. Having fallen from the tree, where *all* the other apples are bright, shiny, and happily married, we feel inferior. We may feel like we just want to lie there and rot. And that is exactly what we might do for a time. We may lie low, experiencing our feelings of inferiority.

When we let ourselves experience our grief and our pain, sooner or later we realize that this fallen rotten apple does have a seed inside it. And inside us, we have the seed of something as well. We don't know what that seed might grow to be. We know that it's in there though, trying to push through and grow.

The seed of our new growth will be related to our old selves. Apples don't have pumpkin seeds inside them. And it will let us grow into something a little different. No two apples are alike. The seed of who we can become is inside us, and all we have to do is feed it, water it, take care of it, and watch it grow.

I carry the seed of who I can be inside me.

AUGUST 23

How are we fal'n, fal'n, by mistaken rules?

—Anne Finch

When our relationship fails, we often feel like we have—and probably indeed we have—mistaken the rules. Maybe the rules changed, and we weren't paying attention. Or the rules didn't change, but we did. And even though we'd changed, we tried to live by old rules.

Trying to live by mistaken rules leads only to more mistakes, to failure. And perhaps the biggest mistake we can make is to fall into the hole of living as if we're the failure. When our relationships fail, we are not failures. Once we're falling, the only thing we can do is to hit bottom.

The way up from the bottom is to acknowledge that the rules will change and so will we. We do that by paying attention to the rules our hearts and our mind are telling us, rather than to someone else's rules about what we should do and who we should be. When we mistake the rules, as we inevitably will—nobody's perfect—we'll know we can pick ourselves up again because we've already done it.

The bottom line is that I'm not a failure just because my relationship failed.

AUGUST 24

*She had trouble defining herself independently of her
husband, tried to talk to him about it, but he said
nonsense, he had no trouble defining her at all.*
                              —Cynthia Propper Seton

One of the great pleasures of getting to know
people is listening to their life story. In their
telling and our listening, we begin to define our
relationship. Defining ends and unhelpful dependence begins when the talker and the listener get
their roles mixed up.

Other people can define us, and many will try,
given the opportunity. Yet, ultimately, the only
definition that will ring true comes from ourselves. If we can listen to other people's life stories, letting them define for us who they are, can't
we grant ourselves the same courtesy?

When we begin to listen to ourselves, we begin
to know who we are, no matter how much our
life circumstances change. We can use the opportunity of changing lifestyles—becoming single
again, changing jobs, moving to a new house or
new city—to listen to new parts of our stories. We
can talk to ourselves out loud. We can take ourselves out to tea. We can write ourselves a letter.

*Getting to know myself better is making a friend I
can depend on.*

AUGUST 25

Why tears! is it? tears; such a melting, a madrigal start!
                                    —Gerard Manley Hopkins

A madrigal is a song sung in harmony. Our tears can open the way for our hearts to sing a song with many parts. As we let ourselves cry, we can begin to hear the many different tones of our feeling. We can cry our grief, anger, pain, frustration, exhaustion, and even our happiness.

Crying can help us figure out what we're feeling. Sometimes we know exactly "why" we started to cry. We were too miserable to do anything else. Sometimes our tears sneak up on us. We see a couple walking hand in hand, and they remind us of our younger married self. We read an inspirational story in the newspaper. We sit down at the end of a long day. And we burst into tears.

Tears are a wonderful gift. We have only to let them come to hear a song sung in multi-part harmony. We may envy the young couple, not want to go through those years ever again, wish we were that age, and admire how beautiful they are together. The tears started with one feeling, and they've taken us to others. And left us feeling at peace for the moment, as if we'd just heard a beautiful, moving piece of music.

Crying releases my feelings.

AUGUST 26

I learned the voice of guilt early; others may learn the voice of blame. They are cousins, both expressions of our emotional "no." Looking outward, we search for someone else to blame. Looking inward, our bad feelings take the form of self-blame, of guilt. —Gabrielle Rico

At the end of a marriage, we may feel guilt about what we did or didn't do. And/or we may blame our partners for causing the breakup and the unpleasant changes in our lives. We can't get beyond guilt, self-blame, or blame, though, as long as we're saying an emotional "no."

What we're saying is "No, I don't accept what is happening in my life. I must be guilty and I must have caused it." Or, alternatively, "No, I don't like that this has happened. It's his fault. He is to blame." The implication is that we or someone else must accept the blame and somehow pay for what has happened in our lives.

To get beyond guilt or blame, our response must change to an emotional "maybe." Maybe, in fact probably, both of us could have done things differently. In time, to truly forgive and forget what is past, our response becomes an emotional "Yes, I accept that this has happened and can let it go."

When I let go of guilt, I say yes to who I am now.

AUGUST 27

Woman must not depend upon the protection of man, but must be taught to protect herself. —Susan B. Anthony

One sense of the word *protect* is to keep away from harm, as one protects a child from a hot stove. Protection is not so much defending ourselves against something as it is shielding ourselves. We need to take care of ourselves so we aren't exposed to cold, hunger, harm of any kind.

Another meaning for *protect* is to conserve. We talk about money this way; we protect our assets and watch them grow. We can choose to protect ourselves from perceived dangers by shutting ourselves in, by not opening up to possibilities. That sort of protection is akin to putting our money in the mattress.

Or we can protect ourselves by choosing wisely to invest our time and energy in projects, relationships, and kindnesses to ourselves that reward us. Protecting our assets might be spending a weekend in bed with a book. Or splurging on a new outfit. Or expending the energy to get to know a new friend better. In that sense protecting ourselves is letting us grow into the person we want to be.

I am my own biggest asset and I can protect me.

AUGUST 28

*It is seldom that the miserable can help regarding their
misery as a wrong inflicted by those who are less
miserable.* —George Eliot

When we're miserable and in despair, it's easy
to say to ourselves—and anyone who will listen—
that it's somebody else's fault—usually our ex-
spouse's. If it's somebody else's fault, we don't
have to do anything to make ourselves less miserable.

Imagine spinning around on a child's merry-
go-round, out of control, perhaps getting nau-
seous. While we're spinning we see signposts: *I
feel terrible. It's your fault. I feel terrible. It's your
fault. I feel terrible. It's your fault.* Over and over
again, stuck in a cycle of blame and despair.

All we have to do to stop the merry-go-round is
to put a foot on the ground. All we have to do to
stop the spinning cycle of blame and despair is
ground ourselves in the present, out of sight of
the *It's your fault* sign. Eventually we see something besides blame and misery. And, eventually,
the spinning stops. We can acknowledge our feelings of misery, sadness, despair. We can own
them without blaming others for them.

*I can lose my misery when I stop finding fault and
blame.*

AUGUST 29

It is astonishing how short a time it takes for wonderful things to happen. —Frances Hodgson Burnett

In the time after our divorce, we may think we can't take time off to renew and refresh ourselves, to let wonderful things happen to us, for any one of a number of reasons. We have too much to do. We have to keep working so we won't feel what's going on with us. We don't have enough money for a vacation. It would be too sad to take a vacation alone or with our children and without our ex-spouse.

These are all excuses. None of them are good reasons for not taking the time for ourselves. It only takes a short time for wonderful things to happen when we take the time to let them happen. If we don't take time, wonderful things won't happen.

If the wonderful thing we want to happen to us is meeting new friends, we're not going to meet them locked up in our kitchens. If we want to get to know ourselves better, we're not going to do it working sixteen-hour days. Of course, we can't force wonderful things to happen in any amount of time. What we can do is to create the time and space in which they might.

Taking time for myself is a wonderful thing.

AUGUST 30

Handle them carefully, for words have more power than atom bombs. —Pearl Strachan

Words are dangerous weapons, at least in part because we don't understand their power to maim and cripple. Words are accessible to all of us; atomic bombs aren't. Bombs can only destroy. Words can create connections as well as destroy them. They can fire and they can backfire.

Arguments often outlive marriages. We must still communicate with our ex-spouses—about children, legal documents, property divisions, any number of details. And we've entered a phase in which we might be likely to use words carelessly as weapons because we don't think we have anything more to lose. We forget the backfire power of words.

Communicating what we want and need without using words that escalate the conflict means choosing our words carefully. Sentences that begin with "You always" or "You never" generally heat things up. Accusing and blaming words have a way of boomeranging and hitting us. The point of an argument is not a direct hit on the other person. The point is to get our needs met.

Fighting for what I want doesn't mean winning a word war.

AUGUST 31

> *Revenge, at first thought sweet,*
> *Bitter ere long back on itself recoils.*
> —John Milton

What goes round comes round. And there's no way to avoid it. We can't avoid it by undertaking revenge and then stopping before it turns back on us. We also can't avoid it by avoiding situations in which we might be hurt and therefore want to take revenge. Nor can we avoid it by denying that sometimes we feel like taking revenge.

We can't control our lives so we won't get hurt. That's an all-too-apparent reality when we're going through the pain of separation and divorce. And even if we can control our impulses to act when we're feeling like taking revenge, we can't control that we have the feeling. Try to repress or deny and it will take on larger proportions.

One thing we do have control over is what "goes round" from us. If we send out vengeance, that's what we're going to get back. On the other hand, if we send out the truth of how we feel, even if that feeling is pain and anger, we're more likely to get back, at the least, truthful acknowledgment of our pain and anger.

Taking revenge is like misaddressing an envelope. It will be returned to sender.

SEPTEMBER 1

Nobody ever said on her deathbed, "I wish I'd spent more time in the office." —Mary Jo Weaver

Most of us have been taught from childhood that working can take our mind off our troubles. Taking our mind off our troubles is not necessarily a good idea. Nor is burying ourselves in work to avoid our troubles. On the other hand, working at something we love to do, something that gives us a sense of accomplishment and makes us feel better, is *not* a bad idea.

When we're feeling we're worthless because our marriage failed, we might work and savor our accomplishments. Or we might use work to try to drown our sorrows, in the same way an alcoholic drinks. It's crucial that we know the difference. When we're using work to bury our feelings, it's time to stop everything and sit for a minute thinking what we might say on our deathbeds.

Do we want to look back and say I should have spent more time at the office or in the kitchen doing more things that didn't make me feel any better? Or might we rather say, "I took care of myself. I took time for myself. I pleased myself."

When I'm working to take my mind off me, it's time to rest and put my mind on me.

SEPTEMBER 2

The idea of strictly minding our own business is moldy rubbish. Who could be so selfish?
—Myrtie Lillian Barker

One meaning of "minding" is to take care of, as in minding the store. In that sense, minding other people's business and our own could be looked at as taking care. When we're totally wrapped up in our own business, it's sometimes difficult to imagine extending our care to others.

Feeling the satisfaction of sharing ourselves with others, of expressing our care, is its own reward, of course. When we step outside "taking care of" and into the realm of "busybodiness," we move from caring to controlling. The recipient of our "care" isn't grateful and we end up feeling frustrated rather than satisfied.

And if we don't take care of ourselves—mind our own business—our ability to mind others' is diminished. Our cares and needs grow, and our energy to do anything about them diminishes. Yet often, and seemingly illogically, if we can get outside ourselves for a minute to see that someone else has a need we can meet, it becomes easier for us to mind our own business as well.

I can, with care, mind my own business and that of others.

SEPTEMBER 3

Any change avoided or left incomplete pulls you back again and again to complete it. —Gloria Karpinski

There's an old saying that a problem is just an opportunity in disguise. A change we're trying to make or avoiding making in our lives is also an opportunity, sometimes well disguised.

If we are having trouble making or accepting a change, we can consider the opportunity this change offers us. That's easy enough if the change is one we know we want to make. When my husband left, I wanted to rearrange my furniture so it would feel like my place. I did it. And for weeks afterward I stubbed my toe on the rocking chair. This was an opportunity to move the rocking chair closer to the couch, out of the traffic pattern, and into a better place for having a conversation with a friend. Now the change *is* complete.

When we face more traumatic changes, we may have to dig to find the opportunity. If we get divorced in our forties, the opportunity is probably not to enter a beauty pageant. It might be the chance to get to know our children, our families, ourselves a little better. To change the way we express our feelings. To change our attitude toward ourselves, our bodies, our work.

I am open to the opportunity to change.

SEPTEMBER 4

The woman whose behavior indicates that she will make a scene if she is told the truth asks to be deceived.
—Elizabeth Jenkins

When we are afraid that the truth will hurt us, our natural instinct is to want to not hear, see, or know it. We may send out nonverbal clues—holding our bodies hunched and closed, refusing to look someone in the eye, drifting off during conversations. Or we say, "I don't want to hear this!"

Our nearest and dearest pick up on these clues. And, maybe because the truth will hurt us, make us angry or sad, those people decide to lie. Maybe our children tell us, "Yes, I have my homework done." Maybe our ex-spouse tells us, "I will be there for you." Maybe we tell ourselves, "I don't have to face this problem and it will go away."

If I'm afraid that knowing the truth may change my life, I can avoid the truth and live in fear. When I know the truth, I can face almost anything, giving myself permission to express my pain, grief, or sorrow. I can begin to make choices for myself based on what I know to be true rather than on what I'm afraid of hearing.

When I'm open to truth I recognize it from myself and others.

SEPTEMBER 5

> *I do not want the peace*
> *which passeth understanding,*
> *I want the understanding*
> *which bringeth peace.*
> —Helen Keller

Understanding is commonly thought of as a mental process. When we understand something, we comprehend it, we have a clear idea of what it means. When we strive for understanding of the "rational" kind, what we're often trying to do is to understand something so we can change it. As in, I want to understand what went wrong in this relationship so I can fix it.

Another component to understanding is emotional, and maybe physical, as well. The word literally means "to stand under." When we stand under something, we not only see it and think about it, we feel it. We're right there under it.

And since we're standing so close, we pretty much have to accept it for whatever it is. When we see, feel, and let ourselves be in the presence of realities in our life, we tend to understand them, and, in the process of standing there, to come to peace with them.

I can find peace in the midst of understanding my life.

SEPTEMBER 6

The best way out is always through.   —Robert Frost

That's fine advice until we find ourselves lost in the middle. Then it *seems* reasonable to think of alternative solutions, also known as creative escape fantasies. How about six months in Tahiti? Not feasible? Well, then, how about a new lover, a new job, a new haircut, a new outfit, a new self-improvement program? If I had those things, I'd be able to escape my present predicament.

Maybe. Until the new outfit gets ruined at the cleaners, my hair grows out, I get bored with my new programs, and I have trouble communicating with my new love or boss. Even if they don't look like escapist fantasies, alternative solutions to dealing with what's going on in our lives in the here and now usually are.

The alternative is "through." Through sometimes means being stuck or lost in the middle. It means not knowing where through leads. It means knowing what it is that we want to get out of and giving up trying to control how we do it. Getting a new hairdo or a new job might help us get through a difficult period in our lives. Yet if we "get" something thinking that it will solve all our problems, we will surely be disappointed.

I can get from A to C by going through B.

SEPTEMBER 7

You grow up the day you have the first real laugh—at yourself. —Ethel Barrymore

Luckily, neither laughing at ourselves nor growing up are something we have only one chance at in our lives. Laughing at ourselves helps us grow, and growing helps us laugh at ourselves. That's especially important to remember at a time when our lives don't seem funny.

Getting divorced can make us feel like we haven't grown up. We're like scared children who see only that the incongruity between what we thought and what turned out to be true threatens to consume us. We don't see the humor in the incongruities. And, in all seriousness, if we can't laugh at ourselves, incongruity can kill us.

Growing up is a process with tragic moments and comic relief. When we look at growth as a process rather than a goal, we begin to see that threats to our carefully guarded, serious maturity are often jokes. Laughing at ourselves is a way to release tension. Holding on to tension requires time and energy. Letting it go lets us spend that time and energy on growing.

Isn't it funny that I'm growing up even though I'm grown up?

SEPTEMBER 8

Pain is no longer pain when it is past.

—Margaret Preston

So hurry up and get it over with already. When we're in the midst of pain it isn't very comforting to hear somebody tell us that someday this too will pass. We'll remember it, but we won't feel it anymore. Big deal, we say. Just make the pain go away.

The only thing that makes pain go away is feeling it. When we get to know our pain, we get to know what's causing it. When we drug ourselves or deny our pain, we run the risk of missing something we should know about ourselves. When we get to know our pain, we can begin to heal the cause, not simply the symptoms.

Another way of not feeling our pain is to remove ourselves from it, to rationalize. "Okay, I must go through this painful time in my life, but I won't let myself feel it, and as soon as it's over, I'll forget it ever happened." Eventually this particular pain might pass. Yet if we try to forget it, the one thing we can be sure of is that it will be back, with a vengeance.

My pain is telling me something, and it will not pass until I listen.

SEPTEMBER 9

My father advised me that life itself was a crap game; it was one of the two lessons I learned as a child. The other was that overturning a rock was apt to reveal a rattlesnake. As lessons go those two seem to hold up, but not to apply. —Joan Didion

The lessons of childhood can lead to the wisdom of now. It's all in how they're applied. Which are totally irrelevant? Which are simply not true? And which can be turned 180 degrees to find the wisdom in them?

So what if I learned that life's a game of chance and nobody likes girls who compete? Maybe those lessons aren't right ones for me now. Maybe competition isn't the lesson. Maybe it's being open to each new roll of the dice. Maybe I can compete without putting myself or others in the loser position.

So what if there's a rattlesnake under the rock? What does it have to do with me? The lesson might be not to pick up rocks. If I think that what's found under rocks is best left there, I might miss a lot in life. If I'm open to the possibility that I might find a beautiful fossil under there instead of a snake, I might be more inclined to turn rocks over.

Wisdom isn't learning my lessons; it's learning how to apply them to my present life.

SEPTEMBER 10

> *Lie down and listen to the crabgrass grow,*
> *The faucet leak, and learn to leave them so.*
> —Marya Mannes

Most of us talk a lot about making, taking, spending time—or our inability to do so. So far nobody has come up with a way to manufacture time or to earn more time. And, most of us, when we're beginning our lives as single people, think we don't have enough time to do everything. Unless we think we have too much.

We don't feel harried and/or bored because we have too much time or too little. We feel that way because we're not living in the present. We're not paying attention to what our inner voices are telling us—that we need time to just be. Overwhelming busyness or unrelenting boredom are signs that we're not letting go and letting ourselves be in the time we're living in.

When we use our time to feel what we're feeling, to dream, to meditate, to play, to listen to ourselves, we let go of what we should do. We have a clearer sense of what we want to do. We know what we want to do and have more energy and—magically—time to do it.

It's time to let go of my boredom and my busyness and be in the time I'm in.

SEPTEMBER 11

It's impossible to be stupid while listening to Bach.
                                        —Ellen Gilchrist

When we feel embarrassed, we feel that we've done something stupid. We might well have. Or that nobody else ever did anything this stupid. Doubtful! Or that we'd better do nothing to embarrass ourselves again. We'd better resolve to do nothing then. The whole world is not watching and judging me. Let's have a little perspective.

Feeling embarrassed to this extent is just a way of being self-absorbed. We think that what we say and do, how we are, is so important that everybody is watching and judging how we're acting. We try to act and react according to what others will think. We try to do nothing embarrassing, to be perfect, a well-known impossibility. So if we're not perfect, we must be stupid.

Giving up our self-absorption doesn't mean we'll never do anything embarrassing again. On the contrary, it means we will. And we will be able to learn from our embarrassment. It means we can pay attention to the world around us without thinking the world revolves around us.

I am so embarrassed—here I thought I was enjoying Bach and it was really Beethoven.

SEPTEMBER 12

Everyone says forgiveness is a wonderful idea until they have something to forgive. —C. S. Lewis

After all, we reason with ourselves, it's not doing me any good to hold on to this hurt or loss inflicted on me by somebody else—or myself. And if I forgive this person (or myself)—false hope springs eternal—we'll all change so nobody ever has to forgive anybody again. Besides, all I have to do to forgive somebody is to say that I do.

"I forgive you"—three of the easiest words in the English language to say without meaning them. Forgiveness seems so simple that we try to do it too often and too soon. We try to forgive without first accepting and letting go. We try to forgive with strings of expectation attached. We attach subordinate clauses: I will forgive you if . . . until we have a contract complicated enough to keep three attorneys busy for years.

To forgive, when we're ready, is to give over. When we give something over to someone else, we need to know what we're giving—and to accept that it's real. We must let it go, not harbor it in our hearts. We may not forget the incident or the pain in our minds, yet we do in our hearts.

When I forgive, I create a place for something new in my heart.

SEPTEMBER 13

> *"Did you exchange embraces of any kind?"*
> *"No. She was always in a hurry."*
> —Elizabeth Bowen

Affection for others or ourselves cannot be hurried. We must have time to spend with the object of our affection—including ourselves—time to go to a concert, to stroll in the park, to exchange simple pleasantries and profound ideas. And when we are sharing, we must remain in that time, not mentally rushing off to do the laundry, finish the project, cook the dinner.

The old saw might be rewritten: History makes the heart grow fonder. Old friends can be especially important when we are going through the crisis of divorce. Spending time with old friends can give us perspective on what's happening to us. We can draw on their affection as a respite from all the changes around us.

Rushing from task to task, or away from our feelings, is not conducive to affection. Taking time to express affection increases affection. This is true when we're expressing affection for others and even more true when we're nurturing affection for ourselves.

Can I be in such a hurry that I don't have time to embrace myself affectionately?

SEPTEMBER 14

No one can make you feel inferior without your consent.
                                        —Eleanor Roosevelt

"No one" includes ourselves. The big news is that we can refuse our consent to make ourselves feel inferior. Who besides me spends as much time as I do judging my actions, reactions, intelligence, wit, and accomplishments? Who gave me permission to say that because I didn't achieve what I set out to do today, or get as far in life as fast as someone else did, I am inferior?

And what is it to say that I feel inferior? Is it to say, "Oh, woe is me, I'm not as good, rich, smart, well-educated, as she is—so don't expect as much of me"? Or, "I'm less worthy than she is; give her the job, the relationship, the happiness. Feel sorry for me." Or, "I'm not proud of my accomplishments because they're not as good as hers." All of this is idle comparison. It implies that what we do, buy, win is who we are.

And what if someone tells me I'm inferior? My ex-spouse, for instance, in so many words, or by choosing someone else to be in a relationship with. That isn't the same thing as feeling inferior. That doesn't mean I'm an inferior person.

Permission denied, today, to call myself inferior.

SEPTEMBER 15

Any two of us are smarter than any one of us.
                                        —Wayne Paulson

Two heads are better than one. When we consult someone else to help solve or accomplish something, two people can think up more ideas or work faster. Two are also better than one because when we share a problem or a project with another, we're enhancing our relationship.

Following our separation and divorce, we often feel unconnected. Old connections aren't there for us anymore, or they and we have changed so that we don't recognize them. We might think we have to prove something, doing everything right all by ourselves. Or we may withdraw into ourselves. We might feel that we are somehow not worth connecting with.

When we think we need to do it all ourselves, the smart thing is then to make a connection. We might call an old friend to help us think of fun things to do. We might meet with a colleague to brainstorm ways to get a project done. We might enlist our children's ideas for ways to feel like a whole family again. The benefits of connecting are getting something done *and* feeling connected.

I can support myself by connecting with others.

SEPTEMBER 16

In the face of an obstacle which it is impossible to overcome, stubbornness is stupid.

—Simone de Beauvoir

Scarcely had our heroine scaled the mountain when she discovered that she was not at the top at all. The mountain magically seemed to grow higher as she climbed. We've all had obstacles in our lives that seemed to grow just as we thought we might surmount them. And haven't we all persisted in climbing without map or compass, sure that the top is just a step ahead of us?

To continue to try to overcome our obstacles, whatever they are, through sheer willpower is stupid. Yet our stubbornness often prevails, mocking any urge to sit still where we are, to admit our powerlessness, to wait for a different solution.

Admitting that we can't get to the top opens the way. My obstacle might be that I keep trying to make a dead marriage live. I try communication, accommodation repeatedly, and it just won't work. I can keep trying, or I can stop to assess the situation and turn to take a new path out of the marriage. I might well find a sunny meadow in which I can be myself.

It's smart to stop and plot an alternate route for my life.

SEPTEMBER 17

The brain is not, and cannot be, the sole or complete organ of thought and feeling.   —Antoinette Brown Blackwell

If all our thinking and feeling came from our brain, we wouldn't need this too big, too small, complicated, clumsy, unreliable body. We wouldn't need to eat or exercise. We wouldn't suffer physical illnesses. And we wouldn't be who we are.

We all know our brains alone don't taste food, smell flowers, see beauty, hear music, or feel physical pain or pleasure like burns or back rubs. It's not quite as easy to see that our brains aren't the source of all our thoughts or our "nonphysical" emotions—sorrow, anger, grief. That becomes obvious when we try to *think* our way out of pain or into pleasure. We simply can't.

We can try to use our brains to block information from our bodies or to tell our bodies they don't feel something they do feel. We can try to use our bodies to turn off our brains—by ingesting substances that numb us or by working ourselves to exhaustion. Or we can look at ourselves as a whole thinking, feeling, doing entity, greater than the sum of the parts. Alone they're nothing; together they're more than either.

Trying to use my body without my brain is like trying to use my brain without my body.

SEPTEMBER 18

For hatred does not cease by hatred at any time; hatred ceases by love. This is an unalterable law.
                                        —The Dhammapada

Hatred is fecund and self-fertilizing. It is always "in season" and has a short gestation period. The only thing hatred can breed is more hatred. And it can do so with rampant productivity in an amazingly short period of time. What you get when you hate somebody or something is more hatred.

The worst part about it is that hatred not only breeds hatred, it destroys practically everything else, including—especially—the person in whom it lives and breeds. Hatred feeds on our fear, our anger, and our sense of injury. And when we act on our hatred, trying to get even, it goes into a feeding frenzy.

Given all that, it seems the best thing to do might be to try to abort it or kill it in infancy. Yet hatred is an emotion, a feeling. And we can't kill off one feeling without eventually killing our capacity to feel. When we let ourselves feel our hatred, it's easier to let go of it. When we've let go, we can choose to react in less hateful, more loving ways.

Learning what I hate teaches me about what I love.

SEPTEMBER 19

The reverse side also has a reverse side.

—Japanese proverb

Reverse sides of some weavings are exact opposites. Reversed words can be read in a mirror. Reverse sides of records contain totally different songs and music. Reverse sides of our lives and relationships can be exact opposites, mirror images, or simply different.

Trying to sort out what has happened to a relationship can be like flipping something over and over until we literally don't know which side is up, what really happened. When we look at our relationships to figure out what happened, it's important to know what each side looks like. Knowing that can help us restructure "our side."

What's not important or useful is blaming with cause-and-effect comparisons. If he hadn't walked out, I wouldn't have changed the locks. If he hadn't told me I was stupid, I wouldn't have found someone else. If he hadn't presented the last straw, I wouldn't have broken it. We both did something that resulted in the relationship ending. Only when we can take the blame and reason out of our way can we really begin to look at each side.

Seeing both sides, I can own my own side.

SEPTEMBER 20

Our deeds determine us as much as we determine our deeds. —George Eliot

What we do can help us know who we are. Most of us have had the experience of not knowing why we're doing something. Doing things can be a way to get to know ourselves or a way to deny the same. To know ourselves by our deeds, we need to pay attention to what we're doing.

Volunteering for extra work or cleaning house to keep busy, shopping to distract ourselves from our sorrow, drinking or eating to forget our pain —we let our deeds determine us as we try to blot out feeling who we are. Or, if we decide that we want to be known as a good, loving, caring, nice person, we may do things we don't want to do. Our good deeds will determine we're a good person, at the expense of knowing how we feel and what we *want* to do.

When we pay attention to what we do, we are more likely to choose to do what we want. When we're living consciously, deeds that determine us and deeds we determine to do are like an electric circuit, with the energy flowing continuously and freely.

I know who I am by what I do; I choose what to do by knowing who I am.

SEPTEMBER 21

Many promising reconciliations have broken down because, while both parties came prepared to forgive, neither party came prepared to be forgiven. —Charles Williams

The kernel of the truth is that unless we can be forgiven, we can't really forgive. Oh, sure, we can mouth the words. We can blow it off, "Oh, that's okay. You didn't really hurt me. It doesn't make any difference." Or we can say, "Yeah, sure, I forgive you." And then hold on to our resentment.

To forgive—or to be forgiven by ourselves or others—we have to acknowledge the pain. We have to be open to letting go of the pain. We don't forget it, but its sting has diminished. We have to value ourselves enough to think that we "deserve" forgiveness. We can't be forgiven if we don't value ourselves enough to know that we are hurt.

When we have a sense of our own self-worth, not as perfect human beings, but as people who can make mistakes as well as have them made unto us, we recognize when something has been done to us or we've done something to ourselves that needs forgiving. When we're ready to be forgiven, we'll know it. When we're ready to be forgiven, we're also ready to forgive.

Forgiving myself works better when I'm ready to be forgiven.

SEPTEMBER 22

There is a Zen saying: Put a snake in a bamboo pole. In a sense, that is what structure is. You have all this stuff you want to express—you need to pour yourself into a form.
—Natalie Goldberg

And the form is changing. To start over as a single person is to pour one's self into a new form— as we form it. As the new form emerges we stay loose; we're adapting to new circumstances, new experiences.

We have the stuff of who we are to work with— our past and our present, our experiences and our dreams. That's where the snake in the bamboo pole comes in. If I've been an introvert all these years, I'm not likely to suddenly become an extrovert. If I've worked as a biologist for my entire adult life, I'm not likely to suddenly become a painter. Our new form is apt to bear a strong resemblance to our old one.

The new form grows from the old, though in time it might look quite different. The extrovert may take up meditation. The biologist may take a sabbatical to learn to paint. We may make surface changes that present us differently to the world— new hair, new job, new house. All that, in time, helps us shape and adapt to our single self.

Only I can shape my life into a form that pleases me.

SEPTEMBER 23

*I once read that a fanatic is someone who has lost sight of
her goal and redoubled her effort.*   —Gloria Karpinski

Fanatic, frantic effort toward a goal can lead to
losing sight of the goal, which leads to more frantic effort, which can lead to despair. No matter
how much we do we'll never reach that goal.

Suppose, after my separation, my goal is to feel
better about myself as a person. I decide I can
achieve that by being a better parent and more
successful in my career. I spend more and more
time at my job and more and more time with my
children. I'm desperate to feel better, and no matter how much I work or how much time I spend
with my children, I don't. It's time to stop and
take stock—of both goal and effort.

First, the expectation. Am I really trying to feel
better? Or do I think that divorced women should
be better parents and prove to the world that
they're still "good" people by working harder?
Then the effort. What have I really been doing?
Have I been working toward feeling better about
myself? If I have, why am I feeling desperate?
How can I change my efforts?

*Less effort can mean more when I know my
expectations.*

SEPTEMBER 24

The wish for healing has ever been the half of health.

—Seneca

To wit, we can't get well unless we want to. Our bodies will mend if we, say, break a leg or have abdominal surgery. Yet we probably won't do the leg exercises or change our eating habits, which would make us wholly healthy again, unless we really want to be healthy. When we think about recovering from the pain of a broken relationship, it's pretty easy to say that we wish to be healed— immediately.

The hard part is seeing how our wish might make our dream come true. What is wishing for healing? Wishing things would go instantly back to the time before we broke our legs or our hearts? Wishing we'd feel the same as we did before the break? It isn't going to happen.

We might have abdominal surgery, change our eating habits, and have twice the energy. Yet if we were to go back to our old eating habits, our energy would diminish. Healing from a broken relationship is a process. If I wish to feel better, I might engage in new activities, get to know new people, be kind to myself and be present to my life. As I do that I experience a healthy me.

Each day I wish to heal, I will heal.

SEPTEMBER 25

The mind of the most logical thinker goes so easily from one point to another that it is hard not to mistake motion for progress. —Margaret Collier Graham

I must be getting better. After all, I'm learning a lot—reading books, attending meetings, going to therapy, setting and achieving goals. I'm busy all the time. I can't stop now. I've got too much to do, too many places to go, too many people to meet, too much to learn about myself. After all, getting involved is getting better, isn't it?

When we mistake motion for progress and set ourselves into motion to achieve our goals to get better, we might begin to look like we feel better. Our reasoning seems to be that if we look like busy, happy people, we *will* be busy, happy people. But eventually we find, if the motion is empty, we don't feel any better.

As we work to recover, we gain new insights about ourselves. We put those insights into action. And we progress. We know that getting busy with making ourselves better sometimes means taking time to just be. And we begin to look like busy, happy people because that's what we are.

I make progress sometimes by moving forward and sometimes by stopping to take stock.

SEPTEMBER 26

I cannot and will not cut my conscience to fit this year's fashion. —Lillian Hellman

Our beliefs inform the "I cans" and "I cannots," the "I wills" and the "I won'ts" of our lives. Sometimes the consequences for stating our beliefs, for saying we can't do something against our conscience, hurt like hell. We can lose a spouse, a house, money, work, friends. If we act according to our integrity, the one thing we can't lose is what we came with—ourselves.

When my marriage was ending, I said to myself, just about every day, I will do anything I can to stop this from happening, to make my marriage work. As time passed, I realized that sentiment had an important qualifier. Anything *I can* is not the same as anything at all. There are some things I am just not willing to do in order to preserve a long-term relationship.

To act with conscience is by definition to be conscious of our beliefs and to act in accordance with them. To act blindly, unconsciously, is to act while keeping our beliefs locked in a dark closet of our mind. To keep our beliefs in the dark is to create dark monsters in that closet.

There's no time like the present to discover my beliefs and to act on them.

SEPTEMBER 27

Solitude vivifies; isolation kills.   —Joseph Roux

Other people—perhaps we can't live with them, but we can't live without them. None of us can live a healthy, happy life in utter isolation, cut off from feeling connection. Numerous studies on everything from monkeys who died of loneliness to murderers who kill because they can't connect with others confirm this fairly obvious truism.

Our tendency when we're feeling isolated and cut off is to try to connect. Mostly we try to connect with other people. We tend to ignore the fact that unless we're connected with our own emotional lives—with how we really feel, with what we really want—we're not going to be able to satisfactorily connect with others.

Solitude is simply spending time connecting with ourselves. Solitude means we do it alone, spending time in reflection—perhaps talking to ourselves, writing a journal, meditating. When we practice solitude regularly over a period of time, we develop a deep and abiding connection with our self. We can use that connection to alleviate isolation—from ourselves and others.

When I practice solitude, the life I save will be my own.

SEPTEMBER 28

*Talking about oneself can also be a means to conceal
oneself.* —Nietzsche

We can say a lot without saying anything that's
true. We can lie to ourselves. Or we can say a lot
without saying anything essential, maybe starting
with an ingrown toenail and working our way up
to the three pounds we lost. Maybe throwing in
that the dog threw up and ending with a mono-
logue on today's headlines.

Often when we're self-absorbed, we're keeping
secrets—from ourselves and others. We may not
want to acknowledge our feelings of sadness, despair, anger, rage, grief over the loss of our marriage. So we say over and over how great things
are—or how great they will be any minute. We
may want to hide our actions. So we spend hours
talking about nothing essential.

We may be so self-absorbed that it takes a while
for us to absorb the fact that nobody's listening—
even ourselves. It's high time to stop talking and
to listen to our inner self. One way to do that is to
make an inventory of our secrets—no excuses, no
explanations, just the secrets, please.

When I know what I'm hiding, I can begin revealing.

SEPTEMBER 29

It is not your obligation to complete your work, but you are not at liberty to quit.   —The Talmud

There are two ways—at least—to look at this injunction. It's like a bad news/good news joke. The bad news is that we have to go on making an effort. The good news is that we don't have to complete our work. This truly is good news for those of us who demand perfection and set impossible goals for ourselves. And it's great news if we're the sort of people who, faced with our own standards of perfection and accomplishment, paralyze ourselves.

If we can make our goal a process, we can keep working on the tasks we've set for ourselves—indeed, at our life itself. We empower ourselves to do something, anything, rather than to give up in despair. That *is* freeing.

And it's particularly liberating if we look at our life as our work. Suppose we can't make something happen. We can't repair our broken relationship. We can't complete it in the way we thought we might when we began it, for instance, by growing happily old together. Our relationship has ended; should we quit our lives?

I am at liberty to continue living my life.

SEPTEMBER 30

Our challenges come because it is time for us to learn to crawl, then walk, then run. Without them we'd be continually stuck in infancy. —Gloria Karpinski

Growth is, quite simply, pushing against and adding to. As we are growing from childhood, we add to our height, our weight, our general fund of knowledge. As we are growing in our understanding of our lives, we're adding new experiences every day.

Ending our marriage certainly provides challenges to grow. It provides new experiences and knowledge to add to our general fund for us to examine, reexamine, and push against. We might reassess everything from our standards of housekeeping to what we do for a living to how we handle conflict. In so doing, we'll push against old beliefs and ways of doing things.

Adverse experiences challenge us to grow. Conversely, if we don't look for the opportunity to grow from these experiences, we get stuck: challenges arise, we don't meet them and grow from them, and they keep coming back.

As I grow into my new single role, I add today's experience to the new me and push against the old me.

OCTOBER 1

The good life exists only when you stop wanting a better one. It is the condition of savoring what is, rather than longing for what might be. —Marya Mannes

Well, now that I'm single again I'll be able to really live my life as soon as—my kids leave home, I get a new job, I find the real love of my life. Then there's the flip side—"I didn't know how good things were until . . ." Longing for what might be and lamenting what was are two sides of a coin that won't buy so much as a cup of coffee.

If we make a resolution to savor the present, and think that because we so resolve things will be just fine, we are fooling ourselves. We might as well go back to singing past blues and future pie in the sky. We can't prevent pain and control damage in our lives simply by saying we're savoring the present.

However, just about any situation in our life offers something to be savored. It might be small. The house burned down, but I saved Grandma's teapot. It might not seem like much to others. My husband left me in the lurch, but now I can watch late-night movies in bed.

When I live in the present, I always have a present to savor.

OCTOBER 2

The world is divided into people who think they are right.
                                              —Anonymous

If our rightness is a righteousness that proclaims loud and clear, "I am right and you are wrong," then there is nowhere for us to be but divided from others. Being right causes famine, wars, fatigue, and the end of relationships. If right is looked at as a rigid half of a dualistic principle, there is no way to stop dividing the world into people who think they're right.

Maybe we didn't end our relationship for months, even years, and went along thinking there was something wrong with us because our ex-spouse was right. And then one day we decide we're right. The other person is wrong. The relationship ended, maybe in part because we wouldn't give up being totally right or totally wrong.

This is not to say that any of us should give up our strongly held beliefs of right. Nor is it to say that we should not try to tell others, particularly in intimate relationships, what we think is right. It is to say that we all might give up trying to control—to make others act according to our idea of right.

I can give up the controlling seesaw of right and wrong for the connecting balance beam of what is.

OCTOBER 3

*Let her swim, climb mountain peaks, pilot airplanes, battle
against the elements, take risks, go out for adventure, and
she will not feel before the world . . . timidity.*
—Simone de Beauvoir

Timidity or fear stops us from taking risks. And
taking risks can allay our fear. When we're hurt
and fearful about what the future might bring is
the best time to take a few risks.

I imagine my newly single self as a ball of yarn,
all tangled, rolled tightly in on myself. If only I
could untangle this yarn, I could weave a whole
new piece of fabric. Yet how am I going to untangle the yarn when I fear that pulling one strand
will unravel the whole into a hopeless mess? The
first small risk is straightening out one bit of yarn.
The more risks I take, the more untangled yarn I
have.

We might join a dance class, invite a new friend
to lunch, walk farther than we ever have. By the
time we get into the habit of risks, we've got a lot
of yarn to work with. And we might decide to
dye the whole thing passionate purple—or climb
in the Himalayas, go back to school, move across
country, get involved with a new love.

*Taking risks can be habit-forming and dangerous to
my fears.*

OCTOBER 4

> *And at some time*
> *in your life*
> *trying to be good*
> *may be to stop running*
> *and take time . . .*
> *to be quiet*
> *and discover who you are*
> *and where you've been . . .*
> —Corita Kent

It's often difficult in our fast-paced lives to find time to stop and take stock. It's especially difficult if our lives consist of too much "trying to be good" by running to meet the never-ceasing, ever-increasing demands of others.

When we reach a starting-over stage in our lives, our inclination may be to keep going. We're often given advice to keep busy—it will help us forget, dull the pain. Or we think our accomplishments will "prove" to us that we're still good people.

And, starting over, as painful as it may be, offers us an opportunity to sit back, take stock, and contemplate who we are, what we've done, and what we'd like to do. The loss in our lives has created a space we can fill with contemplation.

When I sit in the silence, who knows what I might hear?

OCTOBER 5

Beware of over-great pleasure in being popular or even beloved. —Margaret Fuller

We all like to be liked. We all want to be loved. Ergo, we should do all we can to make ourselves liked and/or loved by those in our lives. And if we don't, we are miserable failures. Or they are. When we are in the midst of the end of a relationship the last thing we might think about is taking over-great pleasure in being loved. Or perhaps in taking over-great pleasure in anything.

We don't need, truly, to be wary of too much pleasure. We do need to be wary of taking too much pleasure at the risk of not being true to ourselves. When we invest in others the ability to give us pleasure at the expense of our own ability to please ourselves, we risk losing our integrity and our self.

Suppose, instead, I had an opportunity to take pleasure in loving myself and being popular with myself. What if that gave me permission to do what I always wanted to do but wouldn't because my beloved wouldn't approve? What if that made me unpopular with someone else? Could I, would I, do it?

My integrity and my popularity belong to me.

OCTOBER 6

*Uncoupling is more than a leavetaking. It is also a
transition into a different life. This transition is marked by
the coincidence of departure and arrival—the intermingling
of going from and going to.* —Diane Vaughan

At the end of a marriage we're probably con-
fused about where and what we're going from
and to. Whether or not we wanted the separation,
we're going away from something we'll grieve,
no matter how bad it was. We're going to a new
single self. And we often haven't a clue to who
that self is.

As we try to sort things out, we may feel like
we're living in one of those cartoons where a kid
loops around and around, back and forth,
through the neighborhood, to get next door. The
dotted line in those cartoons traces the route. We
may feel like we're trying to follow—if only we
could find them.

We don't feel comfortable in transition, yet the
only way to get out of transition is to be in transition. Even if we have a pretty good idea where
we're going, we need to sort out our past—possessions, children, pets, legal papers. We need to
negotiate each day: the up days, the down days,
the birthdays, anniversaries, and holidays.

When transition is where I am, that's where I am.

OCTOBER 7

Whether living alone is adventure or hardship will depend entirely upon your attitude and your decisions. Become friends with yourself; learn to appreciate who you are and your unique gifts. Be patient with yourself and use your sense of humor to keep things in perspective.
—Dorothy Edgerton

Going on an adventure means keeping our wits about us, being flexible in response to new developments, being curious and willing to look beneath the surface, creating new ways to use our gifts and skills.

Finding ourselves single again most often means finding ourselves. That can be the biggest adventure of all. Who is this person who can balance a checkbook through her tears? Laugh because she finally remembered to put the garbage out early enough—on the wrong day. Congratulate herself for simply getting through the day.

Who is this person who's willing to begin the quest? Who's willing to map uncharted internal terrain? Who's willing to try new things? She might be able to leap buildings in a single bound, converse engagingly at the Mad Hatter's tea, or convince the plumber to come within the hour.

I might, in fact, be someone I love to live with.

OCTOBER 8

Everything that happens is either a blessing which is also a lesson, or a lesson which is also a blessing.
—Polly Berrien Berends

Accepting what happens to us is the key to understanding the blessing and the lesson in what's happened. Some blessings and some lessons are harder to take than others. Accepting doesn't mean denying that they're hard—that we feel sad, angry, discouraged, that they happened.

Until we accept the fact that we're getting divorced, we can't do anything about getting on with our lives. The lessons and blessings in divorce are different for each of us. And they may not be immediately apparent to any of us, particularly if we try to complicate our lives with "rational" explanations of why it happened.

When we accept, we open ourselves to what we might learn about how we interact with others, how we react to stress, how we act to support ourselves. As we act, we find the blessings. Perhaps it's that our lives are no longer filled with shouting matches, that we no longer have to live with someone who belittles and demeans us, that we are free to pursue our own interests.

Accepting life's blessings and lessons simplifies my life.

OCTOBER 9

As soon as you trust yourself, you will know how to live.
—Goethe

Trust encompasses the impulses of our minds, hearts, and bodies. When we trust, we think and feel and do. Trust, as a verb, means doing something without fear or misgiving. Trusting is not knowing that everything we do will come out perfectly, the way we expect it to. It is knowing that we can act and react to the circumstances of our lives and things will be okay.

The ways of the world often seem to contra-indicate trust. We are born trusting (albeit not at a conscious level) that people will take care of us. As life happens, our ability to trust can diminish as we become conscious that somebody we trusted—ourselves or others—failed us. And then, often, we begin to act as if trust resides in a small container inside ourselves. We act as if once it's used up, it can't be replenished. We'll soon run short of it if we don't conserve it.

Trust takes practice. We can't trust others until we trust ourselves. And how we'll know we're trusting ourselves is that we're trusting ourselves. Trust decreases when we hoard it. Trust increases with use.

Trusting myself is a good practice to live by.

OCTOBER 10

*I was talking to a psychiatrist friend about the importance
of memory, and he said that many of his patients are afraid
to remember, because they are afraid to learn who they
really are.* —Madeleine L'Engle

We learn by memory and by association. Once
we discover what we like and what we don't,
what hurts us, what feels good, we remember that
for the next time. If we try to shut down our
"bad" memories, we're inevitably going to shut
down our "good" ones, too. And if we were able
to shut down all our memories, we'd lose the lessons they taught us.

When our marriages end, we're likely to want
to shut down. It's painful to remember the bad
times. And it's even more painful to remember
the good times. Could that really have been me?
Happy? Secure in my relationship? If it was, who
am I now? I'm still me, and I'm different.

We can try to shut our memory down, or we
can feel our memories and use them to discover
who we really are. We can remember and we can
use those memories to accept that we are people
who make mistakes, who are capable of loving
and hurting, and who are able to change.

*Remembering who I am can help me discover who I
want to be.*

OCTOBER 11

I take it as a prime cause of the present confusion of society that it is too sickly and too doubtful frankly to use pleasure as a test of value. —Rebecca West

How do we know when we're on the road to recovery—from a physical illness, an addiction, the end of a marriage? One answer is that if we have to ask, we aren't. Only we can answer that question if we trust ourselves to be in touch with how we're feeling.

Often when we ask ourselves this question, we're looking for an ultimate either/or answer. If I feel so good today, I must be recovered. Or if things go wrong, I'll never feel better. What's really going on is that we don't know and don't trust how we feel. We can't use our pleasure or our pain as a guide because we aren't in touch with feeling either.

When we begin to let ourselves feel, we begin to trust our feelings. We stop trying to mask our pain with alcohol, food, sex, drugs, keeping busy. And we begin to notice what does give us pleasure. We stop looking outside ourselves for what we're supposed to do and what we're supposed to value.

I treasure and trust my pain and my pleasure to lead me on the road to recovery.

OCTOBER 12

Meditation is the steady flame of a lamp sheltered in a windless place. —The Bhagavad-Gita

In order to benefit from the light of meditation, we need to create the windless place. A windless place can be fifteen minutes in the bathtub or sitting silent behind our closed bedroom door. It can be in a church or synagogue. It can even be at the windy beach. When we begin to create windless places for ourselves in our hectic, windy lives, it becomes easier. The more we do it, the easier it is —and the brighter the flame of the lamp gets.

Regular meditation can shed a lot of light in pretty dark times. Sometimes it gets so dark in our lives that we're afraid of making a move for fear of stepping off a cliff or into a pile of mud. It's time to find the sheltered place and wait for a little illumination.

Yet to meditate only when our lives have become dark and murky is to risk not having a steady flame when we need it. To burn steadily and brightly, lamps need a steady source of fuel or energy. What feeds the lamp of meditation is, of course, meditation.

If I can see my way to meditate, meditation can help light my way.

OCTOBER 13

We may be a long time learning that life is, at best, "a dream controlled"—that reality is built of imperfect conditions. —Judith Viorst

Most of us pay intellectual lip service to the idea that we live in a less-than-perfect world. Yet in reality we waste a lot of time and energy either railing against injustice or trying to control our lives so that they reflect a rational reality. Reminding ourselves that reality is built of "imperfect conditions" we can't control can be a comfort.

Acceptance allows us to cease expecting perfection from ourselves or others. It can lead us to see the paradoxes that allow us to make sense from the senseless, to laugh at absurdity, to make plans and decisions without specific blueprints. So what if I don't know exactly how much money my spouse will provide for child support? So what if I don't know where I'm going to live five years from now?

Once we accept that reality is not perfect, we can accept that our lives are real (and valid) to us just as they are. We can use the absurd and imperfect conditions to help us piece together the parts of our lives. We can begin to dream (sleeping or waking) about what we want our lives to be.

My dreams guide my changing reality.

OCTOBER 14

Healthy guilt leads to remorse but not self-hate. Healthy guilt discourages us from repeating our guilty act without shutting down a wide range of our passions and pleasures. We need to be able to know when what we are doing is morally wrong. We need to be able to know and acknowledge our guilt. —Judith Viorst

Guilty people are bad people because *(a)* they did something wrong, *(b)* they might have done something wrong, *(c)* it's bad to feel guilty, *(d)* they can't accept themselves, *(e)* all of the above. This is a silly little test, with an obvious right answer: none of the above, because people who feel guilty aren't necessarily bad people. Right?

To feel guilt is to have remorse and to feel distress. The dictionary has an obsolete definition for remorse—compassion. Too bad it's obsolete.

When we do something we feel guilty for, we feel distress, and often we try to pay for the deed. When we try to pay for the deed in the worthless currency of hating ourselves or denying ourselves, we aren't making restitution. And we certainly aren't exercising compassion for a person (ourselves) who's lovable despite the fact that she makes mistakes.

I can admit my guilt with compassion and go on with my life with passion.

OCTOBER 15

*At the moment you are most in awe of all there is about
life that you don't understand, you are closer to
understanding it all than at any other time.*

—Jane Wagner

Some things just *are*. There isn't any rational understanding of why some parts of life are like they are. And, being human, we continue to try to make sense of them. We try to figure out why we're feeling like we're feeling, why our marriages ended, why they didn't end sooner, why we're not happy, why we are.

Then, in fleeting moments, comes the "aha" of awe. Yes, things are crazy, upside down, and senseless. Things are happening too fast for me to figure them out. Or they're not happening at all, and I'm stuck in a mire. There's so much I don't understand, and I suddenly know I am not required to understand everything. I can, in fact, stand in awe of the things I don't understand.

In awe, I can understand that I am not in charge of everything that happens. An impulse to understand is so often an impulse to try to control things, to make them right for ourselves, our children, those close to us, the whole world.

*Understanding that I don't need to understand
everything is awesome.*

OCTOBER 16

You don't get to choose how you're going to die. Or when.
You can only decide how you're going to live. Now.
—Joan Baez

There are some things we don't get to choose. Choosing to live doesn't mean we get to choose the perfect life for ourselves. It means choosing from the alternatives available to us now, whatever our circumstances are. Today, tomorrow, and so on. One day at a time.

Making decisions to live means responding to life as we find it. We got divorced and we can decide whether we're going to grieve our losses. We can decide to be open to our feelings of pain, sadness, anger—and whether we're open to the possibility of letting them go. We can also decide where we want to live, who we want to befriend, and what we want for dinner tonight.

Sometimes we make decisions we can live with over time. And sometimes we make decisions we find we can't live with. Then we can make new and different decisions that reverse or ameliorate the effects of those first decisions. When we consciously choose to live we make and remake many decisions every day. We make them as consciously as possible being as aware as possible of where we are in life—one day at a time.

Only I can choose to live my life.

OCTOBER 17

. . . if you do not clear a decent shelter for your sorrow, and instead reserve most of the space inside you for hatred and thoughts of revenge—from which new sorrows will be born for others—then sorrow will never cease in this world and will multiply. —Etty Hillesum

The world works against us when we grieve, and we work against ourselves when we don't. The world wants us back, to get on with things, to carry on with business as usual. And that's what we seem to want too. Grief can be hard, painful, boring, and seem to have no end.

Indulging in hatred and scheming revenge might give us some grim pleasure. We might amuse ourselves by imagining what we will do or say to our ex. We might even act to escalate our conflict—over children, settlements, taxes, the weather. While this may make us feel bad, we sincerely hope it makes him feel worse.

We often think and are told that getting on with life means carrying on. Truly getting on with life means sitting in the present with our feelings and letting ourselves feel them. Letting ourselves just be with sorrow, giving it time to die a natural death, lets it become the mulch to feed new growth in our lives.

Sheltering my sorrow is getting on with my life.

OCTOBER 18

Their lives had intertwined into a comfortable dependency,
like the gnarled wisteria on their front porch, still twisted
around the frail support which long ago it had outgrown.
—Beatrice Conrad

Intertwined dependence, or interdependence, can
add a richness and ease to our lives that a fierce
independence never will. Interdependence begins
slowly and grows over time. Shared interest supports growth, like the rail on a front porch, but it
is not what holds the balance.

If only half the wisteria plant got the light, water, and nourishment it needed to grow, the balance of interdependence would be short-lived. In
order for two adults to have an interdependent
relationship, their dependence on each other must
be fairly equal and reciprocal.

As any of our relationships moves beyond the
first stage, we need to perform the balancing act
of leaning and being leaned on. If we don't keep
things balanced over time, one half falls down.
That can be the one who depended overly on the
other, when the support is suddenly withdrawn.
Or it can be the one who is depended upon, who
falls under the weight of being depended on.

I can depend on myself to build reciprocal
dependence with others.

OCTOBER 19

Helping a child develop that "internal guidance system" is what our work is all about. —A. D. Thompson

Some of us have children. All of us have a child within us. The stress of change can provide the ideal workshop for developing the "internal guidance system" of our children and the child within us.

There will be different teachers, parents, friends, bosses, who want something of us. There will be different pressures, temptations, alternatives, and pleasures to choose from. What will stay the same, even as it grows and assimilates new experiences, is the internal voice.

The best way to develop an internal guidance system is to recognize situations in which we can exercise it. This can mean giving a two-year-old the choice of walking or being carried to bed. It can mean giving a seven-year-old the option of picking up his toys or giving them up for a week. It can mean giving a teenager the option of doing her homework or explaining to the teacher why she didn't. It might mean giving ourselves the option of taking time off or getting sick.

Relying on my inner self to act in the outer world takes practice at any age.

OCTOBER 20

You know you're in crisis when you can't tell if the bathroom lightbulb is burned out or the house is burning down. —Margaret Welshons

So what went wrong today? Surely something must have. Everything does these days, doesn't it? When we're in a period of traumatic change, the littlest thing can seem like the house burning down. And what's more, a smarter, better woman would surely be able to see that it's only a light bulb and change it.

Sometimes the best thing to do about a crisis in our lives is just to sit in the dark for a while. To wait. To see what happens. To give ourselves the time and the permission to see what the crisis is really about and to see if we need to do something to solve it, rather than to rush around trying to put out a fire that may or may not be burning. When we think we're having a crisis, we can sit and drink a glass of water while we determine whether or not this is a crisis.

And what if there really is a fire? We can trust ourselves to know. We can trust ourselves to put out little fires by ourselves and to get help putting out the big ones.

Knowing I'm in crisis helps me know what to do about it.

OCTOBER 21

Eat chocolate now; after you're dead there isn't any.
                                        —Jean Powell

It doesn't make any difference whether it's eating chocolate, taking a walk on the beach, getting together with friends, climbing into bed with a good book, taking a day off. And it doesn't make any difference whether we feel like celebrating. Celebrating something, no matter how small, even when we don't feel like it, can make us appreciate that being alive is something to celebrate.

If we live in the present moment every single moment of our lives, if our eyes, ears, and hearts are really open, sooner or later we'll stumble across something to celebrate. If we are open to feeling sadness, rage, anger, loss, we are also open to feeling celebratory moments. If we're closed to one, we're closed to both.

When we lose a relationship, we might find a bird in our backyard. If we lose our backyard, we might find a flower in the park. If we can't walk to the park, we might feel the sun through our window on a warm spring day. When it's winter and everything seems dead, we might rejoice to see a spider in the corner of our living room.

When I notice what might be celebrated, I can celebrate it.

OCTOBER 22

I'm so angry that my body's all but bursting into flame.
—Alamanda

Imagine the tabloid headline: Woman Self-Combusts in Anger at Ex-Spouse. When we're this angry, we're often afraid of our anger. We're so angry that we are afraid we might inflict severe bodily damage on others or ourselves. So angry that we might lose control. So we try to reason ourselves out of anger before we go beyond reason.

We might try to deny that we're angry. Or we might try to bury it in work, food, alcohol. Or we might lash out at somebody—or ourselves—who is not the object of our anger, but a "safe" outlet.

The only thing to do in the heat of anger is to stop and let ourselves feel the anger. We can find safe ways of burning off our anger before it burns us—screaming into the wind, hitting pillows, crying, stomping around the block. And once the danger of setting ourselves or someone else on fire has passed, we can let the person with whom we are angry know that we are angry and that we won't tolerate whatever has been done to evoke such an angry response.

My anger is a barometer, indicating what I will and won't put up with in myself or others.

OCTOBER 23

Without this self-approving voice within us, the applause of shouting millions is idle, empty praise.
—Sarah Josepha Hale

Ssh! Sit very quietly and listen. It's in there, somewhere. Our self-approving voice may have been drowned out by the self-critical sounds we've learned to make over the years. It goes something like this. "I'm okay the way I am." "Oh, no, you're not. How can you say that? But you might be okay if you lose thirty pounds and clean up the garage."

If we lose thirty pounds and clean the garage, the loud critical voice still won't be satisfied. Then we'll only be okay if we buy new clothes and clean the basement. And so on. Even if the world says I'm great—my boss loved my presentation, my mother praised my Sunday dinner, and my kids gave me a handmade card—I won't be able to hear them if I can't hear the self-approving voice inside me.

My self-approving voice isn't impressed by thundering applause. I don't need to do every laudable thing I ever thought of or possess every positive trait I aspire to in order to hear it. I only need to sit and listen.

Only I can accept myself.

OCTOBER 24

It is good to have an end to journey towards; but it is the journey that matters, in the end. —Ursula K. Le Guin

Achieving our goals is both easier and more rewarding if we pay attention while we're on the way to reaching them. As we journey along, if our eyes are focused only on the prize, we're likely to miss much of our daily lives. If we're paying attention to what's happening to us as we go in search of our goal, we notice when a particular goal no longer suits us.

Suppose our goal was to grow old together with our spouse, enjoying the fruits of our combined labors. Maybe we were so focused on saving money for an early retirement that we didn't notice we were no longer talking to each other. Or maybe we worked so hard that we never took the opportunity to enjoy each other's company. We got so far off the track that not only didn't we retire together, we got divorced instead.

Many of us have experienced the feeling of flat dejection when we reach a long-held goal. We thought we would feel proud, elated, satisfied, anything but dejected. But somehow, in our relentless pursuit of one thing or another, we failed to notice that we didn't want that thing anymore.

Staying in touch with today lets me stay in touch with my goals for the future.

OCTOBER 25

*Relationship addicts . . . have selective amnesia. In order
to maintain or be in a relationship, they selectively forget
what it was like last year, last week, or yesterday.*
—Anne Wilson Schaef

Addicts forget things. They have blackouts when
they're drinking or using drugs. When our marriages are ending, or later, when we're beginning
a new relationship, we do well to look at our own
memory about relationships.

If we tried to hold on to a relationship at any
cost, forgetting everything from unmet expectations to battering, we're suffering from selective
amnesia. If we want so much to be in a love relationship that we are willing to ignore or forget
that the person is committed to someone else,
doesn't listen to us, is unreliable about showing
up, then we've got a problem.

We can do some things about recovering our
memories, recovering from our capacity to forget,
and recovering ourselves. We can join a support
group, talk to a friend, tell ourselves the truth.
When I'm honest about my relationship with myself, I'm on my way to honest relationships.

*When I forget the things that went wrong with my
past relationships, I'm apt to repeat them.*

OCTOBER 26

Nothing in life is to be feared. It is only to be understood.
—Marie Curie

Fear is a great traffic cop. Fear stops us in our tracks. In fact, lots of times, it prevents us from starting out in the first place. To say that nothing is to be feared is not to say that we don't feel fear. Nor is it to say that all fear is unfounded. Yet if we don't attempt to understand our fears, our fears will only increase.

There is fear that prevents us from walking some dark city streets alone. We *understand* that this is inviting trouble, so we don't walk there. We fear a kind of person we've never met, so our fear prevents us from getting to know a potential friend. Or I might be afraid to try roller skating because I broke my leg ice skating. Not understanding our fear prevents us from doing things we otherwise might do—like beginning a new love relationship.

When we deny our fears or act recklessly in the face of them, we are not likely to understand them. And they are likely to rule our lives. We can acknowledge our fears. We can reassure ourselves that we won't act in haste.

I understand my fear and proceed with caution.

OCTOBER 27

Joint undertakings stand a better chance when they benefit both sides. —Euripides

Two things most often get in the way of cooperating in mutual effort for the benefit of both parties: disagreement and disagreement. For cooperative efforts to succeed we need to agree on what the benefits are *and* how we're going to get them.

Suppose we are trying to cooperate with our ex-spouse on dividing our personal possessions. We need to define benefit for both of us. We need to be as clear as we can about what it is we want. And we need to listen to what our ex wants. Having our goal be that our ex gets burned is not of benefit to both of us.

Say we decide that we're going to meet with our ex-spouse to go through photographs and boxes in the basement. Having agreed to appear on a given day to do this, he suddenly remembers he has to stay home to polish his shoes. We seem to be in disagreement, and we won't succeed at our joint undertaking until we agree *how* we're going to do it. Agreeing to working with our ex-spouses doesn't guarantee success. But not figuring out how we can both benefit from the arrangement pretty much guarantees failure.

Clearly, cooperating benefits me.

OCTOBER 28

Everything intercepts us from ourselves.
— Ralph Waldo Emerson

We must spend time alone in order not to be isolated from ourselves. Yet when we're getting used to living without our partners, maybe alone for the first time, we may find it difficult to be alone with ourselves. When we're isolated from ourselves, we're isolated from others—whether we're alone or in a crowd.

The opposite of isolation is, of course, connection. Our impulse at this lonely time of our lives is to build new connections, to keep busy, meet new people, take up new or neglected hobbies, throw ourselves into our children or our work. If we can only find the proper link, we think, we'll feel connected again to our daily lives, not set apart by our pain and sorrow. And for all our efforts, we're exhausted and still feeling isolated.

To connect with others, we must first connect or reconnect with ourselves. Busyness is not going to make us feel better. Too much working, eating, drinking, doing, even fun, is not going to reconnect us to ourselves. Connecting with ourselves can only be done without distractions.

In the quiet of doing nothing with myself, by myself, I find myself.

OCTOBER 29

*I like not only to be loved, but also to be told that I am
loved. I am not sure that you are of the same kind. But the
realm of silence is large enough beyond the grave. This is
the world of literature and speech, and I shall take leave to
tell you that you are very dear.*   —George Eliot

Uncommunicated love is unrequited love,
whether to and for others or ourselves. Love is
kinetic, not static. When it is expressed through
word or deed to others, it flows back to us. When
I express my love for myself by taking care of me
and by telling myself that I love her, the communication of my love creates a flow within me.

It can be risky to express our love for ourselves
or others because we can't control the love that
flows back. Often we express love as a bargaining
chip—I will love you if you take care of me or if
you clean the kitchen. And we find that what
flows back to us is not a mutual expression of
love—or being taken care of or a clean kitchen.

Expressing love as a contract is not really expressing love at all. The truth is that expressing
love, freely and unconditionally, will surprise us.
When we express love for ourselves, we're more
likely to eat right, look prettier, have more energy
and zest for life.

Today is a good day to tell myself "I love you."

OCTOBER 30

Truth is the nursing mother of genius.

—Margaret Fuller

Having a genius for something is having an uncanny talent, a knack, whether it's for inventing new gadgets or making friends feel at home. And we can't know what our genius is if we don't tell ourselves the truth. Telling ourselves the truth about our talents and aspirations won't make us into something we're not—prima ballerinas at fifty or Oscar winners who've never appeared on camera.

Lying to ourselves about what we want and what we can do won't either. One way of lying is to make excuses. I would learn a new language, write a book, or grow prizewinning roses, but I can't because my children, job, responsibilities take too much time. When we lie, we don't become geniuses; we become victims.

When we're truthful with ourselves about what we want to do, we have far more chance of succeeding at doing it than when we lie to ourselves. We're telling the truth and so we're likely to nurture our skills, protect our time, and spend the time and energy it takes to succeed.

I can succeed if I'm truthful about what I want to succeed at.

OCTOBER 31

*. . . until you can free those final monsters within the
jungle of yourself, your life, your soul is up for grabs.*
—Rona Barrett

Who knows what monsters lurk in our psyches?
We don't know what they look like or what they
can do to us, and we're afraid of finding out. Until
we look at them, our fear will continue to grow.

Freeing our monsters means meeting them and
letting them go. We might meet the Monster of
the Unlovable Me. (My marriage failed and no
one will ever love me again.) Letting her go
means giving up the idea that we're unlovable
and loving ourselves. We might meet the monster
Woe S. Me. (She's the one who'll make sure that
bad things keep happening to us.) Letting her go
might mean we start to take responsibility for our
troubles and stop being victims. We might meet
Ann Xiety. (She makes sure we always feel anxious.) Letting her go means we might have to
breathe.

One way of freeing monsters is to acknowledge
the fear they represent. One monster might represent a fear that we won't take care of business if
we don't feel anxious. We can reassure ourselves
by doing the things we need to do.

Freeing my monsters means freeing myself.

NOVEMBER 1

It is only possible to live happily ever after on a day-to-day basis. —Margaret Bonnano

Fairy tales end with the beginning—the prince and princess live happily ever after, without any of the dailiness. We all know that happily-ever-after is not possible. But when our marriages end, we seem to fear the worst—that our unhappy ending guarantees an unhappy beginning. We're sure to live unhappily ever after from this day on.

Living one day at a time does not, of course, guarantee our happiness. Nor are we guaranteed that we won't feel sad, angry, lonely. Or that we won't, at times, feel like we can't cope.

When we live one day at a time we're open to the possibility of being happy. Today I can be happy that it's bright and sunny without worrying about whether it will rain tomorrow. I can immerse myself in today's work without obsessing about what I must do by week's end. I can bear today's grief without wondering how I will bear it in the months to come. And if I'm living in the present, at least I'm there to notice when a small hint of happiness intrudes on my sorrow.

I'm not looking for a prince or a panacea—one day at a time.

NOVEMBER 2

My mind is over-taxed. Brave and courageous as I am, I feel that creeping on of that inevitable thing, a breakdown, if I cannot get some immediate relief. I need somebody to come and get me. —Mary McLeod Bethune

Sometimes the best way to take care of ourselves is to holler "Help!" We don't need to ask for support despite the fact that we're brave and courageous. We ask for support *because* we are. Telling ourselves it's okay to ask is the easy part.

Convincing ourselves that we need help when we do is harder. When we hear a voice inside us saying that a smart, independent, worthwhile, brave, and courageous woman in this situation wouldn't ask for help, it's probably a good time to ask. When that voice nags, "Just buck up and go it alone," holler for help.

Whom to ask for help can seem imponderable as we go through a separation. Will this one or that one help? How will I ever repay people for their help? Am I really asking whether I'm worthy of helping? Or am I too proud to ask for help? Most people who truly want to help don't worry about being "repaid" and know that in the course of your relationship with them, having lent you support, they can, in turn, ask for it.

To ask for help is to get it, and vice versa.

NOVEMBER 3

Just because everything is different doesn't mean anything has changed. —Irene Peters

So everything is different. I used to be part of two. Now I'm one. A single-again woman. When I buy groceries, when I choose a movie, when I get a haircut, when I plan for next week, next month, next year . . . everything is different. Perhaps I've moved. Or the same house feels different. Perhaps when I wake up in the morning, I wonder where my spouse is, then I realize everything is different.

Different circumstances happen to us. There is no way on earth to prevent things being different —children grow, jobs come and go, new presidents are elected, days pass, then years. There's no way we can go back to yesterday. Change, however, is personal choice and personal work. Change takes time, planning, effort.

Do I want to change? Do I want to feel better about myself? To have a clearer sense of who I am in this different world? How do I want to be in it? Would I like to change the way I look, act, make money, am in a relationship? Only I can decide to change my life.

Different is what happens to me; change is what I make of it.

NOVEMBER 4

Things seem to go by the rule of contrary.

—Ellen Wood

There is nothing wrong with wanting things. However, when we try to control ourselves and others—what we do, think, act, feel—so everybody and everything will give us what we want according to our specific expectations, the rule of contrary kicks in. In fact, when things are going contrary to our plan, it's a clue to look at our expectations.

When we married we probably expected to be married for life. Then things began to go by the rule of contrary. Our spouse didn't do the things we expected—make enough money, make us feel loved. The more we tried to make him do these things, the less he seemed to do them. Or, if we controlled our temper, our jealousy, our time, then he would meet our expectations.

When things aren't going the way we think they should, we can try to bring our expectations in line with the way things are going. But that's just another way of trying to control. Or we can try giving up control and go with the contrary flow, which might just get us back in touch with ourselves and our expectations.

I give up to get more of what I want.

NOVEMBER 5

Don't ask the doctor; ask the patient.

—Yiddish proverb

Somewhere out there in the world is an expert who could cure what ails us, if only we knew what ailed us. It's no secret that we spend hundreds of thousands of dollars every year in this country "asking the doctor," searching for the outside expert who will tell us how to be happy, deal with our emotions, resolve our conflicts, reach our true potential, etc., etc., etc.

One of the most frustrating things in caring for sick babies is that they cannot tell us where it hurts, what it feels like, what makes it feel better or worse. But we are not babies. We can ask ourselves what hurts in our lives. We can trust ourselves to know what our feelings are, what makes us happy, sad, crazy, tired, overwhelmed. What pleases us and makes us feel better.

We can ask our own internal patient what ails us. And we can ask our own internal doctor to help cure us. (Sometimes that internal doctor needs the help of a friend, therapist, priest, and we're the only ones who really know when.) Trusting ourselves to know what we think and feel is the first step to making it better.

So, I asked myself, how are you doing today?

NOVEMBER 6

Tact is the intelligence of the heart. —Anonymous

Tact may feel scarce in our lives when we're getting divorced. We find ourselves feeling sad, rancorous, angry, spiteful—particularly toward our ex-spouses. We might feel that being tactful makes us seem weak. And we're feeling so vulnerable, we don't want anybody to think we're weak, particularly our ex-spouses.

We may feel like we stand to lose something if we treat them with tact. We may think that because we have a genuine complaint or grievance, we needn't be tactful about sharing it. In fact, it's at those times when our hurt is worst and our grievance is biggest that it's smart to be tactful. If we ask for something with hostility, hostility is likely what we'll get. If we make the same request with tact, we'll probably get it.

Being tactful doesn't mean not being truthful with ourselves or others. We can tell the truth about how we see things with tact, especially in times of conflict or stress. When we're being tactful we're *not* attacking—ourselves or others. When we're not on the attack, we're less likely to put ourselves or others on the defensive.

Tact can help me win my heart's desire.

NOVEMBER 7

It takes far less courage to kill yourself than it takes to make yourself wake up one more time. It's harder to stay where you are than to get out. —Judith Rossner

Courage comes from *coeur*, the French word for heart. To kill myself is, literally, to stop my heart, to have no more courage. Ergo, it takes more courage, more heart, to go on living each day than it does to stop.

Sometimes people talk about dying of a broken heart, which could also be dying of broken courage. Surely we can't live without courage, and when we face the end of a relationship, living *is* courageous. We get up each morning looking for one heartening thing in our lives. Maybe it's that the alarm clock went off on time. Maybe it's that we spent time on a project that absorbed us. Maybe it's that we said to ourselves, "The life you save may be your own."

Staying where we are is staying in our own bodies, our own lives. We were in a relationship and now we're not. We have got out of something, but not the most fundamental something—ourselves.

When I stay with my heart, I have the courage to stay with my life.

NOVEMBER 8

Sometimes it's worse to win a fight than to lose.
                                        —Billie Holiday

Let's count the ways. We might win a fight and get divorced. We might win a fight and stay in a dead marriage. We might win a fight and lose a friend. We might win a fight and lose our self-respect because we fought dirty. We might win a fight only to discover that we don't want what we fought for. There are more.

When our marriages end, we may feel relieved at not having to count who's winning and who's losing because we've been through so many fights. Yet to give up arguing—with ourselves or others—is often to give up getting what we need or what we believe in. Many of us gave up our marriages to get what we need. Why would we give up fighting?

What we may want to give up instead is how and why we fight. If we're winning arguments by putting other people down, we're not likely to feel good about winning. If we fight to defend ourselves from getting close to somebody, we're going to lose bigger if we win. If we're arguing to prove we're right, we may find ourselves feeling wrong.

Why I fight is more important than winning or losing.

NOVEMBER 9

It is better to wear out one's shoes than one's sheets.

—Genoese proverb

Nearly all spiritual traditions have prayer or meditation that involves walking along a certain path, to and fro, meditative movement. When we're feeling particularly agitated or anxious, or when we've hit a snag, a walk around the office, around the house or the block can accomplish wonders. Sometimes a solution to a problem we've been stuck on will literally present itself.

Wearing out one's shoes needn't literally mean walking. It can simply mean taking action rather than lying around brooding about our problems. Who hasn't experienced times when cleaning closets, washing dishes, running errands, or balancing a budget resulted in calming us down? And maybe it also gave us a renewed sense of satisfaction with ourselves.

There are times when we all need to do something unpleasant, something we're afraid of, something we've got numerous excuses to put off. Sometimes the only way to get it done is to start doing it. We feel better when we start, when we no longer wear out our sheets.

Taking action as if I meant it can change my life.

NOVEMBER 10

> *Sky, be my depth;*
> *Wind, be my width and my height;*
> *World, my heart's span:*
> *Loneliness, wings for my flight.*
> —Leonora Speyer

We can live in the confines we create with our loneliness. Or we can use our loneliness to create wings to soar independently through depths, widths, and heights beyond our imagining.

When we start flying, we don't know where we can go. In the depths, the wind, the wide world, there's bound to be some darkness, some light, some cold, some heat, some disappointment, some passion. When we sit at home in loneliness, we know where we are. We know how dark and cold the space is. We can use artificial means— like drugs, alcohol, sex—to light and heat this little space and drive away loneliness.

That, clearly, is not independence. Being independent is using our loneliness to build up our wings, to explore ourselves and the world around us. We do that by facing ourselves and the world without trying to keep our loneliness at bay. When we face ourselves for what we are, we are likely to discover that we're lonely, and a whole lot more.

I can be independent with my loneliness.

NOVEMBER 11

Loving, like prayer, is a power as well as a process. It's curative. It is creative.   —Zona Gale

It might be said that the power both love and prayer have to cure us comes from the process. When my marriage ends, I may well feel like my power to love and be loved ends as well. I may have prayed for years that my marriage wouldn't end. I may have given up prayer or meditation, thinking they have no place or effect in my life.

It's time for a leap of faith! Simply by engaging in expressing love and practicing prayer and meditation we can begin, once again, to feel the effects of their power in our lives. We can't reason ourselves into loving ourselves, and we can't talk ourselves into believing that if we set aside regular time for prayer and meditation we may feel more effective and powerful in our lives. That's why it's a leap.

The only thing we can do is try it. We have little to lose. It may help to make this our daily prayer: "Help me see the lovable things in myself. Help me act as if I loved myself and others." By admitting the process and power of prayer and love into our lives, we begin to feel their curative effect.

I pray to see that I am a lovable person.

NOVEMBER 12

So much has been said and sung of beautiful young girls, why doesn't somebody wake up to the beauty of old women? —Harriet Beecher Stowe

Beauty and age may well be in the eye of the beholder. But who says that we can't be our own best beholders? Whatever our age when we get divorced, we very often think we are too old and not beautiful enough.

What if we make a list about how old and ugly we are? I'm too old to go to kindergarten. I'm too old to be grounded. I'm too old to believe that I'm not smart. I'm too old to eat food I don't like. I'm too old not to do what I want. Now ugly: I'm too ugly to have to go through the humiliation of entering a beauty contest. I'm too ugly to spend thousands of dollars at the whims of the fashion industry.

What if we turned those lists inside out? I'm getting older . . . I know how to do more things. I have more memories. I have survived. Or beauty . . . I'm beautiful enough to take care of my body. I'm beautiful when I smile. Making lists like this can give us a different way of looking at our old, pretty selves.

Mirror, mirror, on the wall, how am I growing in age and beauty today?

NOVEMBER 13

*In real love you want the other person's good. In romantic
love you want the other person.*   —Margaret Anderson

Wanting another person, when we're talking
about romantic love, is most often wanting that
person to do, be, feel, act in the way we want
them to. Thinking that we can have, possess, or
control another person is a fantasy.

Wanting another person's good is *not* wanting
to control them. If we truly want another person's
good, we're willing to let them figure out what's
good for themselves . . . themselves. We're willing to give up controlling their behavior. We're
willing to negotiate when their good conflicts
with our good. And we're willing to support
them in getting what they want.

Oh, and one more thing . . . Before we can experience real love for another person, we have to
love ourselves in a way that wants our own good.
It may seem strange to think of loving ourselves
in the romantic love way, wanting ourselves. But
that's exactly what we do when we say we'll love
ourselves only when we are happy, do our work,
act nice, live up to all sorts of expectations. That's
control, not love.

I love myself enough to discover what's good for me.

NOVEMBER 14

Fear not those who argue but those who dodge.
—Marie von Ebner-Eschenbach

Arguing, at its best, is a way to get out into the open what each party truly believes and feels. When we argue, the worst thing that can happen is that we decide we can't continue the relationship. If we're willing to argue, at least we'll know that.

Dodging disagreements is cause for fear because people who dodge disagreements are, by definition, keeping secrets. When we keep secrets or people keep secrets from us, our fear is going to increase. We don't know what might happen. If we dodge or deny our feelings to avoid engaging in arguments, we can end up not knowing what we're thinking or feeling. And what we don't know can hurt us.

The only way to alleviate our fear is to be willing to engage ourselves and others. Engaging means openly admitting our own thoughts and beliefs. That may mean confronting ourselves or others about behavior that's not in line with those beliefs. It may mean disagreeing on what's important. It may mean arguing.

Engaging in open arguments with myself or others is nothing to be afraid of.

NOVEMBER 15

And it is still true, no matter how old you are, when you go out into the world, it is best to hold hands and stick together. —Robert Fulghum

One of the most heartening sights ever is a flock of children on a field trip. There they are, in slickers or snowsuits, clinging to each other for dear life. Not one of them would dream of crossing the street or turning the corner without holding to the hand of the next one. They know that if they hold on, they won't get hurt or lost.

Holding on to the support of friends is an art learned in childhood, and often lost along the way. We think we don't need it anymore. Of course we can, most of the time in our adulthood, cross the street by ourselves. Yet many of the things we do would be easier if we'd let our friends or family help us.

When we separate from our spouses, it can feel like we don't have anybody to hold hands with anymore—or to help make those decisions about work, home, life. We might not feel like going out into the world, especially with groups of people, and this is a good time to do it.

When I can't cross a street alone, I can find someone to cross with me.

NOVEMBER 16

In every parting scene there is an image of death.
— George Eliot

The world is gearing up to winter. Scenes of loss are all around us. Trees have lost their leaves. The sky and landscape may be gray. The days are getting shorter and darker. The images of death are concrete and abundant—as they are when we're ending our marriages.

A marriage, whether we deem it good or bad, whether it lasted two years or twenty, is a living thing. It has the energy of connection, the promise of growth together, the bloom of love. Divorce kills all that off. And we're reminded of it in all the little parting scenes. The last night we spent together, the day the truck arrived and one of us actually moved, the day our divorce is final.

No wonder we might feel like a November landscape. It can be so dark that we believe we've forgotten what light looks like. We can look outside at November and remember what will happen next. Things will lie fallow for a while. It will get even darker, and then, inexorably, the light will return. To the world and to our lives.

With my divorce something died, and I hold tight to my belief that something may grow out of it.

NOVEMBER 17

The trouble is not that we are never happy—it is that happiness is so episodical.   —Ruth Benedict

And in the time after our separation those episodes may seem entirely too far apart. Days go by, or weeks or months, when we think we'll never be happy again. Our lives may play like advertisements for a soap opera we wish we weren't part of: "In our next episode, look for tears, sadness, rage, despair, worry, hard work. If you're looking for happiness, change the channel to *The Days of Someone Else's Life.*"

Happiness is not something we can beg, buy, borrow, steal, or will. It is not, and this is very important, something someone else can give us. The best we can do, when happy episodes are few and far between, is to be on the lookout for them, recognize them when they come, and savor them for every bit they're worth.

We can't will ourselves to be happy, *and* we can allow ourselves to feel happy when we do. It only stands to reason that if we bury our feelings over time, we bury *all* our feelings. Refuse to feel anger, sadness, grief, rage, and we'll also be unable to feel our tenderness, our joy, our satisfaction, our happiness.

When happiness comes, I hope I'm there to enjoy it.

NOVEMBER 18

> *It seems as if*
> *I'll never get beyond*
> *the foot-prints that I made*
> —Qernertoq

Of course the way to get beyond the footprints that we've made in this life is to make more footprints. If we've been plodding along in size nine hiking boots, we can't trip away *en pointe* in size five ballerina slippers. Yet we don't have to keep marching along the same well-worn track, sinking in deeper and deeper.

We can exchange our house slippers for walking shoes, get regular exercise and transform our physical condition. We can wear our old work shoes off to a new job. We can change shoes and walk in new directions. That's transformation— getting beyond the footprints of our girlhood, our coupled lives, into our new lives.

As we become who we are in our new single lives, we remember where those old footprints are, celebrating the running, hiking, jumping, twirling, plodding, and dancing that made them. We can remember the paths that served us well and avoid those that ended at a cliff.

Transformation happens as I lay down a new path one step at a time.

NOVEMBER 19

When we are unable to find tranquility within ourselves, it is useless to seek it elsewhere. —La Rochefoucauld

Serenity is learning to live with myself, warts and all. No one else can give me serenity. I won't find it in a bookstore, a self-help program, or a relationship. If I don't have it, I will always be anxious, on edge, looking for it. And I won't find it until I stop looking for it outside myself.

When we're getting divorced, our lives can feel anything but tranquil. We may be afraid we won't be able to earn a living, take care of our houses, pay our bills. We may be afraid that because our lives are chaotic we're going crazy. We may overfill our calendars and still not feel fulfilled. Eventually the anxiety will return, and we'll go in search of a new way to take the edge off.

The only lasting way to take the edge off is to jump into the middle of ourselves. When we stop our frantic worrying about money, we can focus our energy and earn our living. When we sit quietly with ourselves, we begin to know what we'd like to do. When we look inside, we see that, while our lives may have been chaotic and crazy, we're not. As we do, our lives become more manageable and our serenity increases.

My quest for serenity leads me back to myself.

NOVEMBER 20

Once you can pump your own gas and take out the garbage, you've got it made. —Jane Quade

It doesn't matter what it is—hanging pictures, hiring a plumber, painting the kitchen. What can happen to us when divorce turns our world upside down is that we lose our confidence in our ability to do things. Add to that the knowledge that we have to do things we never did before, and we easily come up with a self-confidence rating less than zero.

A way to gain or regain our self-confidence, of course, is by doing those things. Whether it's something relatively simple like taking the garbage out, or something more complicated, like filing income tax on our own, we'll feel better about ourselves when we do it.

Doing things only builds our self-confidence, if we do them *and* give ourselves credit for doing them. Who hasn't watched a small child crow with delight when she first learned to climb stairs? Can we find that small child in ourselves? Can we give the person we are now any less credit for learning to do new things no matter how little those things might seem?

I credit me where credit is due for doing what I have to do.

NOVEMBER 21

The eyes of others our prisons; their thoughts our cages.
—Virginia Woolf

To look to others for approval of our appearance, our actions, our very being, is to trap ourselves. We imprison ourselves when we live as if our lives depended on their approval.

When we don't like the way we look, think we're making the wrong decisions, or know we'll never be attractive again, we're vulnerable to imprisoning ourselves behind the bars of other people's approval. During a divorce, we do need to make many decisions and do many new things. It's important to ask ourselves if we're trapping ourselves by looking to others for approval.

If my mother tells me I'll never get another man until I lose twenty pounds . . . And my best friend tells me it wouldn't hurt if I did something about my hair . . . And my boss says I'll feel better if I get involved in several new projects . . . And my kids say I'm a better mom when I make homemade lasagna . . . I can win the approval of all these people only if I make lasagna but don't eat it while I am churning out work and sitting at the hairdresser's.

When things get complicated in approval prison, I can let myself out and throw away the key.

NOVEMBER 22

. . . you cannot fire up, cannot manufacture desire, when there is no spark at all to build on. —Judith Guest

At the end of a relationship we may feel like we've lost ourselves. We not only lose the relationship, we lose interest in the things that make our lives interesting. We may lose our passion for work, for play, for pleasure, for relationships, for food, for sex. We feel as if there is no spark, nothing inside us that will ever be roused again.

Thinking and determination will not make us interested in living. We cannot will ourselves to be interested in living. No amount of doing things works either. We can get involved in self-improvement programs, new friends, new hobbies, new work. We can do, do, do until we're exhausted and still feel no passion for living.

We're not dead yet, and there is a spark somewhere in us—even if we can't find it. What we can do is to bring ourselves into a warm, dry place and wait. It's impossible to light a fire from a single match in a wet and windy forest. When we protect our spark, no matter how small and weak, from the elements of willpower, control, overdoing, denial, it will eventually begin to burn again.

If I find it and feed it, the spark within me blazes.

NOVEMBER 23

> *you can see forever*
> *when the vision is clear*
> *in this moment*
> *each moment*
> *i give thanks*
> —Harriet Kofalk

Thanksgiving as a major family holiday is almost guaranteed to be difficult. We may have bad memories of holidays while we were married—alcohol, overeating, arguments. Or we may have good memories and feel the loss particularly at this time of family togetherness.

Whatever arrangements we make for family holidays after our divorce, it's important to keep our expectations low and our vision clear. Deciding that we're going to have the perfect holiday now that we're out of a bad marriage is as dangerous as deciding we'll never have a "real" family holiday again.

We have different things to be thankful for than we did when we were married. And we need to find new ways of celebrating our thanks, in this season and every day. When we live every day and every moment to its fullest, we're likely to see our way clear—to what we're truly thankful for.

When I live in the moment, I recognize the moments I'm grateful for.

NOVEMBER 24

Most men experience getting older with regret,
apprehension. But most women experience it even more
painfully: with shame. Aging is man's destiny, something
that must happen because he is a human being. For a
woman, aging is not only her destiny . . . it is also her
vulnerability. —Susan Sontag

Shame is free-floating, all-encompassing embarrassment and guilt—for nothing we did wrong.
The older we get, it seems, the less we're valued,
so we must not be worth valuing. And that's
something we're ashamed of.

To get older, especially as a woman alone in
this society, is to be vulnerable to a variety of statistics: that we might or will earn less money than
our male counterparts, be unsafe alone on certain
streets, and be seen as dotty old women.

The vulnerability and the shame are real; so are
the statistics. Denying them won't make them go
away. Nor will trying to talk ourselves out of
them. Yet if we admit our shame and our vulnerability, we can begin to release them. Releasing
them makes room in our lives. And we can use
the energy we were expending on keeping and
hiding our shame to explore new territory.

Living as an aging, vulnerable woman is pretty good
when I consider the alternative.

NOVEMBER 25

*I've never sought success in order to get fame and money;
it's the talent and passion that count in success.*
—Ingrid Bergman

The second biggest success we can have in this
life is discovering our own unique talents. The
biggest success we can have is using them passionately. No matter how successful we are in
anybody else's eyes or how much fame and
money we accrue, if we're not using our own
unique talents, we'll never feel successful.

Yet knowing what our talent is and even using
it doesn't ensure that we'll be or feel successful.
That takes passion—the feeling that will let us define our own terms of success, recognize them
when we get there, and bask in the light of doing
what we want. Just because we're good at doing
something doesn't mean we'll enjoy doing it.

To embrace our talents passionately is to engage in an ongoing relationship with them, to celebrate them, and to exercise them. Just using
them feels like a success. Our internal negative
voice can't stop us. The measures of the world
can't stop us.

*When I start using my talent passionately, nothing
can stop me.*

NOVEMBER 26

Dependence invites encroachment.
—Patricia Meyer Spacks

And vulnerability invites interlinking, or inter-dependence. As we go through a separation, vulnerability and dependence can both seem like words we'd just as soon expunge from our vocabulary and our lives. It's hard to tell whether our dependence on our ex-spouse was dependence or *inter*dependence. Differentiating is crucial to our ability to open ourselves to others.

When we're dependent, we turn ourselves over to the other person, body and soul. We invite him or her to take responsibility for what is rightly ours—our decisions, our feelings, our actions. We are bound, sooner or later, to feel invaded. In interdependence, we do not relinquish responsibility. And we do not feel invaded.

When we're suffering feelings of loss, we may react to dependence and vulnerability as if they were the same thing. As we attempt to redefine our territory of self, we may close our borders completely. We do need to know our boundaries. Vulnerability is the ability to know our boundaries and to invite others to come inside for a time.

When I know my boundaries, I won't be invaded.

NOVEMBER 27

My parents gave us a fantastic sense of security and
worth. By the time the bigots got around to telling us we
were nobody, we already knew *we were somebody.*
—Florynce Kennedy

Some of us were lucky enough to get a sense of
security, worth, and confidence in childhood. We
knew we were somebody, not because we could
read faster, jump higher, work harder.

Others of us have to learn the hard way that we
are who we are and who we are is somebody.
We've had to give ourselves the sense of security.
And some of us never have experienced the feeling of being somebody, of having the confidence
and conviction that we are okay as we are.

When tough things happen to us, our sense of
confidence in who we are is in danger of eroding.
Maybe my mother said I was somebody, but she
doesn't count. Maybe my ex-spouse said I was
somebody, but he doesn't count. Maybe my
friends, family, and coworkers think I'm somebody, but they don't count. We can learn to listen
to them. And in fact we are the only ones, ultimately, who can give ourselves a sense of worth,
security, and confidence in ourselves.

I can count on myself to know my own worth and to
listen when others recount it to me.

NOVEMBER 28

Nevertheless we must recognize that while guilt deprives us of numerous gratifications, we and our world would be monstrous minus guilt. For the freedoms we lose, our constraints and losses, are necessary losses—part of the price we pay for civilization. —Judith Viorst

Often when we talk about feeling guilty, we talk about what we can't do. And we talk about how other people make us feel guilty. They—usually beginning with our parents—tell us we can't do a myriad of things. And when we do them—or are tempted to—we feel guilty.

Yet our guilt can stop us from doing truly monstrous things—for instance, murdering our ex-spouse. It can stop us from doing things that are against the law and from doing things we believe are wrong—maybe lying to our boss about being sick. We lose the opportunity to act on an impulse because our guilt stops us. And that usually keeps us out of a whole lot of trouble.

The good side of guilt can help us decide which impulses not to act on—now or again. Feeling guilty when we act against our own or society's best interests—or are tempted to—means we lose some freedom. And we gain the freedom of being able to live with ourselves.

Feeling my guilt can guide my choices.

NOVEMBER 29

. . . the smooth mind of each is everywhere present to the other, and as received and unchallenged as the falling snow. —Annie Dillard

There is little in nature that is more clean, quiet, or peaceful than the falling of first snow. It covers the ground, cleaning away the gray dinginess, and there's no stopping it. The landscape takes on a kind of glow. Good time spent sharing and connecting with a friend can be like a first snowfall. It lightens the gray landscape of our hearts.

When we're sharing we are with each other in each other's sorrow, joy, pain, celebration. To make the way for spending open time with another, we must open to spending such time with ourselves. We must be able to be present to the moment of our lives, whatever we're feeling.

When we make connections with friends or family, we share part of our lives with them. When we spend time with them, that's where we are. We're not off somewhere in the hinterlands of our mind worrying about work to be done yesterday, next week, or next year. We can feel it when we're "clicking" with another person. We are open, honest, and trusting, and we can feel their reciprocation.

Sharing my life with a friend puts it in a new light.

NOVEMBER 30

Any change in one part of your life affects all other parts.
                                            —Gloria Karpinski

Things can change so much and so fast when we're going through a separation and divorce that we may have trouble remembering what's changing, let alone having time and space to integrate those changes into our lives. Being single again involves the obvious changes of living arrangements, household duties, socializing in different circumstances.

They lead to changes in the way we feel, maybe the way we look, the way we look at the world. Perhaps we discover that we want to paint the living room green after so many years of living with someone who hated green that we forgot we liked it. Or that we can read the Sunday paper in the order we want. Pretty soon our whole lives are different.

When changes spin my life topsy-turvy, I can remind myself that change and life happen only one day at a time. When it seems like everything is changing so fast that I'm apt to forget who I am, I can know that today is the only day I live in. And, after a time, I realize that the changes happening every day are a transition to a new me.

I am who I'm changing to be today.

DECEMBER 1

The future is made of the same stuff as the present.
—Simone Weil

If we are enduring the present with gritted teeth, thinking that the future will be made of the same stuff can bring on despair. If we patiently and passively await future solutions to today's problems, a future made of the stuff of the present can bring only more problems. If we spend our time and energy worrying about the future, the future can bring only more devastating worries.

If, however, we live fully open to the present, the horror of a future made up of the same stuff gradually dissipates. If our present is full of the complications, fears, and ravages of ending a relationship, we can ensure that the future is not more of the same by dealing with today's problems today. Yes, we will still have problems, and we'll have resources for dealing with them.

With each moment we let ourselves feel what we are feeling, with every small decision we make, we are living in the present. With every bit of credit we give ourselves for doing well in the face of adversity, we establish credit for the future. We can change our future only by changing our present.

If I attend to today today, I can do so tomorrow, too.

DECEMBER 2

By blaming ourself, we can believe in our life-controlling powers. By blaming ourself, we are saying that we would rather feel guilty than helpless, than not in control.
—Judith Viorst

Sometimes we go to great lengths to deny—even to ourselves—that we feel like helpless victims. We might blame ourselves—if I had been a better wife, he wouldn't have . . . become a drunk, gone out with others, buried himself in work, turned away from me. The implication is that we had control.

If we had control, then we're guilty of not using it. If we didn't have control, we can always blame ourselves—and feel guilty—because we didn't. The more we try to rely on control, the more out of control our lives can get.

Pretty soon we start to feel guilty *and* helpless. Our lives *are* out of control *and* we blame ourselves because we're not doing anything about it. This is a pretty nifty place to live if we don't want to take responsibility for our own lives. The alternative is admitting that sometimes we aren't in control. It's only then that we can figure out what our accountability was for the situation.

I am not in control and I can account for my own actions.

DECEMBER 3

If only I believed all I believe. —Anonymous

To believe is to hold a firm conviction, based on faith or trust, and not necessarily on rational thought, that something is true or right. When we say we believe something or someone, however, we often have something further in mind. We think that an action is required of that belief.

It is through actions—those of ourselves and others—that we test our beliefs. If we persist in saying we believe in something and our own actions don't bear out that belief, we may examine and change or discard the belief. Or if we come to believe in something, we may change our actions to align with the belief. Looking at our actions is a way of seeing if we truly believe what we say we do.

If we are coming to believe that we will have the moral and psychological strength we need to live singly, it can be frustrating when we find ourselves acting as though we're really helpless. Now is not the time to beat up on ourselves because our actions aren't congruent with our new belief. Changing actions and/or changing beliefs is a continuous process of discovery.

Seeing, being, and doing lead me to what I believe.

DECEMBER 4

*The minute you or anybody else knows what you are you
are not it, you are what you or anybody else knows you
are and as everything in living is made up of finding out
what you are it is extraordinarily difficult really not to
know what you are and yet to be that thing.*

—Gertrude Stein

Knowing who and what we are is a process.
Very often the definition or articulation of who we
are lags behind actually living it out. We were
somebody's spouse. While that may not define
the whole of who we are, it surely informs many
facets of it. We are different if we are part of two.
Suddenly we become single.

So we have to redefine the part of us who was
wife—and all the rest of us too. And in the process of that definition we come across lots of who
we are this minute and might not be the next.

We are living proof that it truly is difficult to
not know who we are and yet be that thing. In
time, living from one day to the next without being sure who we are leads us to live in the present
of who we are *and* to be open to the who we are
becoming.

*Finding out who I am is a way of life, one day to the
next.*

DECEMBER 5

Why, sometimes I've believed as many as six impossible things before breakfast.
    —The White Queen, in *Through the Looking Glass*

What's belief? What's impossible? What's real? And when's breakfast? There are days when our lives seem to be an impossible Wonderland, every bit as scary (and frustrating and fascinating) as the original one was to Alice. Part of ourselves is saying, "Believe this is happening to me, it's true." And part of us is saying, "This can't be real. I didn't expect this. It's impossible!"

When I began my marriage, ending it seemed improbable, if not impossible. Yet here I am at the end of it. At first I don't believe my marriage is ending, and then I don't believe a lot more—like how I could have believed it wouldn't, how I'm going to go on, who I'm going to be. Yet the impossible is happening, so I might as well make like the White Queen and believe in it.

The White Queen is, in fact, quite pleased to believe in the impossible. Being open to believing impossible things can bring us to wonder and adventure, depending on how we look at them.

Believing the impossible about myself brings me a whole new perspective on who I might be.

DECEMBER 6

If one does not have a relationship with the self, it is truly
impossible to have a living process [healthy] relationship; it
will not be possible to be honest with the "other" if one is
not in contact with oneself.   —Anne Wilson Schaef

I would tell the truth, I really would, if only I
knew what it was. The first step in an honest relationship with ourselves, not to mention somebody else, is being in touch with our feelings,
bodies, and actions enough to know what's honest for us and what isn't. If we're not in contact
with ourselves, we simply don't know what's true
and what isn't.

Getting in contact with ourselves is sort of like
hanging flypaper up inside ourselves. The truth
begins to stick to it. And once we've caught the
truth, we can take a look at it. We can begin to
know what it feels like, what it looks like, what
it's called. We can tell ourselves the truth. We can
be honest in our relationship with ourselves.

When we're honest with ourselves it's almost
impossible not to be honest with people we're in a
relationship with. Having come into contact with
honesty, we stick to it. When we stick to our own
honesty, other people can stick to theirs.

Honesty in relationships is catching.

DECEMBER 7

Warning: Laughter may be hazardous to your illness.
—Nurses for Laughter

Vegetables and laughter are good for what ails us. If nothing ails us, they're good for us anyway. Nobody seems to know exactly why, yet it's been documented time and again—watching funny movies and laughing out loud helps cure physical ailments. And what's good for our bodies is good for our minds and spirits.

So we're feeling down in the dumps. We can wallow around in the garbage. We can try to climb out. Or we can sit back and laugh at all the things our psyche has thrown into the pit. If our own lives seem hopelessly unfunny and we can't look inside to find something to laugh at, we can look outside ourselves.

The only caution is that reading a funny book, listening to an old friend tell a joke—even one we've heard before—or going to a funny movie might be detrimental to our ability to hold on to our grumpy moods, our desolation, our ill feelings about our lives.

If I can catch myself laughing, I must be on the road to recovery.

DECEMBER 8

If you can take one peaceful step, you can take two. You
can take one hundred and eight peaceful steps.
                                        —Thich Nhat Hanh

Anybody who has ever watched a baby learn to walk has seen this miracle. Babies aren't sure at first. They pull themselves up on a piece of furniture. They let go with one hand, they take a step. Then they step back to the supporting table. After a while, they find they can step away from the table, one step at a time. And soon they can toddle, then walk, then run.

When we reach a point in our lives where conflict and chaos seem to reign, we'd do well to watch and imitate babies. First, we pull ourselves up on something that will support us. Then we take that first step toward creating peace in our lives. But we don't let go of the support just yet. We take another step and another. If we take these steps, one at a time, walking this way will start to seem normal.

When we're learning to walk a new path in our lives, there's another important lesson we can learn from babies just learning to walk. Babies know when to rest.

I can learn to walk a peaceful path with rest stops.

DECEMBER 9

When the situation is desperate, it's too late to be serious.
Be playful. —Edward Abbey

Only a fool would fool around when her life is falling apart. Get serious and get real. There are problems to be solved here. New identities to be forged. Living arrangements to be figured out. Bills to be paid. Projects to be completed. And I'm supposed to be playful?

Yes, and no but about it. Sometimes all the hard work and clever thinking in the world won't solve a problem. No amount of serious consideration can make us feel as good as a barefooted romp along a beach can. Or eating an ice cream sundae for dinner. Or watching a hokey movie with a happy ending. Or riding on a carousel. Or all of the above plus add your own.

The funny thing about getting playful is that it puts our problems in perspective. We might figure out something about who we are as we walk along the beach. We might figure out how to finish that project that has us running around in circles while we ride the carousel. And we can go back to serious considerations with new energy.

Taking a play break can help me see my problems from a different angle.

DECEMBER 10

Solitude is un-American. —Erica Jong

To take time alone, in quiet, to reflect, to rejuvenate ourselves, is especially important when we are feeling weak or vulnerable or just plain sad. Young children, who sometimes want to be left alone or who cry because they just need to, seem to know this instinctively. And in this culture, we have done what we can to bury that instinctive knowledge.

Feeling lonely? Feeling blue? Feeling down? Feeling at loose ends since you and your ex are no longer together? Never mind. Get up, get out, see people, do things, take on projects. Get going! How many times have we heard that advice? Maybe even given it to ourselves.

And while it's true there is a time to get up and get outside our self, what we often don't tell ourselves is that there's a time to sit down and get inside our self. What would happen if we treated solitude as an antidote for loneliness? If we spent our lonely time exploring our own hearts? Meditating, daydreaming, walking, just sitting. Practicing solitude doesn't mean we won't be lonely. It does mean we'll have resources for dealing with our loneliness.

My solitude connects me to my life.

DECEMBER 11

One face to the world, another at home makes for misery.
　　　　　　　　　　　　　　　—Amy Vanderbilt

Showing one face to the world, another to our families, and yet a third to ourselves is all too common. We may be miserable, but what will the neighbors, our colleagues, our friends think if we let them know that? We may be hurting and worried, but what will our families think if we share our worries? We may be angry, scared, and feeling like life is barely worth living. But what will happen if we admit that to ourselves?

What will happen if we do not? If we continue to put on a mask each day before we look in the mirror to brush our teeth? What will happen is the mask will become implanted, impossible to remove, even in the privacy of our aloneness, and it will do its job. It will mask our feelings—all of them.

The longer we wear the masks, the more difficult it becomes to think, feel, speak, or act honestly with others or ourselves. Certainly we all need to wear masks in some situations. We can hardly, for instance, go around crying all day at work. Yet if we don't make the attempt to bring our true face out into the light of day, the day will come when we don't know what our true face is.

Taking off my mask allows me to recognize myself.

DECEMBER 12

Truth is not discovered by proofs but by exploration.
                                        —Simone Weil

Exploration is, by definition, a process of trial *and* error. Discovering the truth of our new single lives means that we need to try things out. And we need to allow ourselves to make mistakes. If we don't, we will probably never discover who we can be.

I can never prove to myself that I am a lovable and capable person. In fact, since my marriage ended, the "proof" seems to point out that I'm not. Maybe I'm cranky and despondent. Maybe I can't get simple things like cleaning the house and paying the bills done. Besides, maybe I tried something new, like going to a singles dance, and it didn't feel right or true for me. Well, so what?

Making an error in action or judgment—whether it's something simple like purchasing a dress we'll never wear or something more far-reaching like taking a new job we hate—can throw us off the course of actively exploring. Or it can give us information to use in our quest for truth. I didn't like that. Okay, now I know it. I can do it differently next time. As I continue to explore, I discover new truths about myself.

Trial and error reveal my true self.

DECEMBER 13

For people who live on expectations, to face up to their realization is something of an ordeal.

—Elizabeth Bowen

Living on expectations is living only for what will be. When we live for what will be, we are by definition never satisfied with what we have. And if by some miracle we realize our expectations, we're not satisfied with what we get either.

I lived my life for a long time thinking that if only I had a better job and more time alone with my spouse, I'd be happy. I got them both, a job people envied in a city far away from friends and family. My job was picture perfect, except I didn't like it. Not having lots of old friends around meant my husband and I had plenty of time to spend together. Time we spent discovering that we didn't really have a lot in common. Facing up to the realization of my expectations was, need-less to say, something of an ordeal.

When a marriage ends, an opportunity presents itself. We can turn our energy to living our lives as they are now—maybe not pleasant. We can choose how we spend our time, who we hang out with, what work we do for the simple pleasure and process of doing it.

Giving up expectations gives me energy to live now.

DECEMBER 14

*One doesn't discover new lands without consenting to lose
sight of the shore for a very long time.*   —André Gide

Sailors don't need to see land to keep their bearings. We don't need to see the familiar landscape
of our old life to know how we feel now. Explor-
ers don't need to know what the new land will
look like in order to find it; and we don't need to
know what our future life is going to be like in
order to get there.

We may feel like we don't have much choice
about setting out on our journey. Our old life is
over, it's true. We can't choose that. However, we
could choose to repeat our old life as closely as
possible. We could choose another relationship as
much like our marriage as possible. We could
choose not to change old patterns, habits, and
traits. We could also choose to lose our bearings,
to be at sea, lost in our anger and grief.

Or we can consent to set out on a journey in the
spirit of discovery, which means we don't kno
where it will take us. We can get our bearing
observing what's going on inside and arou
—paying attention to our feelings, adjusti
course, and, above all, being where we
we're there.

I'm not lost; in fact, I'm finding mysel

DECEMBER 15

And when is there time to remember, to sift, to weigh, to estimate, to total? —Tillie Olsen

If it's true that a woman's work is never done, it's time to count time for reflection, remembering, examining our lives, where we've been and where we're going, as part of woman's work. It's also probably time to settle for less than done with regard to our workload. Taking time for ourselves is often difficult, particularly if we base our identity and self-esteem on the things we get done.

Reflecting on where we've been, who we are, and where we're going doesn't mean dwelling on the past and longing for what was or might have been. Nor does it mean putting our now on hold until a mythical better future. Taking time for reflection is simply a way of taking stock.

No one else is going to tell us where and when this time is, give it to us, or find it for us. We might have to give up doing things for others. We might have to make choices to leave other things undone. We might have to give up a self-esteem based on how well we do everything. Sooner or later, we have to claim time for ourselves.

The longer I wait to take time for myself, the more time it's going to take me to claim myself.

DECEMBER 16

*When you befriend yourself, you discover that there's
somebody home, and when you've been knocking at the
door for years without getting an answer, that's very
reassuring.* —Geneen Roth

There are times when I don't even know where
to find a door to knock on, let alone know the self
who answers the door. Yet I know that if we don't
start knocking on internal doors, we never will
find out who we are.

It's quite probable that nobody answered our
doors of self-knowledge during our marriage because we stopped knocking. We probably even
nailed some doors shut. The process of opening
them can be painful. The nails of "what if" take
some time to pull out: What if I don't find anybody there? What if I don't recognize her? What if
I don't like her? What if she doesn't like me?

There is only one way to answer those questions—knocking on the doors. Pulling nails out as
we go. And mostly what happens is we welcome
ourself home. We see some parts of ourself that
we like, some that we don't, some that we want to
change. If we break down a door or two, we're
left with archways to our new life.

*Coming home to myself opens doors to new
experiences and a new me.*

DECEMBER 17

It's not love that is blind, but jealousy.

—Lawrence Durrell

Blind love overlooks what's there—or sees faults, bad habits, or quirks and makes allowances for them. Blind jealousy looks and sees what isn't there and often misses or misinterprets what is there. Jealousy of a loved one's time and attention to people and things besides ourselves can blind us to their care for us. Jealousy also blinds us to ourselves. When we're jealous we don't see anything but the objects of our jealousy.

In fact, what we call blind love might well be called blind jealousy of a sort. In overlooking traits, behaviors, or addictions in our love partner, we're often jealously guarding the continuation of the relationship at the expense of the truth.

When we're jealously guarding a relationship, we're not seeing the forest for the trees. What our jealous selves aren't seeing—or aren't admitting to seeing—is that we're not getting what we need out of this relationship. And rather than risk seeing that and saying it, we're overlooking things that are there and seeing things that aren't.

My jealousy can keep me safely in the dark about what I want in love.

DECEMBER 18

*If you fear something, you set yourself up to experience it
again and again. As Job said, "What I have feared has
come upon me."* —Gloria Karpinski

Skydivers who are afraid of heights and keep on
jumping. Children who are afraid of the dark and
frequently dream of dark monsters. People who
are afraid of rejection and repeatedly apply for
jobs they're not qualified for. Consciously, sub-
consciously, or unconsciously they all keep encountering their fear.

When we deal with our fear by repeatedly
banging up against it, the object of our fear often
simply changes. Jump out of planes enough and
we might find ourselves afraid of driving a car.
Avoiding the fear is another way of trying to deal
with it. Avoided fears have a way of multiplying.
We find ourselves spending most of our time—
waking and sleeping—avoiding them.

If we can't kill them and we can't avoid them,
how can we break the grip our fears hold us in?
Making friends with our fears, acknowledging
them, having a conversation with the fearful part
of ourselves is a beginning. If we are afraid of
being rejected, for instance, are we also afraid of
asking for what we want or need?

Meeting my fears is a way to meet myself.

DECEMBER 19

Thinking of myself as a sort of superwoman, I felt worthy only when I produced—which meant working harder, running faster, juggling more and more balls—and almost always denying: denying a hunger for something, denying emptiness, denying anger, denying pain. Denying opportunity.   —Gabrielle Rico

We often have no sense that we are running, doing, and accumulating to fill a void in our lives—because we deny that we have a void to fill. Even if we "know" that our divorce left a void to fill, we think we can fill it by doing more.

Our unnamed hunger can lead to trying to fill it with more food, activities, relationships. Our denied pain can lead to illness. Our denied anger can lead to frustrated outbursts. Our denial can lead to chronic fatigue. In any case, we reach the point where we just can't keep up.

And there comes a time when we must realize that more is less. When we reach this point, we can stop denying that we feel loss, pain, anger, hunger for meaning. And we can stop denying ourselves the opportunity to discover what's truly important to us.

I can try to be everything to everybody or I can be somebody to myself.

DECEMBER 20

It takes a whole village to raise a child. —Bill Moyers

Children need love, wisdom, humor, discipline, and nurture from as many related sources as possible. Children, both those we may be raising and the child within each of us, need to feel connected to their "village."

Unfortunately, most of us don't live in a village with grandmothers, aunts, uncles, and cousins just down the path. Perhaps when we were part of a couple we just got by. Now each of us must choose and create the "village" that will help us raise our children and nurture our child within. We can rely on family, friends, our ex-spouses, support or self-help groups, social services, schools, any of a number of sources.

The first step—admitting that we can't do this alone—gives us permission to ask for help. Then we need to figure out what help we need. It might be finding someone to help with a child's algebra homework. It might be finding someone to pamper us. It might be somebody to share a meal with us and/or our children. Whatever it is, we're the only ones who can figure out what it is, and we're the only ones who can ask for help.

I support my own efforts to find the support I need for my child within and for my children.

DECEMBER 21

> *Only with winter-patience can we bring*
> *The deep-desired, long-awaited spring.*
> —Anne Morrow Lindbergh

People who live in northern climates know it's futile to plant flowers outside in February. And in some parts of the world, spring begins in February. Each of us lives through times of winter-patience. Spring might come sooner and it might come later. It will come, and it won't come any sooner if we try to force it.

Getting a divorce is almost certainly a time like winter. It's cold, lonely, dark, and we feel like it will go on forever. Even if we're feeling good about starting off on our new lives, we have to wait until the proper time to plant the seeds that will blossom into what that life will be. Winter-patience is a time for us to lie dormant, which doesn't mean we aren't doing anything.

Living in winter-patience is not living for spring, for the future. It's listening to our inner selves so that we know what we want our spring garden to look like. It's giving ourselves time to ponder and reflect, perhaps to lay out a plan for our spring garden. It's giving ourselves time to heal so that our spring garden can grow.

If I'm patient with myself, it won't always be winter.

DECEMBER 22

*Before we can move into a new ar-rangement, we must
first go through a period of de-rangement.*
— M. C. Richards

Sometimes our deranging seems to be done for
us. Things just won't go right no matter what we
do. Every machine we touch breaks. Every project
we start lies in an unfinished heap. We're at odds
with our friends. Our lives are totally out of balance—not to mention our bank statements.

When we're in transition, it often seems like
we're never going to get out of the deranging
part. Since nothing ever goes as we've planned it
or seems reliable anymore, we may begin to feel
crazy. We may try to explain what's happening to
ourselves or others and feel like we're speaking a
language neither of us understands.

Yet if we look at the derangement, we may begin to see a pattern. Perhaps our inner self is telling us we're not finishing our work because this
isn't the right work for us to be doing anymore.
We're not getting along with our friends because
they belong to an old life we don't want anymore.
We're distracted from taking care of everyday
business because there's a deeper inner business
we need to attend to.

In my derangement I can find new arrangements.

DECEMBER 23

Humor is emotional chaos remembered in tranquility.
—James Thurber

Almost all of us have had experiences about which we might say, "Looking back on it now, I can see that it was funny." We didn't see the humor in the situation as it was happening, probably because our feelings were pretty intense.

Being able to laugh at intense feelings as we recollect them is not a way of denying them. It is a way of getting to know them better. It is also a way of putting them into proper perspective. When we're going through a separation, our feelings tend to run pretty strong and close to the surface. We may be meeting new feelings—panic, independence, contentment, rage.

Seeing the humor helps us see our feelings. For instance, I panic when my hot water heater starts spewing all over the basement floor. I call my brother and he suggests that I could turn up the flame and poach eggs on the basement floor, or I could buy him a plane ticket and he'd come turn off the water spigot leading into the heater, or I could turn the water off myself. Laughing at his suggestions, I begin to see my options. My panic subsides.

Humor helps me see the patterns in my chaos.

DECEMBER 24

I have the power to make truths of my beliefs.
—Beryl Markham

Perversely, most of us believe we have the power to prevent or stop things being true—and we exercise it. Consider the woman who believes she'll never have another intimate relationship. She believes that she is not young enough, attractive enough, that there is no one in the world to love her. She makes no effort to act contrary to her belief and actually creates a scenario in which she never meets anyone with whom she might develop an intimate relationship.

Believing something can come true can empower us to act as if it is. If I believe that I am a lovable person, and act as if that's true, sooner or later, it will be true. It may or may not follow that I will begin a new intimate, loving relationship.

It will follow that people will notice a change in me. It will be easier for anyone—my family, my friends, an as-yet-unknown other—to love me. When we own our power to make our beliefs into truths, we also own the power to examine our beliefs and discover which ones are true for us.

I have the power to choose my beliefs, and I have the power to make my beliefs come true.

DECEMBER 25

It can't be Christmas all the time.   —Margaret Sidney

These words were likely written as a caution. They can also be read as a comfort if we're having a difficult time going through this family holiday after our divorce. It won't last forever. It can't be Christmas all the time.

That's true, as well, for any other day of the year. It won't be that day forever. If we stay with the pain we're feeling, the grief, the anger, eventually a new day will come. When we live as fully as we can in that day, we can let go of the expectations that just because it's Christmas or another holiday, it "should" be special and wonderful. No day is going to be as great as we expected or as bad as we dreaded.

When we live without expectations the day might be worse than we thought it would be. And it might be better. Either way, it will only be one day long. When we stay with the present, the presents we get from it transform us. We may always feel a twinge of our losses at Christmas and we won't always feel the way we do today—good or bad.

I can stay with my days and my holidays.

DECEMBER 26

I discovered that when I lived the Light I had, I was given more Light. —Peace Pilgrim

We learn that you can't create something out of nothing in the physical world. To create energy you must use up matter, and vice versa. We often mistranslate that into our emotional and spiritual lives: there won't be enough love, energy, or power for me. If I use up what I have, I won't get any more.

Strength and understanding do not operate under the material law of supply and demand. When we use the understanding and strength we have, we get more strength and understanding. I may understand that I'm not married anymore, and I hurt a lot. I can deny my pain or I can use my strength not to "kill" my hurt but to do things for myself that will heal it.

When we let the light of understanding into our lives, we grow in understanding. This is not the rational understanding of explaining "why." It is the understanding that lets us see and feel what is going on in our lives. When we grow in understanding, we grow in strength that enables us to act and react to our lives as they are.

When I use my strength and understanding, I have plenty of strength and understanding.

DECEMBER 27

And what looks like dark in the distance may brighten as I draw near.   —Mary Gardinier Brainard

When we're in despair, where we are today is dark. No amount of telling ourselves—or having others tell us—that there's light at the end of the tunnel will show us the light. As we go through a separation and divorce, many things can cause us to despair in the dark. We are unsure of the way, and we feel lost and lonely.

We may not have enough money, a satisfying job, any feeling of connection to our friends and family. Even if we tell ourselves we do, we still feel the despair of not believing it's true. We don't know what to do next or where to turn. And we're quite sure that anything we do or anywhere we turn will be wrong. The present is dark and bleak. The future looks, if anything, darker.

When we live with our present feelings, we move toward the future as we drive along a road, paying attention to where we are at that time. If we live for the future, waiting for our despair to go away, it never does. We try to imagine what the light will look like, and instead of moving, we stay stuck in the dark.

When I live with my eyes open to the darkness of my despair, I won't be blind to the light when I see it.

DECEMBER 28

I have so much to do that I am going to bed.
—Savoyard proverb

In the time after our separation, as we tackle the many chores of daily life, anything from setting up a new bank account to having lunch with an old friend can seem like too much to do. At times the prospect of doing anything at all is simply overwhelming.

It's time to retreat—to bed, to a good book, to a good cry, to the bathtub—to anywhere where we can be alone for at least fifteen minutes. Retreat can give us the energy to go on. With renewed energy we can go back to our "overwhelmment" and try to find a way to live with it.

To live with the feeling of being overwhelmed is to acknowledge it: "Hi there, old friend. Back to taunt me again, aren't you? Well, I'm going to sit with you a while. While we rest, maybe I'll figure out how to stop running headlong into you." To simply be with the feeling of too much to do is likely to lead us to new insights about what we're expecting of ourselves—perfection? Or of how we see ourselves—inadequate? Of what we're missing—time to retreat into ourselves?

Meet, greet, retreat—three things I can do in the face of too much to do.

DECEMBER 29

Let Greeks be Greeks, and women what they are.
—Anne Bradstreet

To live and let live is advice we often give ourselves, thinking—and acting—in large part as if our tolerance is only for others. But if the Greeks might be Greeks, the Romans, Romans, women what they are, should I not be who I am, too? If I am willing to accept others, might I not do the same favor to myself?

Surely anyone who's watched TV, read a magazine or a self-help book lately, has heard the hoopla about accepting one's self. And the reason people are still writing tomes, airing TV programs, and teaching courses on tolerance and self-acceptance is that tolerating—and embracing —others and ourselves is extremely difficult. It is to admit that none of us is perfect but that each and every one of us is the way we are.

In order to change myself I must first tolerate myself, accept whoever I am, however I am at this stage of my life. Then I must begin to act as if I believe that. I am no longer married. That is a fact. I can act, beginning today, as if that's the way I am and it's okay—maybe sad, maybe hard, but me.

Let me be me.

DECEMBER 30

Wisdom is the courage to live in the moving resonance of the present. —Sam Keen

Wisdom is knowing in our heads *and* our hearts that time travel is impossible, that the only place we can live is the present. It's also knowing that the present constantly moves and changes.

It's important to remember that today is not yesterday or tomorrow when we suffer from the "if onlys." If only I could get it once and for all that I don't have to control everything, that I'm not responsible for everyone, that I'm not perfect, that I'm strong and capable. . . . "If only" thinking erroneously assumes that the present lasts forever and that once we've discovered the trick of living in it, we'll be set for life.

To live in the present is to listen when the resonance of the moment is a reverberating discordance that we can't understand and can barely stand to hear. And it's marching merrily along when the present is a nice, steady drumbeat easy for us to follow. It's having the courage to listen to our internal music and to follow it as one present moment leads to the next.

Wisdom is knowing that the present is ever changing; courage is living in it.

DECEMBER 31

*Instead of seeing the rug being pulled from under us, we
can learn to dance on a shifting carpet.*

—Thomas Crum

On the last day of the year we might take time to reflect on all the changes in our lives. Just to remember them—not to judge them, not to beat ourselves up because we thought surely we'd have gotten this, that, or the other done by now.

The truth of the matter is that the years are all shifting carpets, uneven floors, and sometimes, even, the floor falling out from under us. How we look at the changes in our lives can make all the difference in how nimbly we're able to dance through them. If we think the rug is about to be pulled out from under us, we're likely to move very cautiously and stiffly. If we know the rug is about to shift, we may be alert in our movements, yet relaxed and loose enough to change our step.

When we reflect on changes, we mourn losses and we celebrate gains, growth, and new beginnings. We might think we have little to celebrate but the end of the year. And if we put a bit of time and energy into reflecting we might find other things to celebrate. We might feel, literally or figuratively, like dancing the new year in.

Hurrah! I change with the changing times of my life.

TOPIC INDEX

Abuse: Feb. 16, May 4, Aug. 5

Acceptance: Jan. 15, Feb. 2, May 2, Jul. 22, Aug. 12, Sep. 16, Oct. 8, Oct. 13

Action: Apr. 17, Jun. 5, Aug. 14, Sep. 20, Nov. 9

Adaptability: Apr. 15, Sep. 22

Addiction: Feb. 13, Oct. 25

Affection: Feb. 16, Sep. 13

Aging: Feb. 8, Mar. 31, Nov. 12, Nov. 24

Anger: Jan. 27, Apr. 3, Jun. 24, Jul. 3, Oct. 22

Appreciation: Jan. 18, Jun. 26

Approval: May 26, Aug. 18, Nov. 21

Arguments: Aug. 30, Nov. 8

Attitude: Mar. 2, Jul. 27, Oct. 2, Oct. 7

Attractiveness: Jul. 21

Avoidance: Nov. 14

Beauty: Feb. 8, Nov. 12

Beginning: Mar. 16

Being Right: Feb. 22

Belief: Jan. 2, Jan. 19, May 18, Sep. 26, Dec. 3, Dec. 5, Dec. 24

Blame: Apr. 13, Aug. 26, Aug. 28, Sep. 19, Dec. 2

Body: Mar. 14, May 19, Jun. 8, Jul. 24, Sep. 17

Boredom: Jan. 5, Jul. 9

Caring: Jun. 2, Sep. 2

Celebrating: Apr. 25, Jun. 21, Jun. 29, Oct. 21, Dec. 31

Centering: Jan. 14, Jun. 8

Change: Jan. 31, Feb. 20, Feb. 28, May 3, Jul. 8, Sep. 3, Nov. 3, Nov. 30

Childhood: Apr. 22

Children: Feb. 20, Jun. 10, Oct. 19, Dec. 20

Choices: Mar. 4, Aug. 15, Oct. 19

Communication: Mar. 23, May 3, Jul. 10, Oct. 29
Compassion: Feb. 1, Aug. 6, Oct. 14, Nov. 6
Confidence: Jun. 25, Nov. 27
Conflict: Feb. 22, Jul. 29
Connected: Jan. 12, May 14, Sep. 15, Nov. 29
Contradiction: Jun. 30, Jul. 14, Sep. 19
Control: Feb. 22, Apr. 9, Apr. 26, Jun. 12, Jul. 12,
    Aug. 20, Aug. 31, Oct. 2, Nov. 4, Nov. 13, Dec. 2
Cooperation: Feb. 19, Jun. 17, Aug. 2, Oct. 27
Courage: Feb. 7, May 9, Jul. 20, Nov. 7, Dec. 30
Craziness: Jan. 26, Dec. 22
Crisis: Feb. 11, Mar. 17, Apr. 4, Oct. 20
Criticism: May 24
Deception: Mar. 5, Sep. 4
Denial: Nov. 14, Dec. 19
Dependence: Feb. 10, May 21, Aug. 24, Oct. 18, Nov. 26
Depression: Feb. 17, Jun. 22, Aug. 14
Despair: Feb. 18, Apr. 16, Aug. 28, Dec. 27
Discovering: Jan. 31, May 10, Jun. 4, Jul. 6, Oct. 10,
    Dec. 12, Dec. 14
Divorce: Feb. 5, Mar. 6, Jun. 10, Jun. 18, Aug. 8,
    Nov. 16
Dreams: Jan. 3, Jul. 18
Effort: Jan. 10, May 30, Sep. 23, Sep. 29
Embarrassment: Mar. 25, Sep. 11
Emotions: Jan. 24, Mar. 24, Jul. 25, Sep. 17, Dec. 23
Envy: Jun. 3
Escape: Mar. 7, Sep. 6
Expectations: Jan. 9, Feb. 20, Jun. 12, Aug. 11, Sep. 23,
    Nov. 4, Dec. 13
Experience: Jul. 31
Failure: Jan. 28, Jun. 28, Jul. 2, Aug. 23
Fear: Jan. 17, Apr. 27, May 15, Oct. 26, Oct. 31,
    Dec. 18

Forgiveness: Mar. 24, Mar. 26, Jul. 27, Aug. 12, Sep. 12, Sep. 21

Freedom: May 13, Jul. 4, Jul. 7, Oct. 31

Friends: Feb. 9, Nov. 15

Getting Needs Met: Mar. 10, May 25, Aug. 2

Goals: Sep. 25, Oct. 24

Gratitude: May 20, Nov. 23

Grieving: Jan. 23, Feb. 26, May 17, Jul. 6, Oct. 17

Growth: Feb. 11, May 14, Jul. 22, Aug. 22, Sep. 7, Sep. 30

Guilt: Jan. 4, Jun. 16, Aug. 26, Oct. 14, Nov. 28

Happiness: May 16, Jul. 26, Nov. 17

Hate: May 22, Sep. 18

Healing: Mar. 8, May 12, Sep. 24, Nov. 5, Dec. 7

Help: Jul. 28, Aug. 2

Holidays: Dec. 25

Home: Mar. 22, Dec. 16

Honesty: Jun. 13, Jul. 7, Dec. 6, Dec. 11

Hope: Mar. 21, May 8, Jun. 29

Humor: Apr. 1, Apr. 8, Jun. 28, Aug. 9, Sep. 7, Dec. 7, Dec. 23

Inadequacy: Feb. 15, Jul. 14

Independence: Jan. 25, Apr. 27, Jul. 26, Nov. 10

Inferiority: Aug. 22, Sep. 14

Inspiration: Feb. 25, May 11

Integrity: Sep. 26, Oct. 5

Intimacy: Jan. 11, Apr. 7, Aug. 13

Isolation: Jan. 13, Jan. 29, Apr. 6, Sep. 27, Oct. 28

Jealousy: Apr. 8, Jun. 24, Aug. 10, Dec. 17

Kindness: Nov. 6

Knowing Myself: Jan. 12, Jan. 21, Apr. 25, Apr. 28, May 12, Jun. 23, Jun. 27, Aug. 16, Aug. 24, Sep. 20, Nov. 5, Dec. 4, Dec. 16

Laughter: Apr. 1, Apr. 8, Sep. 7, Dec. 7

Letting Go: Jan. 16, Feb. 28, Apr. 2, Apr. 30, Jun. 24,
   Aug. 21, Sep. 10, Oct. 15
Living in the Future: Apr. 23
Living in the Past: Jan. 20, Jun. 1
Living in the Present: Feb. 3, Apr. 21, Apr. 23, May 1,
   Jun. 21, Aug. 1, Oct. 1, Oct. 21, Nov. 23, Dec. 1,
   Dec. 25, Dec. 30
Loneliness: Jan. 6, Feb. 4, May 10, Jun. 7, Nov. 10,
   Dec. 10
Loss: Mar. 28, May 17, Jun. 22, Jun. 27, Nov. 16,
   Nov. 22
Love: Feb. 14, Mar. 19, Jul. 17, Aug. 11, Oct. 29,
   Nov. 11, Nov. 13, Dec. 17
Making Decisions: Feb. 29, May 1, Oct. 16
Making Mistakes: Jun. 1, Jul. 2, Aug. 23
Meditation: Jan. 2, Oct. 4, Oct. 12, Nov. 11
Memory: Jan. 19, Feb. 24, Apr. 5, Jun. 6, Oct. 10
Needs: Jul. 11
Newness/New Beginning: Jan. 7, Mar. 16, Apr. 14,
   Apr. 30, Jun. 4
Nurture: Jan. 15, Feb. 26
One Day at a Time: Jan. 1, Jan. 30, Apr. 15, Oct. 16,
   Nov. 1, Dec. 8
Opportunity: Feb. 12, Mar. 31, Sep. 3
Overwhelmed: Feb. 15, Aug. 20, Dec. 28
Pain: Jan. 13, Mar. 8, May 12, May 16, Jun. 9, Sep. 8
Passion: Nov. 22
Patience: Jul. 23, Dec. 21
Peace: Sep. 5, Dec. 8
Perceptions: Feb. 23, Mar. 6, Apr. 11, Sep. 19, Dec. 5,
   Dec. 25, Dec. 27, Dec. 31
Perfection: Jan. 8, Mar. 11, Oct. 13
Perspective: Jul. 8, Dec. 9
Play: Jul. 15, Dec. 9

Power: Mar. 1, Jun. 19, Nov. 11, Dec. 24
Powerlessness: Mar. 17, Sep. 16
Prayer: Jan. 2
Problem Solving: Jan. 23
Quarreling: Aug. 30, Nov. 8, Nov. 14
Rage: Oct. 22
Reality: Apr. 4, Apr. 11, May 7, Jul. 17, Oct. 13
Recovery: Jan. 30, Apr. 20, May 29, Sep. 25, Oct. 11
Regret: Jan. 20, Mar. 11, Apr. 5, Jun. 26
Relationships: Mar. 13, Aug. 9, Oct. 25, Dec. 6
Remembering: Jan. 15, May 31, Sep. 8
Resentment: Mar. 15, Jul. 27
Resistance: Apr. 19
Revenge: Feb. 21, Mar. 26, Jul. 29, Aug. 31
Satisfaction: Feb. 13
Secrets: Apr. 12, Apr. 20, May 6, Jul. 19, Sep. 28
Self-Absorption: May 21, Jun. 9, Jun. 11, Aug. 6, Sep. 11, Sep. 28
Self-Acceptance: Jan. 18, Feb. 3, Mar. 28, Jul. 10, Oct. 23, Dec. 29
Self-Blame: Apr. 13
Self-Confidence: Mar. 3, Apr. 29, Nov. 20
Self-Deception: Mar. 5, Sep. 4
Self-Esteem: Jan. 21, May 25, Jul. 10, Jul. 21, Sep. 14
Self-Expression: Apr. 17
Self-Pity: Mar. 12
Serenity: Mar. 9, Nov. 19
Sex: Feb. 8, Mar. 14, Mar. 27, Jun. 15, Jul. 30
Shame: Feb. 27, Aug. 3, Nov. 24
Sharing: Jun. 11, Nov. 29
Silence: Jul. 5, Aug. 17
Simplicity: Mar. 20, Apr. 24, Oct. 8
Singleness: Sep. 22, Oct. 7
Solitude: Feb. 4, Sep. 27, Dec. 10

Sorrow: Oct. 17

Space: Jul. 13, Aug. 16

Starting Over: Jan. 1, Apr. 2, Aug. 7, Oct. 4, Dec. 4,
Dec. 8, Dec. 22

Strength: Jan. 16, Jan. 22, Jun. 20, Jul. 26, Dec. 26

Success: Jan. 28, Oct. 30, Nov. 25

Support: Mar. 18, Jul. 13, Sep. 15, Nov. 2, Nov. 15,
Dec. 20

Taking Care of Me: Jul. 28, Aug. 27, Sep. 1, Nov. 2

Taking Risks: Mar. 3, Mar. 25, Jul. 16, Jul. 20, Aug. 17,
Oct. 3, Oct. 29

Talent: Nov. 25

Tears: Mar. 9, Apr. 10, Jul. 6, Aug. 25

Time: May 27, Aug. 29, Sep. 10, Dec. 15

Transformation: Jan. 26, Feb. 13, May 23, Nov. 18

Transition: Mar. 30, May 23, Jul. 1, Oct. 6, Nov. 30

Trapped: Apr. 19, May 22

Trust: Jan. 6, Feb. 12, Mar. 22, May 7, Oct. 9, Oct. 11,
Nov. 5

Truth: Feb. 6, Aug. 4, Oct. 30, Nov. 6, Dec. 12

Understanding: Jan. 17, Jan. 24, Jun. 5, Sep. 5, Oct. 15,
Dec. 26

Unwilling: Apr. 18

Vacation: Aug. 29

Vulnerability: Jun. 14, Jul. 16, Nov. 26

Wants: Jul. 11

What If: Mar. 29, Apr. 26, May 28

Willing: Apr. 18

Wisdom: May 5, Jul. 31, Sep. 9, Dec. 30

Wishing: Mar. 29, Apr. 26, May 28

Work: May 30, Sep. 1, Sep. 29

Worry: Apr. 21, Aug. 19